Changing English

Parts of this book were published previously as:

Graddol, D., Leith, D. and Swann, J. (eds) (1996) *English: History, Diversity and Change*, London, Routledge/Milton Keynes, The Open University.

Titles in the series:

Book 1 *Changing English* (edited by David Graddol, Dick Leith, Joan Swann, Martin Rhys and Julia Gillen)

Book 2 *Using English* (edited by Janet Maybin, Neil Mercer and Ann Hewings)

Book 3 *Learning English* (edited by Neil Mercer, Joan Swann and Barbara Mayor)

Book 4 *Redesigning English* (edited by Sharon Goodman, David Graddol and Theresa Lillis)

Series editors: Joan Swann and Julia Gillen

Changing English

Edited by David Graddol, Dick Leith, Joan Swann, Martin Rhys and Julia Gillen

Published by

Routledge
2 Park Square
Milton Park
Abingdon OX14 4RN

in association with

The Open University
Walton Hall
Milton Keynes MK7 6AA

Simultaneously published in the USA and Canada by

Routledge
711 Third Avenue
New York NY 10017

Routledge is an imprint of the Taylor & Francis Group

First published 2007

Edited and designed by The Open University.

Typeset in India by Alden Prepress Services, Chennai.

Printed and bound in the United Kingdom by CPI, Glasgow.

This book forms part of an Open University course U211 *Exploring the English language*. Details of this and other Open University courses can be obtained from the Student Registration and Enquiry Service, The Open University, PO Box 197, Milton Keynes, MK7 6BJ, United Kingdom: tel. +44 (0)870 333 4340, email general-enquiries@open.ac.uk

http://www.open.ac.uk

A catalogue record for this book is available from the British Library.

Library of Congress Cataloging in Publication Data
A catalog record for this book has been requested.

ISBN 978 0 415 37669 3 (hardback)
ISBN 978 0 415 37679 2 (paperback)

1.1

Contents

Preface to the series

The books in this series provide an introduction to the study of English, both for students of the English language and the general reader. As Open University course books, they constitute texts for the course U211 *Exploring the English language*. The series aims to provide students with:

- an understanding of the history of English and its development as a global language
- an appreciation of variation in the English language across different speakers and writers, and different regional and social contexts
- conceptual frameworks for the study of language in use
- illustrations of the diversity of English language practices in different parts of the world
- an understanding of how English is learnt as a first or additional language, and of its role as a language of formal education
- introductions to many key controversies about the English language, such as those relating to its position as a global language, attitudes to 'good' and 'bad' English, and debates about the teaching of English
- explorations of the use of English for new purposes and in new contexts, including multimodal texts.

Parts of these books were published previously as:

Graddol, D., Leith, D. and Swann, J. (eds) (1996) *English: History, Diversity and Change*, London, Routledge/Milton Keynes, The Open University.

Maybin, J. and Mercer, N. (eds) (1996) *Using English: From Conversation to Canon*, London, Routledge/Milton Keynes, The Open University.

Mercer, N. and Swann, J. (eds) (1996) *Learning English: Development and Diversity*, London, Routledge/Milton Keynes, The Open University.

Goodman, S. and Graddol, D. (eds) (1996) *Redesigning English: New Texts, New Identities*, London, Routledge/Milton Keynes, The Open University.

The editors for the previously published books were listed in alphabetical order. The list of editors for the present series retains this original order, followed by the additional editors who have worked on the present series. Production of this series, like that of the previously published books, has been a collaborative enterprise involving numerous members of Open University staff and external colleagues. We thank all those who contributed to the original books and to this series. We regret that their names are too many to list here.

Joan Swann and Julia Gillen
Series editors

Biographical information

Book editors

David Graddol is Director of the English Company (UK) Ltd, which produced 'The Future of English?' for the British Council in 1997, an influential report on trends in global English. He was formerly a Lecturer at The Open University. His books include *Describing Language* (1994, 2nd edn, Routledge) written with Jenny Cheshire and Joan Swann.

Dick Leith is a freelance writer, whose books include *A Social History of English*, (2nd edn, 1997, Routledge). He is co-author, with George Myerson, of *The Power of Address: Explorations in Rhetoric* (1989, Routledge & Kegan Paul). He was formerly a Senior Lecturer in Linguistics at Birmingham Polytechnic (now University of Central England).

Joan Swann is currently Director of the Centre for Language and Communication at The Open University. She has many years' experience producing distance learning, multimedia materials on linguistics and English language studies. Her research interests include language and gender and other areas of sociolinguistics. Recent publications include *The Art of English: Everyday Creativity* (co-edited with Janet Maybin; 2006, Palgrave Macmillan).

Martin Rhys is a Staff Tutor at The Open University in Wales, and a member of the Centre for Language and Communication at The Open University. He has recently contributed to an Open University Level 3 course, *English grammar in context,* and is involved in research into bilingualism and teacher education. His interests include prosodic phonology and Anglo-Welsh literature.

Julia Gillen is Chair of the Open University course *Exploring the English language*, and a member of the Centre for Language and Communication at The Open University. She is author of the book *The Language of Children* (2003, Routledge). Her interests include discourse analysis, the history of literacy research and children's communication skills.

Additional contributors

Liz Jackson, now an Associate Lecturer at The Open University, was a Senior Lecturer in English at the University of South Africa and she has also taught in the USA. She has a particular interest in the boundary between orality and literacy in the early medieval period and has published a series of papers on Old English and Old Norse.

Lynda Mugglestone is a Fellow of Pembroke College, Oxford, where she tutors in English. She has published widely on language in the late eighteenth and nineteenth centuries, including *'Talking Proper': The Rise of Accent as Social Symbol* (2nd edn, 2003, Oxford University Press) and *Lost for Words:*

The Hidden History of the Oxford English Dictionary (2004, Yale University Press).

Indra Sinka is a Staff Tutor at The Open University and a member of the Centre for Language and Communication at The Open University. Her research interests include: bilingualism (bilingual first language acquisition and teacher-training issues); mother tongue and second language teaching and learning; inclusion (supporting effective inclusion and communication); the pupil's voice (deaf pupils in mainstream education).

Introduction

Julia Gillen and Martin Rhys

'Where shall we look for standard English, but to the words of a standard man?' wrote the American writer and poet, Henry Thoreau in 1849. Perhaps one of the main themes of this book is the impossibility of pinning down a standard, fixed version of the English language – ultimately as elusive a quarry as the 'standard man' or, indeed, 'standard woman'. The English language is presented here in aspects of change at various levels. The most dominant is that of time, with chapters devoted to tracing the English language as it has moved in history, consequent upon social, political and cultural changes. The relationship of language to history is not one of dependence, however, but rather one of opposing forces in which we must not lose sight of the influence of individual activities on the overall process. Hence the interplay between external change from social forces and individual activities, which lead in practice to language change. And that change can be viewed both across time (diachronically) and as diversity within any one period (synchronically).

This is not only a book about the history of English. The editors of the predecessor volume, *English: History, Diversity and Change*, believed that a fruitful approach to the study of the historical change of a language is not to view this as the study of 'things that happened in the past', but also to see change at work in contemporary regions, societies, networks and indeed individuals. We share that belief and it is reflected in the present book. The first chapter provides an introduction to diversity. The chapters that follow present the large-scale geographical, historical and political factors of the development of the English language. Alongside this roughly chronological thread runs one that traces the concerns and even methodologies of linguists interested in change and variation. The focus on diversity at the level of physical geography and across time, which accommodated the interests of linguists concerned with dialects, broadened over time to include variables such as class, age and gender – in short, we can say that sociolinguistics emerged out of dialectology. Such new perspectives on the English language have led to an academic challenge to the very notion of '*the* English language' by more viable conceptions of varieties of English or Englishes, as we shall trace. The final chapter studies change and variation at the individual level, while presenting that individual as a social being, subject in many ways to the very large-scale factors discussed at the beginning of the book. We see how the individual user of English is constantly drawing upon a changing repertoire of resources, as they renew and reshape their own identity as a speaker of English varieties.

- Chapter 1 takes diversity as its main theme and raises issues and questions that recur in later chapters. How do varieties of English differ from one another? How is the language used in different parts of the world?

- Chapter 2 introduces the origins and early history of English. Where did it come from? What have been the major influences that caused it to develop into its modern forms?
- Chapter 3 begins with the introduction of printing in England. It examines processes of linguistic standardisation as well as the cultural debates that surrounded English during its development as a 'national' language.
- Chapter 4 traces the spread of English throughout the British Isles and in various parts of the world in relation to colonialism. It explores the subsequent development of new varieties of English.
- Chapter 5 follows the case study of Received Pronunciation within the UK as a means of exploring the ways in which accents of English throughout the world are imbued with values external to language and become social symbols.
- Chapter 6 asserts that all varieties of English – Standard and non-Standard – have grammatical rules which determine their structure, and it examines some of the social and regional factors which influence who speaks which variety.
- Chapter 7 turns to the language use of individual speakers: how speakers routinely switch between different varieties of English, or between English and other languages, to represent different aspects of their identity.

Each chapter is accompanied by at least one reading, which represents an additional 'voice' or viewpoint on one or more of the principal themes or issues raised in the chapter. The volume's overall coherence is enhanced by the readings, which serve to broaden the reader's understanding of the rich range of perspectives available in this dynamic field of study.

Each chapter includes:

activities to stimulate further understanding or analysis of the material

text boxes containing illustrative or supplementary material

key terms which are clearly explained as soon as they appear in order to increase the reader's familiarity with the subject.

A note on representing the sounds of language

This book is about spoken and written English, and so deals with the sounds of speech as well as the letters of the alphabet. The distinctive sounds of a particular language, or more precisely of a particular variety of a language, are known as phonemes, and phonemes are conventionally signalled by being enclosed in diagonal brackets / /. The sound of each phoneme is always clearly explained or illustrated by placing it in a familiar context. The important thing to remember is that when you see diagonal brackets, the symbols inside represent sounds and not letters. Hence the (written) word *cool* would be transcribed by the sequence of phonemes /kul/.

You will also (more rarely) come across instances of symbols inside square brackets [ ]. These symbols are from the International Phonetic Alphabet and are meant to convey an accurate transcription of speech sounds from potentially any language, allowing comparison of subtle differences in pronunciation between different accents or different speakers.

English voices

Joan Swann

1.1 Introduction

Since you are reading this book, the chances are that you are quite fluent in English, though it may not be the only language you speak and it may not be your first language. Different readers will speak, or be familiar with, different varieties of English; they will have different experiences of using English, and maybe different feelings about the language.

Such diversity is a major theme running through this chapter, and in fact through the whole of this book. Here, I look at some of the ways in which the English language varies and changes, at the diversity of speakers of English, and at how English is used and what it means to its speakers in different parts of the world.

1.2 What counts as English?

The Scots, the Irish and the Welsh all speak English, and some also speak a Celtic language, so that one can talk of 'Scottish Gaelic' and 'Scottish English', as well as 'Irish Gaelic' and 'Irish English'. These lead on contrastively (and inevitably) to 'English English', a term now common among scholars of the English language. Furthermore, varieties of the 'same' language can be mutually incomprehensible: in England, a Cockney from London and a Geordie from Newcastle may or may not always understand one another; in the United States, a Texan may not always grasp what a New Yorker is saying; and in the wider world a Jamaican may not be transparent to someone from New Zealand. Yet all have used 'English' all their lives.

(McArthur, 2002, p. 7)

[O]ur *Grammar* aims at ... comprehensiveness and depth in treating English irrespective of frontiers: our field is no less than the grammar of educated English current in the second half of the twentieth century in the world's major English-speaking communities. Only where a feature belongs specifically to British usage or American usage, to informal conversation or to the dignity of formal writing, are 'labels' introduced in the description to show that we are no longer discussing the 'common core' of educated English.

(Quirk et al., 1972, p. v)

> The language I speak
> becomes mine
> Its distortions, its queernesses
> all mine, mine alone.
> It is half English, half Indian
> funny perhaps, but it is honest,
> It is human as I am human
> Don't you see?

(Das, 1973, quoted in Verma, 1982, p. 178)

The first quotation above comes from Tom McArthur's book *The Oxford Guide to World English*. As the title suggests, the book is about English around the world – the varieties of English used in different regions, often alongside other languages. The book takes account of the diversity of different 'Englishes', in terms of their linguistic characteristics and the sociopolitical contexts in which they are used.

On the other hand, the grammar produced by Randolph Quirk and his colleagues emphasises a 'common core' of English. This kind of grammar may give the impression that English is relatively fixed, something unified and discrete, playing down the diversity highlighted by McArthur. This is hardly surprising because such grammars provide a model that can be consulted, that will tell the reader what structures are possible in English and what are not possible. In this case, although the grammar is meant to cover 'the world's major English-speaking communities' it focuses, in practice, on 'educated' British and American usage.

Quirk's grammar was produced thirty years before McArthur's guide. A more recent successor, the *Longman Grammar of Spoken and Written English* (Biber et al., 1999) does provide more evidence of different uses of English. The editors of the Longman grammar consulted a substantial corpus of written and spoken English: texts taken from conversations, fiction, newspapers and academic writing that together amounted to over forty million words. The grammar deals with differences in the way English is used in these contexts (e.g. forms of English found in conversation may not occur in academic writing). In terms of regional variation, however, the grammar restricts itself, like Quirk's earlier grammar, to (standard) British and American English. Such usage has frequently been taken as a model for teaching and learning. If you learnt English in school as a foreign language, this is the kind of model you will probably have encountered.

Kamala Das's poem, *Summer in Calcutta*, focuses on what English means to the poet, writing in an Indian context. Speakers and writers of English in different parts of the world respond to the language in particular ways, and may sometimes seek to emphasise the distinctiveness of regional varieties.

In the remainder of this section, I look more closely at some of the ways in which English varies. Later in the chapter I return to the different meanings English may have for its speakers and writers.

ACTIVITY 1.1

Allow about
10 minutes

Please read through the extracts which follow. Which look to you like recognisable varieties of English? How many do you understand?

1   Yu noken draivim kar long sipid nogut. Igat bikpela tambu long dispela. Maksi tingim igat tambu long winim 30 mail tasol. Nogat. Sapos yu ron long 20 mail na planti manmeri wokabaut, em tu i tambu.

You are not allowed to drive a car at an unreasonable speed. This is strictly forbidden. It does not matter, for instance, that the official limit is 30 miles per hour. If you drive at a speed of 20 miles per hour and many people are walking in the street, this is illegal.

(quoted in Mühlhäusler et al., 2003, pp. 159 and 161)

2   Maist aw fowk that nou uises email will be acquent wi emails that's been sent athoot invite adverteesin guids an services, or willin fowk see it on tae ithers thay ken for tae cairy on some kin o steer an stour anent thair guids or services ... Thir kin o spam mails reenges fae offerin help in reddin credit tae peels that gars bits o fowk growe. Maist o thir guids an services is o coorse o a quaistenable naitur.

(Eagle, 2004, p. 103)

3   Shutyorgob

Please keep quiet

    Yegotnehyemteganti

Please leave

    Letshowaydoonthabooza

Allow me to take you for a drink

    Broonsaalroond

Drinks on me

(Douglas, 2001, p. 35)

4   Trust chi. Ry. Jaggu has safely landed at Gainsville. We heard that he landed safely at New York and had to stay there for the night as he did not have time to catch his flight to Orlando. Perhaps he must have reached his destination safely by Saturday evening (American time). He may join his duties as per schedule on 23/5/94 by the grace of God.

5   This Banaras very old city. Nobody know how old. Varanasi our very oldest city in India. Varuna plus Assi both jointed called Varanasi. The most important temple the golden temple.

(quoted in Mehrotra, 1998, p. 107)

6   Having destroyed the gang's 'iron and steel and hat factories' and condemned its crime of savagely attacking and persecuting them, our cadres are displaying renewed revolutionary spirit.

(quoted in Cheng, 1992, p. 170)

7 The ECMS **must** support the association of alternative content object renditions to a content object.

   Content object renditions are alternative digital file formats of a given content object. For example, a Microsoft Word document may own an XML document as one rendition and an Adobe PDF document as another rendition (i.e. different file formats of the same content). In another example, a bitmap image may own a JPEG file as one rendition and a GIF file as another rendition (i.e. different quality format of a given image).

Comment

1 This is a brief extract from the first (1969) translation of the Highway Code into Tok Pisin, a language variety based on English that is spoken in Papua New Guinea. Tok Pisin began life as a pidgin, a contact variety that develops between people who do not share a common language. Pidgins, at first, may be quite rudimentary, but they may develop as lingua francas, and eventually become the mother tongue of a group of speakers, in which case they are usually referred to as creoles. Tok Pisin began as a contact language in the European colonial period when people from Papua New Guinea worked as indentured labourers on European-run plantations. It is now often regarded as a creole, serving as a lingua franca within a multilingual community; it has an official orthography and a standardised variety (you will read more about pidgins and creoles in Chapter 4 Section 4.4).

   Can varieties such as Tok Pisin be referred to as English? They have taken a lot of their vocabulary from English (if you look at the extract and its standard English translation you can see connections between *draivim* and *drive*, *mailand* and *mile, yu* and *you*, etc.), but their structure is rather different. They are sometimes referred to as 'English-related', but also sometimes as 'Englishes'.

2 This example comes from an article on email spamming, written for the Scots Language Association's journal, *Lallans. Lallans* refers to the Scots language; it has sometimes been termed 'literary Scots' or 'new Scots' (Aitken, 1984, pp. 530–1). The journal is written entirely in Scots. Scots looks similar in some ways to English, although there are distinctive words (*athoot, acquent*) and spellings (*adverteesin, quaistenable, naitur*). Spelling may be intended to reflect different pronunciations, but it also has the effect of making Scots look different from English on the printed page.

   Scots, like (English) English, developed from Anglo-Saxon or Old English. It has been regarded by some as a dialect of English, by others as a separate language. The Scots Language Association has as its aim the promotion of Scots in literature, drama, the media, education and everyday usage.

3 This is an extract from a booklet entitled *Geordie English*. Geordie is a variety of British English spoken in the north-east of England. The booklet contains

Geordie words with translations into Standard English, as well as sections on grammar and pronunciation. The main readership for the booklet, however, is local Newcastle people rather than those who do not understand Geordie. While some of the entries look serious, the phrases above are clearly humorous, playing on stereotypes of a macho, beer-swilling culture.

Geordie has quite a distinctive pronunciation, but in terms of vocabulary and grammar there isn't an enormous difference today between the variety many people speak and Standard English. However, the phrases suggest – again, humorously – that Geordie is quite distinctive, almost a 'foreign language'.

4　This is an extract from a letter my friend Jayalakshmi received from her father in India. 'Jaggu' is my friend's brother, Jagadish, who left India to work in the USA. The family's first language is the south Indian language Kannada; they also speak other Indian languages.

The English in the letter should seem familiar to most readers of this book, though the phrases *join his duties* and *as per schedule* may seem unusual in this context to anyone who is unacquainted with Indian English. Some words and phrases also carry Indian cultural associations. To Jayalakshmi, *duties* has some of the connotations of the Kannada *dharma* (originally a Sanskrit term), which it is frequently used to translate. It refers here to Jaggu's new job, but also has the sense of doing a job well or to the best of one's ability. The phrase *by the grace of God* is a translation of the Kannada expression *devru dayadinda*; the expression *chi. Ry.* stands for the Sanskrit phrase *Chiranjeevi Rajeshwari* ('may he live a long and prosperous life').

Extracts 5–7 are all varieties of English intended for wider, international communication.

5　This is another example of Indian English. It comes from a commentary given by a boatman to foreign tourists in Varanasi, and is transcribed by Raja Ram Mehrotra. The speaker is multilingual and is likely to use English only in this restricted context. The English is simplified; Mehrotra argues that it is characterised by 'limited vocabulary, simplified structures, a reduction in the number of grammatical devices and shifts and manipulations in meaning' (Mehrotra, 1998, p. 142). Mehrotra is here focusing on the extent to which the text differs from a standard variety of English, but the commentary is designed for an international audience.

6　This comes from the English edition of the Chinese weekly *Beijing Review*. It appeared in 1978, shortly after the end of the cultural revolution. The *Beijing Review* is translated from Chinese into English by professional Chinese translators, with 'finishing touches' added by native English speakers. The intended audience for the review is the international community.

The review claims to follow a British model of English. It does, however, contain several expressions and idioms related to cultural and social conditions in China in the 1970s. Chin-Chuan Cheng comments: 'Iron and steel and hat factories (from the Chinese *gangtie gongchang maozi gongchang*) are where cudgels are made to beat (to criticize), and caps are fabricated to force upon someone's head (to label); hence the phrase means "wanton attack"' (Cheng, 1992, p. 170). (I feel perhaps that 'wanton attack' does not do full justice to the original!) Cheng argues that, with moves towards 'modernization' after the cultural revolution, such idioms became less common.

7　This final example is an extract from an invitation to tender for an Enterprise Content Management System (ECMS). This is a software system that would be used by an organisation to store, process and retrieve information, and the invitation is directed at potential suppliers. While the document is undoubtedly written in English it may be hard for non-specialists to follow. This is partly a question of technical terms, including acronyms such as XML and GIF, but also of words that may look familiar but that have a technical meaning in this context ('alternative content object renditions'). This is a variety of English sometimes known as a register, associated with a particular context or situation (in this case, information technology).

These extracts are indicative of some of the complexity of English: the language is highly variable and continually changing. There is a long history of academic interest in language variation and change, which has broadened out recently with increasing attention paid to the newer varieties of English spoken in many parts of the world.

Like other languages, English varies in several different ways. For instance, most of the examples above were produced as written texts. They might be rather different if spoken (if one speaker was telling another about the ECMS tender, or if Jayalakshmi's father was chatting to her on the phone). Example 5 is transcribed speech, but you may still feel that it has a certain written quality: it is a rehearsed speech which has probably been delivered with some variations on countless occasions; it would be different in a spontaneous form of speech such as an impromptu conversation. Language also varies in relation to different speakers or writers, where they come from and what social groups they belong to; and it varies for the same individual in different contexts (for instance, depending on whether the speaker perceives a context as formal or informal, and depending on the purposes for speaking in that context).

The fact that I've referred to someone speaking in different contexts is not unusual. Linguists have tended to accord priority to speech over writing: sometimes 'language' and 'spoken language' become conflated in linguistic analyses, with language users routinely referred to as 'speakers'. Empirical studies of regional and social variation in contemporary English are often based on spoken language. But linguists' relationship with spoken and written language is rather ambivalent. Authoritative grammars of English, even those that are based on spoken and written usage, tend to rely more heavily on written sources.

Linguists concerned with different regional and social varieties of English often distinguish between **accents** (varieties that differ only in terms of pronunciation) and **dialects** (varieties that differ also in terms of grammar and vocabulary). This is a distinction we observe in this book for convenience, but we should admit that it is not clear-cut. I mentioned above that the variety of English of many Geordie speakers differs from the standard mainly in terms of pronunciation – but how many non-pronunciation features (particular terms or grammatical structures) does it take before an accent becomes a dialect? I have made frequent use of the term 'language variety', which is a device for letting linguists off the hook by avoiding the need to specify whether they are talking about a language, a dialect, an accent, or indeed a register associated with a certain professional or technical field.

Language varieties are not simply linguistic phenomena. They carry important social meanings. The Geordie in *Geordie English* is sometimes humorous (though it is rather an insider joke). The magazine *Lallans* uses Scots for more serious purposes. But Scots and Geordie are used by their speakers to a wide range of effects – and in each case, social meanings will differ in different contexts. The different social meanings attached to English resurface throughout this and later chapters.

However we describe language varieties, it's worth bearing in mind that the idea of distinct varieties is itself an idealisation. It is not possible to draw neat boundaries that delimit English. There is no obvious cut-off point beyond which we can say that variability and change within English have given rise to new languages. In practice, even what counts as an identifiable, distinct variety of English (e.g. Indian English or Geordie), or what distinguishes English from another language (e.g. from Tok Pisin or Scots), is likely to be decided on social or political grounds rather than according to purely linguistic criteria.

1.3 Who speaks English?

Today, English is used by at least 750 million people, and barely half of those speak it as a mother tongue. Some estimates have put that figure closer to 1 billion. Whatever the total, English at the end of the twentieth century is more widely scattered, more widely spoken and written, than any other language has ever been. It has become *the* language of the planet, the first truly global language.

(McCrum et al., 2002, pp. 9–10)

[English is] a language – the language – on which the sun does not set, whose users never sleep.

(Quirk, 1985, p. 1)

If the diversity of forms taken by English has provoked considerable, and increasing, academic interest, so too has the diversity of its speakers (as the comments from McCrum et al. above and Figure 1.1 illustrate). Quirk's remark,

Figure 1.1 English co-exists with other languages in Tokyo.

quoted above, comes from a conference 'English in the World', held to celebrate the fiftieth anniversary of the British Council, an organisation which itself has done much to promote (British) English in different parts of the world. Moreover, several recent books about English have as their project (or part of their project) the emphasising of its 'global' spread, and its role in different cultures and as an international language. This is a complex project, not least because it is difficult to detach oneself from the values with which English is associated (Figure 1.2) and to present a dispassionate account of its spread and its use. The frequent focus on the large number of English speakers is interesting in itself: is the implication that this makes the language more powerful, or somehow better than others? And there is more than a hint of triumphalism in Quirk's assertion of the global nature of English.

Even grappling with the sheer number of people who speak English turns out to be somewhat problematical. The figures quoted in McCrum et al.'s *The Story of English* at the beginning of this section are similar to those quoted in several other sources. To that extent they are representative of current beliefs about the number of English speakers worldwide. But what is surprising about these figures is their lack of precision. How can there be such uncertainty about who does, or doesn't, speak a language?

Figure 1.2 'No worries. If it can't be said in English, it ain't worth saying at all.'

ACTIVITY 1.2

Can you think of two or three reasons why there should be discrepancies between different estimates of the number of speakers of English?

Read now 'The English language today' by David Crystal (Reading A). Crystal is a British linguist who has written a great many books and articles on various aspects of English. Here, he discusses different types of English speakers, and why it is difficult to compile reliable statistics.

Crystal draws what is a common distinction between three different types of speaker: those for whom English is a **mother tongue**; those for whom it is a **second language**; and those for whom it is a **foreign language**. Some writers make a simpler distinction between **native** (mother-tongue) and **non-native** speakers. Such distinctions have frequently been made by those concerned about teaching English to different types of learners, but distinctions may be made on different bases. In this book, Dick Leith distinguishes Englishes spoken outside the British Isles according to colonial settlement patterns (see Chapter 4, Section 4.4).

In practice, it is difficult to draw hard and fast boundaries between 'second language' and 'foreign-language' speakers, and even the 'native'/'non-native' distinction can be questioned in contexts such as India and Singapore, where some (notionally) non-native speakers become familiar with English from an early age and use the language routinely. Furthermore, many non-native (at least 'second', and perhaps 'foreign') varieties of English are now recognised as 'new Englishes' in their own right. Despite these difficulties, however, there is general agreement that English continues to spread, and the spread is most extensive among non-native speakers.

The spread of English is generally seen in positive terms. Crystal comments that English gives access to a range of media, international business, scientific and other academic communication. Braj Kachru is equally favourable in his assessment:

> ... the acquisition of English across cultures has broad promise and is not restricted to a language specialist. It is a symbol of an urge to extend oneself and one's roles beyond the confines of one's culture and language. English continues to be accepted in this role, ever since and despite the depressing colonial experience ... The language has no claims to intrinsic superiority; rather, its pre-eminent role developed due to extra linguistic factors. The importance is in what the medium conveys about technology, science, law, and (in the case of English) literature. English has now, as a consequence of its status, been associated with universalism, liberalism, secularism, and internationalism. In this sense, then, English is a symbol of concept that Indians have aptly expressed as vasudhaiva kuṭumbakam (the whole Universe is a family). True, not everyone may agree with this perception, but that there is such a positive reaction towards English cannot be denied.

> (Kachru, 1992, pp. 10–11)

Not everyone, as Kachru concedes, would accept such a positive evaluation. P.D. Tripathi has argued that the universal importance of English is: 'an ideological production, the creation of the native and non-native élite with a material and professional interest in the language, its retention and dissemination worldwide' (Tripathi, 1992, p. 3).

Tripathi questions the basis of statistics on speakers of English. He argues that in many contexts they are based on impressions rather than empirical evidence (this is conceded by Crystal in Reading A). He also suggests that they fail to take into account how the language is used: can someone who uses English for only a restricted set of activities be deemed a 'user of English'? In India, for instance, where Hindi is the official language, English has also been retained as a language for official communication. It is used for several institutional purposes and for communication between people from different states, each of which has its own state language or languages. But several Indian institutions (the education, legal and civil administration systems) have been reducing their dependence on English. And at the interstate level it is used mainly by an elite:

> To think of [English] as the language of inter-state communication (except, perhaps, at the minuscule top) is to ignore the reality of everyday life and to assume that before its advent there was no communication, and there cannot be any now without it, between one part of the country and another. The lowly worker from Bihar based in Calcutta or Bombay does not use English, which he does not know, but some local language instead, to relate with fellow workers, equally deficient in English, from other parts of the country.
>
> (Tripathi, 1992, p. 7)

The apparently straightforward question of who speaks English, then, raises complex issues to do with how English is used by its speakers in different contexts, and what social and cultural meanings are ascribed to it. I turn to some of these issues in the following section.

1.4 When, and when not, to speak English

> Consider the range of items which can be used to fill the slot in the kind of question frames a social psychologist might use: 'If he speaks English, he must be ...'. Depending on where you live, ... the answer might be 'British/American/an imperialist/an enemy/one of the oppressors/ well-educated/a civil servant/a foreigner/rich/trying to impress/in a bad mood ...'. There is a long list of possible clozes [i.e. words to insert], and not all make pleasant reading. This conference is concerned to evaluate progress in English studies, in which case we must not forget those areas where the spread of English is bad news, and where people are antagonistic towards the language, for a variety of social, economic or political reasons.
>
> (Crystal, 1985, p. 9)

He smiled. This, he knew, was his true self, a dichotomy of east and west that he had not quite yet managed to balance. Usually he found himself blending into the mainstream, blinded by the uniform colour of the multitude and submerging himself to becoming one of them. When in Asia, he saw himself as Chuan, his mother's son and when he in England, he saw Russell, his father's son.

Unfortunately, it was never that cut and dry with people like him. His English relatives insisted on calling him 'Chuan' to demonstrate they are liberals, while his Singaporean relatives took great pride in being able to pronounce 'Russell'.

In the mire of confusing personalities, he salvaged his own identity through the acceptance of others. So it was in Singapore, he spoke English with a distinctive Singlish lilt while in England, he slipped into the short clipped public school accent of the English upper class. Yet he knew he could never fool himself all the time. After a week of grilled lamb chops and peas, he hankered for a bowl of century egg porridge. Come Sunday, no matter how sumptuous the spread his Grandma Chen cooked for him, his day is not complete unless he has had roast beef and Yorkshire pudding.

(Wee Kiat, 1992, p. 196)

Precisely how, or whether, English is used, and what it means to its speakers, will vary considerably in different contexts (the quotations above give just a flavour of this – they include Crystal's comments from the British Council conference 'English in the World', and an extract from Wee Kiat's novel *Women in Men's Houses*). English may be welcomed, or resented, or rejected. It may bring considerable social and material benefits to its speakers. But its historical spread has also been at the cost of other languages (and of speakers of those languages). In many countries today, English is regulated: its use may be officially restricted by formal language policies or language planning in order to protect languages, cultures and speakers seen as being under threat.

As an illustration of this I shall look now at the use of English in three different countries: patterns of language choice in Kenya, particularly the capital, Nairobi, where English is used alongside several African languages; the problematical relationship between English and French in Quebec and Ontario in Canada; and attempts by the authorities in France to limit the influence of English.

Language choice in Kenya

Kiswahili (Swahili) and English are the two official languages of Kenya, a country where there are more than forty indigenous languages. Kenya was a British colony from the late nineteenth century and achieved independence after a bitter struggle in 1963. English might be regarded as part of the colonial legacy, but in fact its current position is rather ambiguous.

Mohamed Abdulaziz (1991, p. 392) pointed out that English is the language of civil service correspondence, of the legal system (jointly with Kiswahili), of the armed forces and police, of most of the media, and 'generally of all modern sectors of socio-economic activity, including the commercial and industrial sectors' (Figure 1.3). It is, then, a language with high status, whose use is associated with social and economic success – nevertheless, Musimbi Kanyoro suggests that it is not universally welcomed:

> Kenya's capitalistic system, whose success depends on foreign investment, creates a climate for dependence on the English language. However, its pro-English policy has not been without challenge. In Kenya it is widely felt that English should not receive special attention or be promoted over any other language, but rather it should be on an equal footing with other languages in the country. It is also sometimes heard from this or that group, 'why can't Luo or Kipsigis or Kamba or Gikuyu etc. be a national language?' or 'why can't we have several Kenyan languages promoted to national status?' The argument made is that, after all, the number of English speakers of any one of these languages equals or surpasses the number of English speakers in the country. The argument continues further that those unfamiliar with any of the regional languages would need to expend no more effort to learn any other local language than they would to learn English. On the other hand, those who prefer English to Kiswahili or indigenous languages point out that English is neutral, with no ethnic or emotional attachments and, in addition, it provides a link to the world beyond East Africa. Opponents counter that English is a language foreign to Africa and to African thought, and carries the stigma of colonialism.

(Kanyoro, 1991, p. 415)

Figure 1.3 Street signs in Nairobi, Kenya

The main way in which English is learnt is through the formal education system. During the first years of schooling the medium of instruction is 'mother tongue' or the language of the school's catchment area. Therefore, in urban centres which may draw their populations from a variety of rural areas, the language used is Kiswahili. However, English classes are sometimes begun at the point of school entry, and it is government policy that it becomes the medium of instruction in later levels in primary school. Both English and Kiswahili become compulsory subjects of study with a national system of examination (Njogu, 2005). This pattern of educational policy that follows school induction in an African language with a fairly rapid introduction of the ex-colonial language is a common one across the continent (Makoni and Meinhof, 2003, p. 2).

However, this required bilingualism can be problematical; for example, it appears to demand that teachers be extremely proficient in those two languages, neither of which may be their own or their students' 'mother tongue'. This is sometimes blamed for what is often regarded as a poor standard of results in children's formal assessments at primary level in both Kiswahili and English. In practice, teachers often seem to adopt a pragmatic approach, so that in late primary and secondary classes, where English is the language of instruction (except obviously in Kiswahili lessons) then the teachers oscillate between English and Kiswahili, and indeed a third language where it has particularly relevant salience as the mother tongue of students and teacher (Njogu, 2005). Omulando (2001, quoted in Njogu, 2005) found that, in order to communicate as clearly as possible with their students, secondary teachers would codeswitch (i.e. alternate between one language, in this case English, and another language or languages); for example, always using English for general guidance and counselling purposes. Similarly, Merritt et al. (1992, quoted in Ferguson, 2003, p. 43) found that in Kenyan primary schools, teachers used codeswitching for a variety of purposes, including to reformulate content and for specific classroom routines. (Codeswitching is further discussed in Chapter 7).

In this situation, another creative response has emerged: that of 'sheng' or 'Sheng', which arose as a mode of speaking among urban youth in Nairobi. (As we shall see, the decision on whether to start the word with a capital letter seems to vary according to the degree of regard accorded to it.) In linguistic terms, Sheng is a sociolect, a linguistic variety specific to a section of society. It contains elements of English, Kiswahili and other languages, and has been widely disparaged by powerful sectors of society as merely adolescent slang. For example, Njogu (2005) reports that the Kenyan Ministry of Education regards sheng as a contributor to poor performance in school examinations in both English and Kiswahili and recommends that it should be banned. Njogu, a professor of linguistics, argues:

> Modes of expression such as sheng important in the formation of identities and solidarities will continue to be invented and reinvented. My view has

been unequivocal: we cannot fight and ban a mode of speaking. Rather
we should perfect teaching of standard forms so that pupils can identify
the boundaries between the various forms of language use.

(Njogu, 2005, p. 3)

Some argue strongly that sheng should not merely be tolerated but
appreciated as a coherent and creative response to the conditions of
contemporary youth in Nairobi. Samper (2002b) points to the situation in
which it originated:

> The institutions of family, church, school and popular media present
> Kenyan youth with different possible identities ... The voice of the media
> comes to them in videos, movies, music, radio, and television and is heard
> mostly in English. Each of these languages represents a particular ideology
> of living in the world and young people respond through language. *Sheng*
> gives young people the wherewithal to question and challenge the
> ideologies and identities that attempt to define them. *Sheng* also signifies
> the construction of a linguistic third space between the global, represented
> by a transnational African diasporic culture, and the local, represented by
> tradition.

(Samper, 2002b)

We return to ideas about mixing language varieties with personal identity in
Chapter 7. In the meantime, it is interesting to note that Sheng does appear to
be on the increase, and is showing distinct signs of moving across to the
written mode.

Samper quotes a print advertisement for 'Trust condoms' written in Sheng:

> *Ukifreak bila socks bila shaka nodigity utatrip.*

(quoted in Samper, 2002a, p. 6)

He explains that some English words are combined with Kiswahili
morphemes – meaning-bearing elements of words – to make new hybrids.
This process Samper terms morphological hybridisation. He explains some
of the elements of the slogan:

> In *Ukifreak*, the English word 'freak' is used as if it was a Kiswahili verb
> with pronoun prefix *u-*, you, and the conditional tense marker *-ki-*.
> Similarly, utatrip is also an English verb used in standard Kiswahili verb
> construction. Here, *-ta-* is the future tense marker. *Socks* is a slang term for
> condom and points to the use of metaphor. The word *bila* is standard
> Kiswahili for 'without'.

(Samper, 2002b, p. 6)

The English translation for the slogan in its entirety is:

> If you have sex without condoms, without doubt, no lies, you will die.

Different attitudes, then, may be taken towards new sociolects, such as Sheng, just as they may be taken towards practices such as codeswitching in a classroom situation. Either may be interpreted as evidence of deficiency in a valued linguistic proficiency, in English language for example, or as evidence that in fact high-level bilingual skills are being utilised (Ferguson, 2003, p. 45)

English and French in Canada

In Canada, both English and French have official status, but the relationship between the two languages is an unequal one. Canada is predominantly English speaking, with the exception of the province of Quebec and areas along the border in New Brunswick and Ontario. Ronald Wardhaugh (1987, p. 221) calls Quebec 'A French island in an ocean of English' (see Figure 1.4).

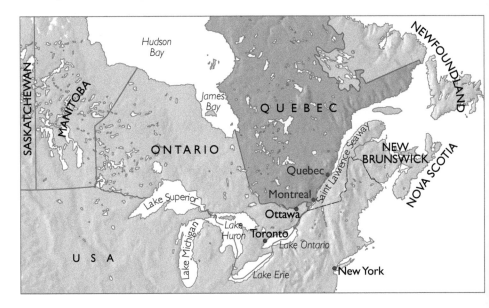

Figure 1.4   Canada: Quebec and surrounding areas

English and French in competition

The English and French competed in colonizing the northern part of North America. That competition was ended in 1759 when the English finally conquered the French in a decisive battle on the Plains of Abraham and captured the city of Quebec. Canada came into existence at that time; it was a British possession to the north of those colonies that were soon to break away from the Crown and unite to form a new country, the United States of America. Canada stayed loyal, and gradually expanded to include other British possessions in North America and to fill the prairies to the north of the United States.

Canada actually dates its origin as a virtually independent state to1867, the year of the British North America Act. This Act of the British Parliament was the last of a series of constitutional arrangements made in London to provide some kind of governing structure for this British colonial possession in North America. The 1867 Constitution established a framework for self-government, but it was actually not until 1982 that the government of Canada and the government of the United Kingdom finally 'patriated' the Canadian Constitution, i.e. gave Canada complete charge of its own constitutional affairs.

(Wardhaugh, 1987, pp. 221–2)

Wardhaugh writes that, with the establishment of Canada as a (virtually) independent state in 1867, French settlers believed they could look forward to an equal relationship with the English. Despite constitutional protection, however, English became the dominant language throughout most of Canada and French speakers found themselves confined increasingly to Quebec. Even here, French language and culture came under threat as the French birth rate fell and new immigrants chose to learn English rather than French.

The 1960s saw increasing political mobilisation of French speakers in Quebec. Successive Quebec governments introduced measures to promote the use of French in the province, and in 1976 the separatist Parti Québecquois was elected to office. In 1977 the government introduced Bill 101, the Charter of the French Language. Among other things, the Bill made French the language of the workplace and imposed tight restrictions on the right to education in English (some of these restrictions were later overturned by the Supreme Court). Outside Quebec, measures were also taken to protect French (e.g. the Official Languages Act of 1969, revised in 1988, and the inclusion of certain rights for French speakers in the constitution in 1982). Despite such measures the position of French in Canada, and even in Quebec, was by no means secure (Figure 1.5). Wardhaugh comments:

Today, Quebec must be constantly on guard if it is to remain French speaking. Regularly losing speakers to English, the province must find ways to replace these. What we see in Quebec ... is a kind of organized rear-guard action to preserve French, one which has had both successes and failures, but one from which the French themselves can seek no respite.

(Wardhaugh, 1987, p. 221)

Monica Heller has argued that the major focus of the political mobilisation of French speakers in Quebec has been the wish to gain access to economic

Figure 1.5   'Of course, it's difficult for outsiders to grasp the subtle complexities of the situation here in Québec.'

resources controlled by anglophones (English speakers) without sacrificing francophone (French-speaking) identity:

> [W]hile through the 1950s and 1960s (and even to some extent, in some places, today) francophones who wished to gain access to management positions in private enterprise had to do so through assimilation, the 1960s saw the beginnings of a collective mobilisation designed primarily to achieve that access for the group as a whole, and used both a sense of collective identity and evidence of collective oppression to achieve that mobilisation.

(Heller, 1992, p. 128)

In this context, the use of either English or French may be an overtly political act. Heller discusses the language choices of people who were somehow involved in the process of mobilisation – whether as supporters or opponents. She cites the case of a man who arrived at the provincial government office in Montreal to take a French language test – under the provisions of Bill 101, members of certain professions were obliged to take this test in order to continue in their profession. (In the following account, French speech is in italics and an English translation is given in the right-hand column.)

Man	Could you tell me where the French test is?	
Receptionist	*Pardon?*	Pardon?

Man	Could you tell me where the French test is?	
Receptionist	*En français?*	In French?
Man	I have the right to be addressed in English by the government of Quebec according to Bill 101	
Receptionist	[to a third person] *Qu'est-ce qu'il dit?*	What's he saying?

(adapted from Heller, 1992, p. 133)

In contrast, French speakers in Quebec in the 1970s attempted to challenge the dominance of English by speaking French where English might be expected. Heller reports that similar strategies were used later by French speakers in Ontario. In the case below she quotes, for example, Louise – a francophone woman living in Ontario, who was interviewed in 1989. This is a verbatim transcript and, like many research transcripts, it is not punctuated. To anyone not used to seeing transcribed speech it may look a little odd – and it takes a while to read! (Note that the French text on the left is the original interview text, with Heller's English translation on the right. Square brackets [ ] indicate brief responses from the interviewer.)

dans les magasins ... je fais ma naïve	in stores ... I act naive
jusqu'au dernier degré 'je ne sais pas	to the utmost 'I don't speak
l'anglais moi' j'ai pour dire à Orléans à	English' to say that in Orleans
Ottawa tu te fais servir en français [oui	in Ottawa you can be served in
c'est vrai] point final [tu peux] c'est moi	French [yes it's true] full stop [you can] it's me
qui perds du temps je veux dire je perds	who's wasting time I mean I waste
énormément de temps parce que je la il	enormous amounts of time because I
faut qu'ils aillent me chercher quelqu'un	then they have to find me someone
que la je fais ma naïve je vais en tout cas	I act naive I'll anyway
si cela ne fait pas je vais protester 'je veux	if that doesn't work I'll protest 'I want
me faire servir en français' l'épicerie ici	to be served in French' the grocery here
e c'est supposé être bilingue tu sais puis	e is supposed to be bilingual you know and
quelquefois il y en a qui ne le sont pas puis	sometimes there are some who are not and
ils sont insultés parce que la je me rends	they're insulted because I then I go
jusqu'à la direction je leur dis 'ça me	all the way to the management I tell them 'I need

prend quelqu'un bilingue' pour {pause} ils
sont supposés [mhum] d'avoir quelqu'un
là toujours une qui parle tu sais je perds
énormément de temps ...

someone who's bilingual' to {pause} they're
supposed [mhum] to have someone there
at all times who speaks you know I waste
an enormous amount of time ...

(quoted in Heller, 1992, p. 131)

It is important to point out that in both these cases the speakers could have
used the other language. The anglophone man was presumably competent in
French since he had come to take a French proficiency test. He was using
English as a language of resistance in a context in which the rights of French
speakers were being asserted. The French speaker, Louise, was also
competent in English – she had taught both French and English. But she was
living in Ottawa, on the border with Quebec, where francophone mobilisation
had come to have an effect and speaking French could be, in Heller's words,
'a major key to upward social mobility'. Heller comments: 'For Louise, and
others like her with whom we spoke, French has become valuable, and the
source of that value has to do with the creation of resources which
francophones exclusively control. It is in her interests to make sure the
boundary is maintained' (Heller, 1992, pp. 131–2).

In other contexts, language may be used in a less antagonistic way – for
instance, bilingual speakers may switch between English and French to level
the boundary between anglophones and francophones.

Franglais in France

France is rather different from both Canada and Kenya, in that English has no
official status there. English is taught as a foreign language in French schools,
but it is intended mainly for international communication. Furthermore French
itself, like English, serves as an international language, spread to various parts
of the world by conquest, colonisation, and as a language of culture and of
diplomacy. This international role of French is in decline, under pressure both
from local languages and from English. And within France itself there are fears
of increasing linguistic and cultural domination – of 'contamination' by Anglo-
American influences (Figure 1.6).

Figure 1.6 Examples of franglais in Paris, Grenoble and Marseille

ACTIVITY 1.3

Now work through 'Franglais', by Marie-Noëlle Lamy (Reading B), noting the points the author makes about the nature of English borrowings in French, attitudes towards English, and official moves by the French state to restrict the use of English and protect French.

English is now used in a range of cultural contexts internationally. Within each of these it will acquire social meanings related to the speakers, contexts and purposes with which it becomes associated. In many contexts (e.g. Kenya and France) there exists a fear of Anglo-American cultural domination, but it cannot be assumed that English always has 'US' or even 'Western' associations, or in fact any one set of unambiguous associations. For many people, English is seen as a language of opportunity, but the examples discussed in this section also suggest that the position of English is often problematical and responses to the language are ambivalent.

1.5 Responding to diversity

No one should underestimate the problem of teaching English in such countries as India and Nigeria, where the English of the teachers themselves inevitably bears the stamp of locally acquired deviation from the standard language ('You are knowing my father, isn't it?').

(Quirk, 1990, p. 8)

We cannot write like the English. We should not. We can write only as Indians.

(Raja Rao, quoted in Mehrotra, 1998, p. 16)

We must note that English does not necessarily mean British English or American English. There are a number of standard Englishes, for there are several English-speaking countries in each of which there is a standard English peculiar to that country.

(Verma, 1982, p. 175)

The quotation above from Randolph Quirk comes from a well-known article in the journal *English Today* (it was originally presented as a lecture in 1988). Quirk was concerned about the view, expressed by a number of people including the Indian scholar S.K. Verma, that 'non-native' varieties of English could be seen as valid in their own terms, and could serve as a model for teaching English. Quirk's view, in contrast, was that non-native speakers needed to maintain contact with standardised, native speaker norms. Non-native varieties were 'deviations' from such norms. Furthermore, Quirk argued, learners of English needed a native standard variety to communicate internationally, to increase their social and geographical mobility and further their career prospects.

Few linguists now would see the varieties of English spoken in different parts of the world as deviations. For instance, verb forms such as *you are knowing* and the invariant tag question *isn't it* are used systematically in Indian English – they are not simply errors, or deviations from the norms of another variety. It is still the case, however, that non-native varieties tend to be described in relation to British or American English, which at least by implication accords them a secondary status. In a discussion of Indian English, R.S. Gupta (2001) recognises that such comparisons are probably inevitable, but argues nevertheless that there is a pragmatic need to accept the existence of Standard Indian English:

> We cannot escape the fact that it is impractical, unrealistic, and even futile to talk of British or American norms or models in such a vast and diverse country where millions of people learn, use and interact in English. ... What we therefore need to do is to accept, recognise and describe adequately all the features of [Standard Indian English] so that a pan-Indian 'norm' can be followed, and to which no 'stigma' is attached.

> (Gupta, 2001, p. 159)

Gupta's argument is based on the fact that Indian speakers of English do not necessarily learn the language to communicate with native English speakers – English is widely used as a language of communication within India (as in the case of Kenya, above). The situation is complex, however: Gupta notes that English is used to communicate with others from the same region; it is also used to communicate more widely with speakers from different parts of the country; and, for some speakers, it is used for international communication – in this case, with other non-native speakers as well as with native speakers. Different varieties of English (from more regional to more international) are often associated with these different speaking contexts. 'Standard Indian English' tends to be used for an educated variety of English that is seen as appropriate for communication at national level (and perhaps also internationally) – hence Gupta's appeal to a 'pan-Indian norm'. As in other contexts, the idea of Standard Indian English (or of regional varieties such as Panjabi English or Tamil English) is an idealisation – the boundaries between such varieties are distinctly fuzzy.

The adoption of Standard Indian English as a norm is a way of marking the distinctiveness, and the validity, of Indian English. But, as the term 'Standard' suggests, it is also an attempt to produce some degree of homogeneity within the Indian context – the appeal is to a single pan-Indian norm over and above different regional varieties.

The establishment of different national norms may suggest that English is in danger of fragmenting – of splitting into quite distinct varieties that will come to be seen as different languages. This is one of the fears that sometimes lie behind the desire for a single, international standardised English. In a discussion of the future of English, however, Crystal (2003) suggests that there is likely to be a brake on continuing diversification:

> Today, we live in the proverbial global village, where we have immediate access to other languages and varieties of English in ways that have come to be available but recently; and this is having a strong centripetal [unifying] effect. With a whole range of fresh auditory models becoming routinely available, chiefly through satellite television, it is easy to see how any New English could move in different directions at the same time. The pull imposed by the need for identity, which has been making New

Englishes increasingly dissimilar from British English, could be balanced by a pull imposed by the need for intelligibility, on a world scale, which will make them increasingly similar, through the continued use of Standard English.

(Crystal, 2003, p. 178)

Furthermore, Crystal argues, there is no evidence that communities of speakers have the kind of strong, common social and political motivation, or the social and economic power, that would be needed to have new varieties of English officially recognised as distinct languages.

Views about the validity of non-native Englishes, and the values attached to these, are central to any discussion of the development of English and its contemporary position in the world; they resurface in later chapters in this book, and in fact in other books in the series.

1.6 Conclusion

In this chapter I have focused on diversity within the English language: formal differences among varieties of English; differences among speakers; different patterns of use, in different contexts; and different (often ambivalent) social meanings with which the language has been associated.

Linguists tend to rely on certain categories as a basis for discussing diversity: they talk about 'British English', 'Indian English' and 'Standard English' (or 'Englishes'). Such categories are useful as a starting point for linguistic description and analysis, but I have suggested that they are idealisations. It is difficult to draw definitive boundaries, according to linguistic criteria, around different varieties of English. (There are further discussions and examples of this point in later chapters.) In fact, diversity cannot be considered purely in linguistic terms: people may desire boundaries between varieties, for social and political considerations are of crucial importance in establishing what counts as distinct varieties of English.

The spread of English to different parts of the world and its use as an 'international' language have provoked considerable debate: the language may be seen as beneficial, purely instrumental, or a threat. I mentioned that English is regulated in several countries in order to protect other languages and cultures. It has also proved difficult for many linguists to write dispassionately about diversity and change. I have tried to give a flavour of different ideological positions taken by those who study and write about English.

READING A: The English language today

David Crystal
(David Crystal is Honorary Professor of Linguistics at the University of Wales,
Bangor, and editor of the Cambridge Encyclopedia of the English Language.)

Source: Crystal, D. (2002) *The English Language* (2nd edn), London, Penguin,
pp. 1–10.

In the glorious reign of Queen Elizabeth (the first, that is, from 1558 to 1603),
the number of English speakers in the world is thought to have been between
five and seven million. At the beginning of the reign of the second Queen
Elizabeth, in 1952, the figure had increased almost fifty fold: 250 million, it was
said, spoke English as a mother tongue, and a further 100 million or so had
learned it as a foreign language.

Fifty years on, the figures continue to creep up. The most recent estimates tell
us that mother-tongue speakers are now over 400 million. But this total is far
exceeded by the numbers of people who use English as a second or foreign
language – at least a further 500 million, according to the most conservative of
estimates, and over a billion, according to radical ones. 'Creep', perhaps, is not
quite the right word, when such statistics are introduced.

What accounts for the scale of these increases? The size of the mother-tongue
total is easy to explain. It's the Americans. The estimated population of the
USA was 284 million in 2001, of whom about 240 million spoke English as a
mother tongue. The British, Irish, Australians, New Zealanders, Canadians, and
South Africans make up most of the others – but even combined they are only
some 115 million. There's no doubt where the majority influence is. However,
these figures are growing relatively slowly at present – at an average rate of
about one per cent per annum. This is not where the drama lies.

A much more intriguing question is to ask what is happening to English in
countries where people *don't* use it as a mother tongue. A highly complicated
question, as it turns out. Finding out about the number of foreigners using
English isn't easy, and that is why there is so much variation among the
estimates. There are hardly any official figures. No one knows how many
foreign people have learned English to a reasonable standard of fluency – or
to any standard at all, for that matter. There are a few statistics available – from
the examination boards, for example – but these are only the tip of a very
large iceberg.

English as a 'second' language

The iceberg is really in two parts, reflecting two kinds of language learning situation. The first part relates to those countries where English has some kind of special status – in particular, where it has been chosen as an 'official' language. This is the case in Ghana and Nigeria, for example, where the governments have settled on English as the main language to carry on the affairs of government, education, commerce, the media, and the legal system. In such cases, people have to learn English if they want to get on in life. They have their mother tongue to begin with – one or other of the local languages – and they start learning English, in school or in the street, at an early age. For them, in due course, English will become a language to fall back on, when their mother tongue proves to be inadequate for communication – talking to people from a different tribal background, for example, or to people from outside the country. For them, English becomes their 'second' language.

Why do these countries not select a local language for official use? The problem is how to choose between the many indigenous languages, each of which represents an ethnic background to which the adherents are fiercely loyal. In Nigeria, for example, they would have to choose between Hausa, Yoruba, Ibo, Fulani, and other languages belonging to different ethnic groups. The number of speakers won't decide the matter – there are almost as many first language speakers of Yoruba as there are of Hausa, for instance. And even if one language did have a clear majority, its selection would be opposed by the combined weight of the other speakers, who would otherwise find themselves seriously disadvantaged, socially and educationally. Inter-tribal tension, leading to unrest and violence, would be a likely consequence. By giving official status to an outside language, such as English, all internal languages are placed on the same footing. Everyone is now equally disadvantaged. It is a complex decision to implement, but at least it is fair.

To talk of 'disadvantaged', though, is a little misleading. From another point of view, the population is now considerably 'advantaged', in that they thereby come to have access to a world of science, technology, and commerce which would otherwise not easily be available to them.

But why English? In Ghana, Nigeria, and many other countries, the choice is motivated by the weight of historical tradition from the British colonial era. A similar pattern of development can be observed in countries which were influenced by other cultures, such as the French, Spanish, Portuguese, or Dutch. French, for example, is the official language in Chad; Portuguese in Angola. But English is an official or semi-official language, or has informal special status, in over seventy countries of the world – a total which far exceeds the range of these other languages.

Does this mean that we can obtain an estimate of the world's second-language English speakers simply by adding up the populations of all the countries involved? Unfortunately, it isn't so easy. Most of these countries are in underdeveloped parts of the world, where educational opportunities are limited. The country may espouse English officially, but only a fraction of the population may be given an opportunity to learn it. The most dramatic example of this gap between theory and practice is India.

In 2001, the population of India was estimated to be well over 1,000 million. English is an official language here, alongside Hindi. Several other languages have special status in their own regions, but English is the language of the legal system; it is a major language in Parliament, and it is a preferred language in the universities and in the all-India competitive exams for senior posts in such fields as the civil service and engineering. Some 3,000 English newspapers are published throughout the country. There is thus great reason to learn to use the language well. Estimates of English awareness in the general population are difficult to make, but an *India Today* survey in 2000 concluded that perhaps a third of the population (well over 300 million) had some competence in the language. And even if we use a very high level of educated fluency, the figures would still be between 5 and 10 per cent (50–100 million), which suggests that English language use in India is now well in excess of the English-speaking population of Britain.

When all the estimates for second-language use around the world are added up, we reach a figure of around 400 million speakers – about as many as the total of mother-tongue users. But we have to remember that most of these countries are in parts of the world (Africa, South Asia) where the population increase is three or four times as great as that found in mother-tongue countries. If present trends continue, within a generation mother-tongue English use will have been left far behind.

English as a 'foreign' language

The second part of the language-learning iceberg relates to people who live in countries where English has no official status, but where it is learned as a foreign language in schools, institutes of higher education, and through the use of a wide range of 'self-help' materials. There are only hints as to what the numbers involved might be. Even in the statistically aware countries of Western Europe, there are no reliable figures available for the number of people who are learning English as a foreign language – or any other language, for that matter. In a continent such as South America, the total is pure guesswork.

Totals cited in the 1990s ranged from 300–400 million to over a billion, the latter (in a British Council estimate) based largely on the figures available from English-language examining boards, estimates of listeners to English-language radio programmes, sales of English-language newspapers, and the like. The figures are vague because it is notoriously difficult to decide the point at which an English learner has learned 'enough' English to be counted as a reasonably fluent speaker. Also, the published statistics are unable to keep up with the extraordinary growth in learning English in many countries. In particular, it is difficult to obtain a precise notion about what is currently happening in the country where data about anything have traditionally been very hard to come by: China.

In China, there has been an explosion of interest in the English language in recent years. One visitor returned to China in 1979, after an absence of twenty years, and wrote: 'in 1959, everyone was carrying a book of the thoughts of Chairman Mao; today, everyone is carrying a book of elementary English'. In 1983, it is thought, around 100 million people watched the BBC television series designed to teach the language, *Follow Me*. Considerable publicity was given in the Western media to the sight of groups of Chinese practising English-language exercises after work, or queuing to try out their English on a passing tourist. The presenter of *Follow Me*, Kathy Flower, became a national celebrity, recognized everywhere. And the interest continues, with new series of programmes being designed to meet the needs of scientific and business users. What level of fluency is being achieved by this massive influx of learners is unknown. But if only a fraction of China's population is successful, this alone will be enough to make a significant impact on the total for world foreign-language use.

And why shouldn't they be successful, in China, Japan, Brazil, Poland, Egypt, and elsewhere? There is enormous motivation, given the way that English has become the dominant language of world communication. Textbooks on English these days regularly rehearse the litany of its achievements. It is the main language of the world's books, newspapers, and advertising. It is the official international language of airports and air traffic control. It is the chief maritime language. It is the language of international business and academic conferences, of diplomacy, of sport. Over two-thirds of the world's scientists write in English. Three-quarters of the world's mail is written in English. Eighty per cent of all the information stored in the electronic retrieval systems of the world is stored in English. And, at a local level, examples of the same theme can be found everywhere. A well-known Japanese company, wishing to negotiate with its Arabic customers, arranges all its meetings in English. A Colombian doctor reports that he spends almost as much time improving his English as practising medicine. A Copenhagen university student comments: 'Nearly everyone in Denmark speaks English; if we didn't, there wouldn't be anyone to talk to.'

Statistics of this kind are truly impressive, and could continue for several paragraphs. They make the point that it is not the number of mother-tongue speakers which makes a language important in the eyes of the world (that crown is carried by Chinese), but the extent to which a language is found useful outside its original setting. In the course of history, other languages have achieved widespread use throughout educated society. During the Middle Ages, Latin remained undisputed as the European language of learning. In the eighteenth century, much of this prestige passed to French.

Today, it is the turn of English. It is a development which could be reversed only by a massive change in the economic fortunes of America, and in the overall balance of world power.

READING B: Franglais

Marie-Noëlle Lamy
(Marie-Noëlle Lamy is Professor of Distance Language Learning at The Open University.)

Specially commissioned for Swann (1996, pp. 32–6). (Revised by the original author.)

Introduction

'Waouh! Super, ton Walkman CD!' shouts a young character in a French educational cartoon. The cartoon is produced by the local authorities in the French city of Nantes for distribution to teenagers on deprived estates in the area. Its aim is to raise teenagers' awareness of the dangers of receiving stolen goods. To achieve this, it features the story of two young men (one a cunning seller and one an unwitting receiver who gets arrested by the police) drawn and told in such a way as to make its young readers identify with the victim character. As seems clear from the quotation above, using vocabulary and syntax borrowed from English is felt to be a good way of reaching out to the young.

The fashion for English words, or for franglais, which is a mixture of English and French, is not new to the French. They have been borrowing from English in this way for at least two centuries, but there are fears among those who want to protect French from Anglo-American influences that the trend is accelerating beyond control. In 1964 a French academic called René Etiemble published the results of the check-up he had carried out on the French language in respect of its 'contamination' by English: his book *Parlez-vous franglais?* (Etiemble, 1964) was a serious linguistic analysis, but it was widely read and Etiemble became a household name. Since the 1960s, many have battled against the trend, most recently by drawing on the French tradition of linguistic interventionism and by using the power of the French state.

Borrowing from English

What is borrowing?

One definition of borrowing is when 'language A uses and ends up absorbing a linguistic item or feature which was part of language B, and which language A did not have. The linguistic items or features themselves are called "borrowings"' (Dubois et al., 1973, p. 188).

At its most noticeable, a borrowing is a word or a phrase that 'feels' to you as though it is foreign. This may be a matter of it sounding or looking different, as when English speakers use French phrases such as *de rigueur* or *haute couture*. Borrowings may also express a familiar meaning in an unfamiliar way: if, as a French speaker talking in English about corruption, I say 'the fish rots from the head', my remark will be recognised as conveying the same idea as 'the rot starts at the top', but it will sound 'un-English'.

However, borrowings only 'feel' foreign if they have not had time to become integrated into the host language. The English language is full of borrowings from Latin (*mansion*, *cart*, *street*), or Danish (place names ending in *-by* or *-thwaite*) (Crystal, 1988). But they have been part of the English language for so long that no one would now point to them as being foreign.

Types of borrowing

There are many degrees of integration of English borrowings into French. At the least integrated end of the scale, words are used with their original pronunciation (or as close to it as speakers of French can manage), and also with their original meaning and spelling. For example, *un scoop, un squat, un one-man show*.

The highest degree of integration is when the borrowed word loses its spelling and its pronunciation. This can only happen over time. It is the case with French words such as *une redingote* (from *riding coat*) or *un boulingrin* (from *bowling green*). The French language needs to invent a gender for these guests that come to it from languages that are not gender based, and this it does in ways which are not always predictable. In the examples above, the ending of each word is derived from imitating the original pronunciation and this provides a pretext for assigning gender: French words ending in *-ote* are often feminine, while words ending in *-in* are masculine. The time taken for complete integration is getting shorter: for example a mere decade has ensured that words like *le Ouèbe* ('Web') and *un mél* ('email') are recognised by all computer-savvy French people, and used alongside their original English versions.

Between these two extremes, there are different ways in which words or phrases can become integrated. Borrowings may retain their spelling (and aspects of their meaning) while the pronunciation is totally gallicised: *une interview* is never pronounced in any other way than (in an approximate rendering) *interviou*, and a *rush* (a stampede for some new film or product) is spelt *un rush* but pronounced something like *reuche*. Sometimes whole phrases and clauses are translated into French: *a blue-stocking* came into French as *un bas-bleu* at the beginning of the nineteenth century; *ce n'est pas ma tasse de thé* ('it's not my cup of tea') was once felt to be an affectation used only by anglophiles. But now it trips off the tongue, at least in younger social groups.

English borrowings are often abbreviated in French, making them easier to pronounce; *un self* is 'a self-service restaurant', *un fast-food* is 'a fast food restaurant' and *le hard* is 'hard-core pornography' (so *un film hard* is not 'a film that's difficult to understand'!). The meanings of such borrowings may also become specialised: *un clip* is not an extract from any video but 'a music video', while *un kit* is not any object sold in parts, to be assembled by the buyer after purchase, but 'a piece of furniture' bought in kit form.

Sometimes the French language adds a new sense to the meaning of one of its own native words, under the influence of a similar word that exists in English. For example, *réaliser*: the French meaning of the word was 'to make real'; at the end of the nineteenth century, but under the influence of the English verb *to realise*, the French *réaliser* acquired the meaning 'to understand'.

English borrowings may bear only a trace of their origins. Thus *un smoking*, a word universally accepted by French speakers, is 'a dinner jacket'. The noun *le flip* refers to a (long-term or transitory) feeling of depression, and its associated verb *flipper* means 'to feel depressed'.

In the case of *flipper* a new verb has been created and integrated into the French verb system. Similarly, the verb *to stress* has found a home within the regular 'first conjugation' of French verbs, yielding everyday phrases such as *je stresse complètement* ('I'm feeling really stressed') and *j'ai trouvé ça vraiment stressant* ('I found that really stressful').

Finally, fake English words are often adopted by large numbers of French speakers, perhaps in the belief that they really are English, or perhaps because they are perceived to fill a gap in the vocabulary, for example, un *rugbyman* and un *tennisman* (with its feminine *une tenniswoman*). *Le footing* means 'jogging' and is now part of the everyday language of everyone. The borrowed form may be a genuine English word, but once imported into French, its grammatical function may change: *parking* becomes *un parking* ('a car park') and *lifting* becomes *un lifting* ('a facelift').

The English language as intrusive neighbour

The dictionary definition I mentioned above (Dubois et al., 1973) makes a clear link between attitudes to borrowing and economic and political power, by saying that borrowing 'is necessarily linked to the prestige enjoyed by a language or the people who speak it or, conversely, to the contempt in which language or people are held'. The borrowing of English words and expressions has to be seen alongside the systematic encroachment of English into parts of French life and culture – a development which may be responded to with enthusiasm, resigned acceptance or outright hositility.

English may be seen as fashionable, particularly by young French people who wish to identify with the prestigious dynamic Anglo-American culture conveyed to them through TV, the Web, pop music and films.

Other groups use English for more utilitarian reasons. For instance, 20,000 members of the staff of IBM France use English as the language of work (*Le Monde*, 1992). International scientific congresses held in France often have to take place in English and budgets aren't sufficient to provide interpreting into French. The Institut Pasteur itself has had to change the title of its *Annales de l'Institut Pasteur* to *Research in Macrobiology, Immunology and Virology and to* publish its articles in English (*Le Monde*, 1990a). There is clearly a feeling among leaders in French industry and research that familiarity with English is a key to staying in the race for world markets. The feeling is shared in other areas, such as the cinema, where producers know that films made in French have little chance of succeeding with Anglo-American audiences, hence the demand made on French actors to use English in French-made productions shot on location in France (*Le Monde*, 1990b).

Among those who fight against the encroachment of English are people who can be described as 'purists', linguistic protectionists who argue for the 'purity of the French language on aesthetic or cultural grounds. One may sympathise with them, or one may feel that there is no such thing as a pure form of French (or of any other language) and dismiss their arguments as unrealistic. However, contemporary France presents us with examples giving purists a sound economic basis for their concerns: French and English announcements on national French flights; French and English displays on cash dispenser screens in areas of France unlikely to be visited by tourists; French and English messages on the telephone answering machines of national service industries; French and English slogans on French railway tickets; job advertisements for posts in France, aimed at French nationals, published in *Le Monde* – in English! A French Minister for Culture has pleaded for a more energetic response on the part of France to the dominance of English both in the world and within the European Union. 'Japan', he said, 'is developing huge research programmes to make sure that, in a world of machine communication, English doesn't eliminate Japanese'. Similarly, 'we, as members of the European Union, must resist the blandishments of arguments promoting a single vehicular language, which would eventually demote all of our languages except one to the rank of a local dialect' (*Le Monde*, 1994).

The English language and the French state

There is a French tradition of state intervention in matters of language. In the sixteenth century, the Ordonnance de Villers-Cotterêts made it compulsory to use French in political and legal documents and thereby established the dominance of the French language over other languages spoken within the Kingdom of France, such as Occitan or Provençal. The creation of the Académie Française in 1635 answered a political need for a monarchy seeking to strengthen its control over a linguistically and religiously diverse country. The Académie's role in modern times is less directly felt, although its prestige is still great. The modern French state started legislating in 1975: the Bas-Lauriol bill laid out a number of prescriptions for controlling borrowings from English, but it was never properly implemented.

In 1994, a major step was taken, known as the 'loi Toubon'. It sought not so much to take up arms against the English language, but to protect French consumers and workers by tackling the problem in the following ways: consumer goods must not be sold without a set of instructions in French; all-English advertisements must not be shown in French cinemas; English job advertisements must not be published in the French press; bilingual advertisements and signs must not display the French part of their message in characters smaller than those in the English part. Documents setting out employee obligations (for example, health and safety or grievance procedures) must be available in French, as must any piece of software that may be necessary for the discharge of the employee's duties, even if the employer is a foreign company. The law didn't touch airlines or companies trading outside France. Nor did it attempt to interfere with the promotion, in English on French territory, of prestige French products like perfumes. Finally, an early amendment inhibited the law from making it compulsory for all bilingual signs to include a third (EU or regional) language. Unlike its 1975 predecessor, the Toubon law had teeth: breaches could be referred by individuals through associations, such as the official pressure group the Commissariat général de la langue française, direct to the police.

However, in this instance, as in many others in the past, resistance to linguistic authoritarianism has been robust. An article in the economic and financial daily *La Tribune* (2005) observed that 'ten years have passed since the implementation of [the Toubon law] and it has been deemed unsatisfactory'. Not only have prosecutions under the Toubon law been very rare, but the law has been unable to cope with the arrival of the internet. As lawyer Thibaut Verbiest asks in an article in *Le Journal du Net* (2005), how can the Toubon law be applied to internet sites created in languages other than French, that may be needed for the discharge of someone's duties? The answer to his question is likely to be ... more of the same, as in March 2005 Jacques Chirac promised a set of measures designed to reinforce the Toubon law (*La Tribune*, 2005).

Rather than turning to the legislative approach, it may be better to look to the advisory approach. Perhaps the most effective aspect of the French state's action has been the creation of the Commissariat, which publishes (and regularly updates) a *Dictionnaire des Néologismes Officiels* (Direction des Journaux Officiels, 1988). Although the dictionary is highly prescriptive in its prohibition against borrowings, it is also constructive in that it offers a wealth of French coinages as alternatives. Some seem doomed in the face of entrenched speech habits (for instance *un bouteur* is unlikely to replace the universally accepted *un bulldozer*), but others are already established (e.g. *un baladeur* instead of *un Walkman*). Some have come from Quebec, where the linguistic struggle against the giant US neighbour is a perpetual preoccupation: for example *un courriel* instead of *un email*, or *un bavardoir* instead of *a chat room* (on your computer screen). The successful coinages are those that have been debated, joked about and generally given much planned or unplanned media exposure. As a result, they have come to sound quite natural, no different from words that have evolved 'organically'. The social status of speakers with access to the media has militated against borrowing in the same way as the influence of a prestigious culture militated in its favour in the first instance. The sociolinguistic mechanism can work both ways, even though its influence is considered too slow and too limited by governments struggling to protect French linguistic sovereignty from a dominant foreign economic and cultural power.

References for this reading

Crystal, D. (1988) *The English Language*, Harmondsworth, Penguin.

Direction des Journaux Officiels (1988) *Dictionnaire des Néologismes Officiels* (5th edn), no. 1468, Paris, Direction des Journaux Officiels.

Dubois, J., Giacomo, M., Suespin, L, Marcellesi, C., Marcellesi, J.-B. and Mével, J.-P. (1973) *Dictionnaire de Linguistique*, Paris, Librairie Larousse.

Etiemble, R. (1964) *Parlez-vous Franglais?* Paris, Gallimard.

La Tribune (2005) Paris, 18 April.

Le Journal du Net (2005) 13 June, http://www.journaldunet.com/juridique/juridique040518.shtml (Accessed 27 June 2005).

Le Monde (1990a) Paris, 12 January.

Le Monde (1990b) Paris, 4 August.

Le Monde (1992) Paris, 10 December.

Le Monde (1994) Paris, 25 February.

The origins of English

Dick Leith; revised and updated with substantial new material by Liz Jackson

2.1 Introduction

Chapter 1 showed how the term 'English language' embraces a rich diversity of linguistic forms used in different places and contexts and by different people. This chapter and the next two examine the historical dimensions of such diversity. Where did the English language come from? What have been the major influences that have caused the language to develop into its modern forms?

In this chapter we examine the history of the English language in its first thousand years of existence – from its original appearance in England in the fifth century AD, following the Anglo-Saxon invasions, to the introduction of printing in the fifteenth century. We see how English has changed over the years and how it has been influenced by other languages spoken by later settlers; that is, the Scandinavian languages spoken by Viking invaders who settled in England between the eighth and eleventh centuries, and the French of the eleventh-century Norman invaders. Various other languages have affected the development of English at different times, in particular Latin, which was used for many centuries by intellectuals and the church, so it's important to trace the history of **contact** between English and other languages.

An important issue in any historical description concerns the evidence that is available to the historian and how that evidence is interpreted. Telling any history is like telling a story which both describes events and gives them a particular interpretation. When studying written sources it is important to ask certain questions. Who is telling this story? Whose perspective does it represent? The traditional view of the early history of English was based on evidence drawn wholly from such sources and the growing evidence from archaeology has been interpreted to fit that view. However, some archaeologists are now offering a different interpretation and genetic studies are making another sort of evidence available. We shall be looking at what these different methods of enquiry can tell us about the history of English.

This chapter thus has two main functions. It describes what is known about the English language in its early stages of development; and it looks at how evidence can be drawn upon to tell particular narratives about the history of English.

2.2 The linguistic background to the emergence of English

When the Romans first invaded Britain in the first century BC it was inhabited by various Celtic-speaking peoples for whom inclusion in the Roman Empire was to provide relative stability and economic growth for more than three centuries. During this time (AD 43–410), Latin was the official language – the language of government and commerce – but Celtic undoubtedly remained the vernacular. Lindsay Allason-Jones suggests:

> By the end of the first century AD the increasingly cosmopolitan flavour of the urban population will have resulted in many languages being heard in Britain with the consequence that a knowledge of Latin would have been essential for efficient communication between people who could have originated as far afield as Scotland, Africa or Turkey. Native Britons will have continued to speak Celtic at home but the increasing number of mixed marriages will have added to the number of families speaking Latin.

> (Allason-Jones, 1989, p. 174)

By the late fourth century the Roman Empire was increasingly under attack and the Romans withdrew their forces from the further reaches of the empire. In AD 410, when the emperor sent word to the British towns that they should take measures for 'their own defence', it seems that the Roman garrisons had already departed. The bilingual Romano-British communities which remained came increasingly under attack from across the North Sea (see Figure 2.1). The newcomers, who began by raiding and who later settled in southern and eastern Britain, spoke a variety of Germanic dialects.

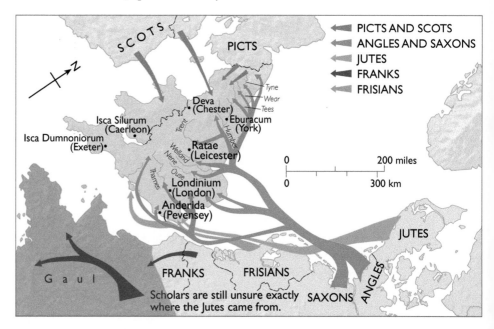

Figure 2.1   Approximation of sources of raiding and settlement in England in the fifth century

It was among this confusion of peoples, origins and languages that the English language first appeared in the fifth century AD. Britain then entered a period from which few documentary records survive. When records appear 200 or so years later, in the form of inscriptions and manuscripts, they indicate that an identifiable language variety had evolved, very similar to Germanic languages such as Old Frisian and with internal dialectal variation between the north and south of England. This language is now called Old English (or Anglo-Saxon) and the people who spoke it are usually referred to as Anglo-Saxons. We will now take a closer look at Old English and its history.

Latin influence on the vocabulary of Old English

There were three 'strands' of influence.

On the continent (before c.450)

Before the Anglo-Saxons migrated to Britain the Germanic tribes were already in contact with Latin, as they had long lived on the borders of the Roman Empire. Indeed, many individuals (e.g. mercenaries and slaves) actually lived within its borders. Several hundred Latin words were borrowed at this time and many of them were brought to Britain by the Anglo-Saxons. Examples are:

> *kettle, kitchen, cheese, butter, plum, pepper, wine, flask, copper, wall, street, mile, cat, bishop, church.*

After arriving in Britain (after c.450)

When the Anglo-Saxons arrived in Britain they found a population familiar with Latin and Roman culture. Some English words of Latin origin date from this time. Examples are:

> *port, tower, mount, -chester* (in place names such as *Chester, Manchester, Lancaster, Leicester*).

As a result of conversion to Christianity (after c.600)

In 597 Pope Gregory sent a mission headed by St Augustine to convert the pagan Anglo-Saxon kingdoms to Christianity. This goal was achieved during the following century and many Latin words were adopted at this time, some relating to the church or to the acquisition of Latin literacy and some to more domestic concerns. Examples are:

> *anthem, candle, relic, shrine, priest, school, verse, sock, cap, silk, lobster, oyster, pear, lily, plant.*

2.3 The early Old English period: problems of interpretation

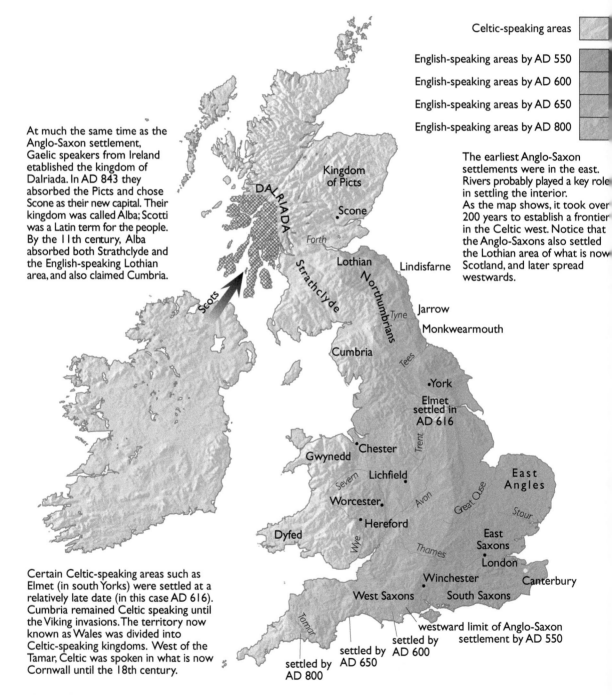

At much the same time as the Anglo-Saxon settlement, Gaelic speakers from Ireland etablished the kingdom of Dalriada. In AD 843 they absorbed the Picts and chose Scone as their new capital. Their kingdom was called Alba; Scotti was a Latin term for the people. By the 11th century, Alba absorbed both Strathclyde and the English-speaking Lothian area, and also claimed Cumbria.

The earliest Anglo-Saxon settlements were in the east. Rivers probably played a key role in settling the interior.
As the map shows, it took over 200 years to establish a frontier in the Celtic west. Notice that the Anglo-Saxons also settled the Lothian area of what is now Scotland, and later spread westwards.

Celtic-speaking areas

English-speaking areas by AD 550

English-speaking areas by AD 600

English-speaking areas by AD 650

English-speaking areas by AD 800

Certain Celtic-speaking areas such as Elmet (in south Yorks) were settled at a relatively late date (in this case AD 616). Cumbria remained Celtic speaking until the Viking invasions. The territory now known as Wales was divided into Celtic-speaking kingdoms. West of the Tamar, Celtic was spoken in what is now Cornwall until the 18th century.

westward limit of Anglo-Saxon settlement by AD 550
settled by AD 600
settled by AD 650
settled by AD 800

Figure 2.2   The Anglo-Saxon settlement

After their arrival in Britain the Anglo-Saxons gradually spread to the north and west (see Figure 2.2) and by the seventh century AD the kingdoms shown in Figure 2.3 had been established. Archaeological excavations from this early period, such as those at Sutton Hoo in Suffolk, have revealed a rich material culture with trading links as far away as Byzantium. There is also evidence of a flourishing oral literature using the alliterative poetic form shared with Germanic peoples on the continent. The Old English heroic poem *Beowulf*, surviving only in a manuscript from *c.*1000, portrays a society with clear links to the one reflected in the spectacular finds from Sutton Hoo.

The major event of this early period was the conversion of the Anglo-Saxons to Christianity during the seventh century. Christianity brought with it renewed contact with Latin and the introduction of literacy using the Roman alphabet. Manuscripts began to be written in England, at first only in Latin but later in Old English, and from about 700 increasing numbers of Old English texts survive.

The main difficulty with writing the history of English in this period has to do with evidence and how to interpret it. The rest of this section examines this problem.

The nature of evidence

The history of any language includes both a linguistic history (the nature of the grammar and vocabulary at different points in time) and an account of who spoke the language, where and when. The former kind of history is often called the internal history, and the latter the external history. Just as there are two dimensions to the history of a language, so there are two kinds of evidence. Broadly speaking, we can distinguish between linguistic evidence (often called internal evidence) and non-linguistic historical, archaeological or scientific information (often called external evidence). Internal evidence comes mainly from texts and documents which provide examples of the language at known points in time. External evidence typically comes from archaeological sites or contemporary written histories. Writing the history of any language involves problems concerning the availability of evidence, the relationship between external and internal evidence, and the interpretation of whatever evidence exists. When we apply these key aspects of evidence to the history of English, we find:

- *Availability*: there is very little internal evidence before the early eighth century.
- *Relationship between the two types of evidence*: sometimes the external and internal evidence seem contradictory.
- *Interpretation*: the evidence that exists can be interpreted in different ways.

Of the seven kingdoms (names in capitals) three dominated the Anglo-Saxon period: Northumbria in the 7th century, Mercia (with its dyke marking the Welsh border) in the 8th century and Wessex from the 9th century.

Figure 2.3   The Anglo-Saxon kingdoms

The external evidence

Let's start by considering what is perhaps the most famous piece of external evidence, Bede's *Ecclesiastical History of the English People* (Figure 2.4), which he wrote in Latin in the eighth century. Bede says:

> [T]he Angles or Saxons came to Britain at the invitation of King Vortigern in three longships, and were granted lands in the eastern part of the island on condition that they protected the country: nevertheless, their real intention was to subdue it. They engaged the enemy advancing from the north, and having defeated them, sent back news of their success to their homeland, adding that the country was fertile and the Britons cowardly. Whereupon a larger fleet quickly came over with a great body of warriors, which, when joined to the original forces, constituted an invincible army ... These newcomers were from the three most formidable races in Germany, the Saxons, Angles, and Jutes. ...
>
> It was not long before such hordes of those alien peoples vied together to crowd into the island that the natives who had invited them began to live in terror.

(Sherley-Price, 1968, pp. 55–6)

Figure 2.4 The first page of Bede's *Ecclesiastical History of the English People*. This is a copy made *c*.820 of the Latin original completed in 731.

According to Bede each tribe spoke its own dialect, derived from its area of origin on the European mainland. These dialects later became identified with the different Anglo-Saxon kingdoms of Mercia and Northumbria (settled by the Angles), Kent (settled by the Jutes), and Wessex (settled by the Saxons).

Bede was writing nearly 300 years after the events he describes and scholars now believe his story to be an oversimplification. He doesn't mention that the Romans themselves used Germanic mercenaries on British soil in defence of their province. He says nothing about the tribe known as Frisians who were among the Germanic invaders, and his account suggests that the names 'Angles', 'Saxons' and 'Jutes' were mutually exclusive, which may not have been the case. Some language scholars have argued that the distinctive dialects used by the Anglo-Saxons were forged not on the continent but in the territory now called England. David DeCamp, for example, argues that:

> ... the origins of the English dialects lie not in pre-migrational tribal affiliations but in certain social, economic, and cultural developments which occurred after the migration was completed. This does not imply that the continental Germanic dialects are irrelevant to the genesis of English dialects ... Only those influences, however, which were felt after

the migrations were relevant to the formation of the English dialects; for I believe that these dialects originated not on the continent but on the island of Britain.

(DeCamp, 1958, p. 232)

Exactly what happened during this period which led to the regional differences in Old English is thus obscure. However, in more recent times there have been perhaps similar linguistic consequences of migration, settlement and the building of new communities. (Chapter 4 looks at what happened when people speaking different kinds of English migrated to America and created a new, shared form of language. Chapter 6 describes the formation of new dialects of English in the southern hemisphere.)

It is possible that Bede's account reflects stories about settlement history that had been passed down through the ages. He may have 'tidied up' the picture in order to construct a coherent history that emphasised the role of his own people, the Anglo-Saxons. In addition, Bede was a churchman and it was the Roman Catholic church, rather than the monarchies, which had the strongest institutions at this time. It has been suggested that the boundaries between the dialects of Old English, though corresponding roughly with those of the ancient kingdoms, might best be seen as ecclesiastical (Hogg, 1992, p. 4). Writing was, for a long time, the preserve of the church, with its various dioceses dividing the land into geographical segments. Our evidence of Old English dialects comes from written texts, and we do not know how well these reflected the spoken languages of the areas where they were written.

The case of Bede demonstrates an important principle in respect of documentary evidence: we need to take into account *who* the authors are, their social position, when they were writing and their reasons for writing in the first place.

Bede's *History* is the earliest English account and the traditional view – that the Anglo-Saxons migrated to Britain in large numbers, pushing the Romano-British population to the fringes of the British Isles – was largely based on it. However, Bede drew on an even earlier Celtic account, *On the Ruin and Conquest of Britain*, written in the 540s by Gildas (it should be noted that reproductions and translations have adopted different titles for this work by Gildas, including the source in the present chapter). The accounts by Bede and Gildas provide rather different perspectives on the external history of English. Seen from the point of view of the Celts, the invasion of the Anglo-Saxons was a disaster. Like Rome itself, their literate, Christian civilisation was being overrun by pagan barbarians. Gildas's first mention (1562 [?540], p. 49) of the Saxons is as 'a Nation odious both to God and man ... (as wolves into a fold of Sheepe)'. Modern Welsh historians such as Gwyn Williams (1985) have perceived negatively the growth in importance of the English language as contributing to the erosion of the Welsh language and Celtic culture. Williams has drawn on passages from Gildas such as the following:

In ſo much as all the townes with the often beatings of the Rammes, and
all the Towneſ-men, Paſtours, Priſts, and People, with naked ſwords that
glittred on all ſides, and crackling flames were together whirled to the
ground; lamentable and dreadfull to behold, there lay the toppes of loſty
Towres now tumbled downe, the ſtones of high wals, the holy Altars, and
rented peeces of carcaces covered with diſtilling & congealed purple
blood, confuſedly in the midſt of the ſtreetes heaped in one, as if they
were to be cruſhed.

(Gildas, 1562 [?540], p. 55)

Williams draws on various kinds of external and internal evidence to cast
doubt on the traditional account of conquest and destruction of the Celts
by the Anglo-Saxons. He emphasises the lengthy resistance, spanning four
centuries, that the Celts put up against the Anglo-Saxon invasions and also the
possibility of cultural 'fusion' between the two peoples. His views have gained
recent support from new interpretations of the archaeological evidence, which
argue against the mass migration of Anglo-Saxons:

[T]oday the world of Anglo-Saxon archaeology is divided over the
question of large-scale invasions in post-Roman times. More conservative
opinion still favours mass folk movements from the Continent to account
for the widespread changes in dress style, funeral rites and buildings.
Other scholars point out that such changes can be brought about by
other means. ... wherever archaeologists have taken a close look at the
development of a particular piece of British landscape, it is difficult to find
evidence for the scale of discontinuity one would expect had there indeed
been a mass migration from the Continent.

(Pryor, 2004, pp. 14–15)

Linguists such as David Crystal now believe that the traditional view is
simplistic and that 'although some Britons fled to the Welsh mountains, the far
north, the Cornish moors ... many – probably the majority – stayed in
subjection, and by degrees adopted the new culture' (Crystal, 2004, p. 25).

The external evidence, however, remains contradictory. For example, recent
support for the traditional view has come from a source quite new to Anglo-
Saxon studies, that of genetics (as you will find from Reading A). At the same
time, stable-isotope analysis, which uses tooth enamel to identify the area in
which a person grew up, suggests that there was no mass influx of population
from the continent in the post-Roman period (Pryor, 2004, p. 214). At present,
then, we cannot establish the facts about the Anglo-Saxon invasion and
settlement from the external evidence. Let's look now at what the internal
evidence can tell us.

The internal evidence

Turn to Reading A, 'The Celtic language puzzle' by David Crystal. It is a contemporary presentation of a key controversy. As you read, try to note sources of internal and external evidence. In your opinion, does the evidence come down clearly on one side or the other?

Comment

You will have noted that Crystal deals mostly with internal evidence: borrowed words, reference to place names and personal names. However, clearly the genetic evidence is external.

This is a genuine debate with adherents on each side. Many scholars take Crystal's view and feel this remains an unanswered puzzle.

Some of the early adoptions from Celtic were used in place names, which are especially difficult to interpret (partly because they were first written down long after the period of naming). These often refer to natural features such as rivers, hills and woods. Celtic forms were frequently combined with Anglo-Saxon ones, and sometimes both elements denote the same thing: *Brill* (in Buckinghamshire) combines Celtic *bre* ('hill') with Old English *hyl* ('hill'). Often included among these Celtic words is *combe* (denoting a valley), which is the example discussed in 'Place-name evidence'.

Figure 2.5   The village of Long Compton in Warwickshire

Place-name evidence

Figure 2.5 shows the village of Long Compton in Warwickshire, taken from the north-eastern side of the combe (shown in the foreground). The high ground in the distance is the southern side of the combe (which marks the border with Oxfordshire).

In modern Welsh *cwm* means 'valley', but there is also an Old English word *cumb* ('cup' or 'vessel'). So place names such as Pyecomb in Sussex or Long Compton in Warwickshire could derive from either Celtic or Old English, or perhaps the Anglo-Saxons decided to adapt the meaning of their own word *cumb* once they had heard the Celtic word used.

Place-name scholars have investigated the actual place or sites where certain names are used (Gelling, 1984). *Cumb* seems to denote a broad, bowl-shaped valley with three fairly steep sides. The name is most common in south-west England, suggesting that it could be an adoption from Celtic. Figure 2.6 shows some of the complex problems involved in interpreting the evidence of its distribution. Notice that it is rare in the north and also in the area of the Welsh border (where we might expect it). Was the Celtic term used in these areas?

Land hilly enough for *combe* to be a relevant name (the areas now known as Wales and Cornwall were not settled by the Anglo-Saxons)

The distribution of *combe*

Offa's Dyke

Figure 2.6   Distribution of *combe* as a place-name element

Or if the term is derived from Old English, was it known to the Anglians who settled in the north and Midlands? Was it no longer used when Anglo-Saxons settled the Welsh border areas?

The problem of interpreting place-name evidence shows some of the difficulties in interpreting the internal evidence in general. I have referred to it as an example of 'internal' evidence. However, we need to draw on so much non-linguistic evidence to interpret place names that we might justifiably wonder how 'internal' to the language such names are. This is part of a larger problem which we will meet again in this book. What exactly counts as part of the language? Where does the boundary lie between linguistic and non-linguistic, between internal and external? The lack of any simple answer to these questions is one reason why it is difficult to define the boundaries of the English language itself.

So far we've looked at some of the problems involved in ordering an external account of Old English. Now let's see what the language itself looked like.

2.4 An example of Old English

The most obvious kind of evidence available for looking at the internal history of Old English (i.e. its linguistic history) is the internal evidence provided by written texts. We deal here with an extract from a story told by the Anglo-Saxons themselves about the poet Caedmon. It also comes from Bede's *Ecclesiastical History of the English People*, which was translated from the original Latin into Old English in the ninth century. As an example of ninth-century West Saxon, it provides *internal* evidence about a dialect of Old English. It is also an example of the rich literature of the Old English period. Caedmon was supposed to be the first person to adapt the ancient Anglo-Saxon poetic form – traditionally used to celebrate the deeds of pagan heroes – for the expression of the Christian message. The gift of verse is miraculously given to him one night when, according to his custom, he absents himself from feasting and revelry because he has no performance skills.

Below is a translation of the extract. Read this now before going on to look at the Old English version in Activity 2.2.

> When he did that on one particular occasion, left the house with the party and went out to the cattle shed (whose care was entrusted to him that night) and at the appointed time he laid down his limbs in rest and fell asleep, then there stood before him a certain man in a dream and he hailed him and greeted him and called him by his name: 'Cedmon, sing me something.' And he answered and said: 'I don't know how to sing; and that's why I went out from this party, and came away here, because I didn't know how to sing.' Again, he who was speaking with him said:

'Nevertheless, you can sing for me.' Then he said: 'What have I to sing?' He said: 'Sing to me about the creation.' When he had received this reply, he began to sing at once lines and words in praise of God the Creator which he had never heard before, their order is this:

> Now we have to praise the guardian of the heavenly
> kingdom, the power and the conception of the creator,
> the deeds of the father of glory, as he, the eternal lord,
> established the beginning of every wonder. He, the holy
> creator, first shaped heaven as a roof for men on earth.
> Then mankind's guardian, almighty and eternal lord,
> afterwards adorned the fields for men.

Then he arose from that sleep and all those things that he had sung in his sleep he had fixed in memory, and quickly he added to those words many words in the same metre of song dear to God.

(quoted in Burnley, 1992, pp. 28–31)

ACTIVITY 2.2

Allow 10–15 minutes

In Old English writing, the Roman alphabet was augmented with extra letters, each with a special name, used to denote some sounds of Old English not found in Latin. These are:

- thorn (þ), used for the sound *th* in words such as *thick*
- eth (ð) used for the sound *th* in words such as *the*
- ash (æ) used for the vowel sound in words such as *tap*.

Some linguists argue that the language of the Anglo-Saxons was the 'same language' as Modern English, contending that there is a continuous development from Old English to Modern English. Figure 2.7 consists of lines from the Old English version of the story of Caedmon from Bede's *Ecclesiastical History of the English People*. Look at Figure 2.7 now. Before referring to the 'Comment' below, see if you can make any sense of it.

Comment

You may have found the text completely unintelligible. Some degree programmes which study the history of English actually require students to learn the language of the Anglo-Saxons as though it were a foreign language. In the section below we look at a selection of the text's linguistic features to see whether the term 'Old English', which emphasises the continuity between old and modern forms of the language, seems justified. One problem for the modern reader is actually recognising the continuity between the Old English words and the modern glossed ones. Let's start with vocabulary, and then examine sounds and grammar.

When he that on a certain occasion did, that he left the house of the

1   þa he þæt þa sumre tide dyde, þæt he forlet þæt hus þæs

feast and out was going to of cattle the shed whose

2   gebeorscipes ond ut wæs gongende to neata scipene, þara

care to him was that night entrusted when he there at

3   heord him wæs þære neahte beboden, þa he ða þær in

the appointed tide his limbs in rest laid down and fell asleep

4   gelimplice time his leomu on reste gesette ond onslepte

then stood him a certain man below in (a) dream and him hailed and

5   þa stod him sum mon æt þurh swefn ond hine halette ond

greeted and him by his name called: 'Caedmon sing me

6   grette ond hine be his noman nemnde : 'Cedmon sing me

something'. Then answered he and said: 'Not know I not (how)

7   hwæþwugu'. þa ondswarede he ond cwæð: 'Ne con ic noht

to sing and I because of this from this feast out went

8   singan ond ic for þon of þeossum gebeorscipe ut eode,

and here came because I nothing to sing not know how'. Again he

9   ond hider gewat, for þon ic naht singan ne cuðe'. Eft he

said, he who with him speaking was: 'However you can for me

10   cwæð, se ðe mid hine sprecende wæs: 'Hwæðre þu meaht me

sing?' Then said he 'What shall I sing?' Said he:

11   singan?' þa cwæð he: 'Hwæt sceal ic singan?' Cwæð he:

'Sing to me (about the) Creation'. Then he this answer received, then

12   'Sing me frumsceaft.' þa he ða þas andsware onfeng þa

began he at once to sing in praise of God the Creator these

13   ongon he sona singan in herenesse Godes Scyppendes þa

lines and these words which he never (had) heard whose order

14   fers ond þa word þe he næfre gehyrde, þæra endebyrdnesse

this is:

15   þis is:

now (we) must praise of heaven's kingdom the Guardian

16   Nu sculon herigean * heofonrices Weard

of the Creator's power and his conception

17   Meotodes meahte * ond his modgeþanc

the work of the Father of Glory as he of wonder every

18   weorc Wuldorfæder, * swa he wundra gehwæs

eternal Lord the beginning established

19   ece Drihten, * or onstealde.

He first made on earth for men

20   He ærest sceop * eorðan bearnum

heaven as a roof the holy Creator

21   heofon to hrofe, * halig Scyppend

	then	the world		of mankind	the Guardian
22	þa	middangeard	*	monncynnes	Weard

	everlasting	Lord		afterwards	adorned
23	ece	Drihten,	*	æfter	teode

	for men	the earth		God	Almighty
24	firum	foldan,	*	Frea	ælmihtig

	Then	arose	he	from	that	sleep	and	all	that	he	sleeping	song
25	þa	aras	he	from	þæm	slæpe,	ond	eal	þa þe	he	slæpende	song

	firmly	in	memory	had	and to those	words	at once	many	words	in
26	fæste	in	gemynde	hæfde,	ond þæm	wordum	sona	monig	word	in

	the	same	metre	to God	worthy	songs	added.
27	þæt	ilce	gemet	Gode	wyrðes	songes	to geþeodde .

Figure 2.7 The story of Caedmon from Bede's *Ecclesisastical History of the English People*.
Above each line is a word-for-word translation (called a 'gloss'). We have used modern
punctuation and capitalisation to make it easier for you to see the sentence structures.
The asterisks in lines 16–24 show the breaks between the verse half-lines of the poem.

Old English vocabulary

The continuity mentioned above is often obscured by the changes in spelling.
If, for instance, you rewrite þ and ð as *th*, and æ as *a*, you'll find some words
become instantly recognisable, for example *þæt, þis, æfter,* or at least close to
their modern form, as in *fæste* ('fast') and *wyrð(es)* ('worth'). Adding two more
rules (*hw = wh, ht = ght*) and we get *what* from *hwæt* and *night* from *næht(e)*.
So there may be more continuity than appears at first sight.

However, the vocabulary of English has been greatly enlarged since Anglo-
Saxon times by adoptions from other languages (often carrying with them the
spelling conventions of those languages). Many of the words in Figure 2.7 are
no longer used today; and some are still used, but in senses different from
those in the extract. *Tide* in line 1, for instance, may make us think of the sea,
but its meaning here is the same as that in the proverb 'Time and tide wait for
no man'. In Old English *tide* meant 'time', but it later came to denote a
particular time or occasion (as in *Whitsuntide*) and it is possible that the
modern sense 'the time the sea either comes in or goes out' derives from this.
Another Old English word, *tima*, retained the meaning of time in the more
general sense. Two other words, *neata* and *scipene*, you might be tempted to
describe as obsolete. But if you have any knowledge of rural speech in
England you may recognise the first word in the East Anglian form *neat-house*
('cattle shed') and the second in *shippon*, a word with the same meaning as
'neat-house' used in dialects of south-west England and parts of the north. So
Old English words are often retained in specialised varieties of English, such
as regional dialects.

Old English sounds

We have looked at some aspects of the vocabulary and the spelling of an Old English text. Is there anything we can say about the *sounds* represented by those spellings? The answer is yes, but first it's necessary to stress that we can never prove how the Anglo-Saxons pronounced certain sounds. What we can do is make an informed guess based on different types of evidence.

Scholars have always assumed that Old English spelling is a closer representation of pronunciation than is the case with Modern English. It follows from this that in Old English 'silent letters' were unlikely, and that a change of sound would be reflected by a change in spelling. Another assumption is that spellings had the sound values originally associated with spoken Latin (it was, after all, the Latin alphabet that the Anglo-Saxons learnt). If these assumptions are valid, quite a lot of information about possible Old English pronunciations may be inferred from spellings. But we also need to know the Old English *system* of spelling. And as well as having unfamiliar spellings, Old English also used familiar spellings to represent unfamiliar sounds, or sounds in unfamiliar positions.

Let's demonstrate this with the letter *h*, familiar both to us and to the Anglo-Saxons. As you can see from Figure 2.7 it occurs initially in Old English in words such as *he*, and it seems reasonable to assume that it sounded much like the modern sound /h/ as in **hot**. But if you consider the use of *h* elsewhere in Modern English, you may find that it's most often used in combination with other letters, such as *th, ph* (and also *gh*, which is either no longer sounded or is pronounced /f/ as in **rough**). So *h* either represents a sound by itself, or in combination with other letters represents different sounds. But in Old English the letter occurs in quite different combinations and contexts from Modern English. It occurs initially before other consonants, as in *hwæt, hrofe*; and as a separate consonant sound (much as in *he*, perhaps). It also occurs at the end of words, as in *þurh*, again as a separate sound related to /h/, but probably closer to the /x/ in Scots *loch* or German *doch*. And in a word like *ælmihtig* ('almighty') the *h* may have sounded like the *ch* in German *nicht*.

So far our account is oversimplified because the Anglo-Saxons had more than one system of spelling, depending on *where* texts were written. Caedmon's poem, for instance, was also written down in the eighth-century Northumbrian dialect. There we find the spellings *uard* and *barnum* instead of *Weard* (line 16) and *bearnum* (line 20). This may be because the sound /r/ in the West Saxon dialect influenced the pronunciation of the preceding vowel, making it a *sequence* of vowels, perhaps pronounced as a **diphthong**. We have no way of knowing precisely why this should have been so – perhaps /r/ was pronounced differently in different parts of England, as it still is today (discussed in Chapter 7) – but we can find similar instances in Modern British English where the same consonant sound has influenced vowels differently in different dialects. In southern English pronunciation *water*, for instance, rhymes with *caught a*, whereas in some northern dialects it rhymes with *matter*. The sound /w/, which is made by rounding the lips, has in the south influenced the pronunciation of the following vowel, which also is rounded, whereas in the north what was probably the original pronunciation, the short *a*, has been retained.

ACTIVITY 2.3

Allow about
10 minutes

The most significant differences in pronunciation between Old and Modern English concern vowels. Here we shall consider just two vowel sounds. First, pronounce to yourself the following two groups of words:

> *holy, so, arose*
> *out, thou, house*

Are the sounds spelt *o* in the first group the same? Similarly, do the sounds spelt *ou* in the second line also form a group with the same sound? And in each case, is the sound a single vowel sound or a diphthong (that is, does the tongue move as you pronounce the *o* and *ou*? You might have to slow the pronunciation right down to feel this). Now look again at Figure 2.7 and find the Old English equivalents of these words, noticing how they are spelt.

Comment

You probably found that the words in the first group shared the same vowel, as did those in the second, although different from that for the first group. In many varieties of English they are both diphthongs, although the actual quality of sounds varies enormously. But the *o* in the first group can also be a simple long vowel for many speakers.

The Old English equivalents of these words are respectively *halig, swa* and *aras*, and *ut, þu* and *hus*. Notice that in both Old and Modern English forms there is a *pattern* in the spelling: where we get *o* and *ou* today we often get *a* and *u* ([aː] and [uː]) in Old English (the diacritic [ː] indicates a lengthened sound). This actually oversimplifies the picture, but it will do for the present discussion.

Spelling patterns can help us predict what Old English might have sounded like if we take them together with another kind of evidence, that of modern dialect pronunciation. The kind of vowel assumed for Old English in words such as *hus* can still be heard in Scotland and some northern dialects of England. Similarly, *a* has developed differently in the same areas, retaining a front articulation in the north, but developing a back one, either a long vowel or a diphthong, further south.

So far we've dealt briefly with aspects of spelling, vocabulary and sound. It's now time to examine the last level: structure.

Old English grammar

In this section, we look at two related aspects of grammar – word order and **inflections** (word endings).

Word order

ACTIVITY 2.4

Allow 10–15 minutes

Look at the first six lines of Figure 2.7 and compare the word order in the gloss with that of the translation. List the differences in terms of the position of the verbs. Can you find a pattern in them?

Comment

You will have found that the words are often in a sequence different from that found in Modern English; for example, *ond ut wæs gongende to neata scipene* ('and out was going to of-cattle the shed') places *ut* in front of the verb phrase *wæs gongende*, instead of after it, the preferred order in Modern English. As you read on, however, you may notice that it is often the whole verb phrase that is positioned differently from today. It is often put last, as in *ond hine be his noman nemnde* ('and him by his name called'). The position of the verb in the sentence tends to vary across the different languages of the world. Speakers of English today usually put the verb immediately after the subject of a sentence, and before any direct object; Modern English is accordingly described as a subject–verb–object (SVO) language. In the last example above, the order is subject–object–verb (SOV).

There was greater freedom in word order in Old English, in comparison with Modern English. This freedom is skilfully exploited in Caedmon's poem (see lines 16–24). To understand this, however, we need to know that Anglo-Saxon verse was based not on rhyme (as became common in later times) but on a combination of stressed syllables (usually four per line) and **alliteration** (repetition of initial sounds). If you look again at the poem you'll find that it is set out in half-lines, with a clear gap in between, with each linked by alliteration. In the example below (line 21) the alliterating sounds are in italic bold and the stressed syllables are in normal bold type:

> *h*eo*f*on to **hr**ofe   **ha**lig **Scypp**end
> heaven as a roof   the holy Creator

If we put this together with the preceding line (line 20) and compare them with the modern translation, we see how radically different the word order is from that of Modern English:

> *He ærest sceop   eorðan bearnum*
> He first made   on earth for men
> *heofon to hrofe   halig Scyppend*
> heaven as a roof   the holy Creator

Perhaps the most natural Modern English word order would be: *He, halig Scyppend, ærest sceop heofon to hrofe bearnum eorðan* ('He, the holy Creator, first made heaven as a roof for men on earth').

Notice, however, that such strange-seeming word-order patterns also occur alongside sequences which are much the same as those found in Modern English. If you look at the dialogue section in the story (lines 6–7), *Cedmon, sing me hwæþwugu* ('Caedmon, sing me something') is virtually identical with Modern English apart from the word *hwæþwugu*. You now know that *hwæt* is the Old English form of *what*, and once you learn that the Old English spelling *sc* corresponds with Modern English *sh*, the clause *Hwæt sceal ic singan?* (line 11) should present no problems. It's therefore possible to say that there are clear lines of continuity between Old and Modern English. But it's also possible to paint a very different picture, as the next section suggests.

Inflections

One reason why word order was freer in Anglo-Saxon times was that relationships between words could also be signalled by the actual 'shape' taken by individual words. If you look at line 26 of Figure 2.7, for instance, you'll see that one of the words we can recognise, *word* ('word'), has two shapes: *word* and *wordum*. The *-um* ending means the same as the modern preposition *to*, and also tells us that the form is plural. So in studying Old English it's very important to learn what endings can be added to a particular word, and what meanings are attached to them.

These endings are known as **inflections**. If you have studied a modern foreign language you may already be familiar with inflections and some inflections even occur in Modern English. One example is the *-s* which is added to the end of many nouns to make them plural. But the Anglo-Saxons had a much richer range of inflections, to mark what linguists call **case**. If we take a noun such as *drihten* ('lord') in line 19 we would find that an *-e* inflection occurs when the word is functioning as an indirect object, as in *to the lord*, for example; whereas an *-es* ending denotes what is called the 'possessive' case, as in *of the lord*. And there is a different range of inflections for the plural cases.

In describing Old English, and indeed other inflected languages, it has long been the custom to use the terminology of Latin grammar. The indirect object case, for instance, is known as the 'dative', and the possessive as the 'genitive'. When a noun is being used as the grammatical subject of a sentence it is in the 'nominative' case; when it is the direct object it is in the accusative case. It is also customary to set out all this information about case endings in the following kind of table:

	Singular		Plural	
Nominative	drihten	the lord (subj.)	drihtnas	the lords
Accusative	drihten	the lord (obj.)	drihtnas	the lords
Genitive	drihtnes	of the lord	drihtna	of the lords
Dative	drihtne	to the lord	drihtnum	to the lords

Linguists speak of this kind of display as a **paradigm**. There are a number of different paradigms (each with different systems of case inflections) according to whether a noun is classified as 'masculine' (as in the case of *drihten*) or 'feminine' (as in *scipene*, line 2 of Figure 2.7) or 'neuter' (as in *hus*, line 1). And case endings vary not only in respect of gender but also according to whether a noun is classified as 'strong' or 'weak'. *Noma* (name), for instance, is masculine like *drihten* but has different endings because it is weak rather than strong (as in *noman* in line 6). (Think of the terms 'masculine', 'feminine', 'neuter', 'gender' 'strong' and 'weak' as purely grammatical ones, referring only to patterns of inflection.)

ACTIVITY 2.5

Allow about 5 minutes

If all this terminology is new or confusing for you, it's worth reflecting on the different forms a personal pronoun, such as *he,* has in most varieties of Modern English.

	Pronoun	Example
Nominative	he	*he* ate it
Accusative	him	I ate *him*
Genitive	his	I ate *his* apple
Dative	him	I gave the apple to *him*

However, the Anglo-Saxons had four forms for the pronoun *he*. They all occur in the first six lines of Figure 2.7; look back at the Caedmon text and make a list of them.

Comment

Three of the Old English forms will already be familiar to you: *he, his, him*. But where today we would use *him* for a direct and also indirect object (as in *I gave the book to him*) the Anglo-Saxons used *him* only in the latter case, that is, the dative. The accusative form was *hine*, which still survives in some dialects of south-west England.

Inflections in Old English were added to adjectives and verbs as well as nouns. But while most modern varieties of English have two forms in the present tense of verbs such as *to sing* (as in *I sing, she sings*), they had four in Old English. The paradigm for *singan* ('to sing') looks like this:

	Singular		Plural	
1st person	ic singe	I sing	we singaþ	we sing
2nd person	þu singest	you sing	ge singaþ	you sing
3rd person	he singe	he sings	hie singaþ	they sing
	heo singeþ	she sings		
	hit singe	it sings		

(There was also an imperative form *sing*, which is used by the night-time visitor in the Caedmon passage.)

Notice that in the paradigm above there is one third-person singular ending *-eþ*, and a plural one *-aþ* (remember that the *þ* was later respelt as *th*). Notice also the forms of the pronouns, and the fact that Old English makes a distinction between a singular *you* (later, *thou*) and plural *you* (later, *ye*). In early Modern English these forms would be *thou singest, ye singeth*.

The evidence of tenth-century Northumbrian texts suggests that, by that time, the inflectional system sketched above was in the process of change. In the next section we investigate why this happened.

2.5 The late Old English period

In Section 2.3 we saw how the vocabulary of Old English expanded as a result of renewed contact with Latin after the conversion of the Anglo-Saxons to Christianity. A more profound linguistic change occurred as a result of invasions and settlement by Vikings (Norwegians and Danes), whose Old Scandinavian language (known also as Old Norse) was closely related to Old English. The invasions started in 747 and continued intermittently until the early eleventh century. In 878, King Alfred of Wessex defeated the Danes, and confined their settlements to an area known as the Danelaw (see Figure 2.8). This led to the dominance of Wessex and the West Saxon dialect in the late Anglo-Saxon period, as Alfred's sons and grandsons retook the Danelaw and established a unified English kingdom. However, renewed invasions in the 990s led to the exile of King Aethelred in 1014, and for the following twenty-five years the whole of England was ruled by Danish kings.

One result of this prolonged contact with Old Norse was another expansion in vocabulary (for examples, see the box on Scandinavian influence on English vocabulary). More than 1500 place names in the north-east of England are of

The southern limit of the Danelaw (shown with the line) coincided in part with the route of the Roman road known as Watling Street, running from London to Wroxeter in Shropshire. North of that line the Danes ruled until the West Saxon kings reconquered the Danelaw in the 10th century. The purple portion represents the area where place names derive from the languages spoken by the Vikings – Danes in the east, Norwegians in the west. Vikings from Norway also settled in Ireland, the north-east and west of Scotland, and along the coast of Wales.

Figure 2.8   The Danelaw

Scandinavian origin and more than 1800 other words entered the language at this time. However, the pattern of adoption is different from the earlier pattern with Latin. This time fewer borrowings were words for new concepts or cultural artefacts. Many of the new adoptions from Old Norse are among our commonest English words today and some replaced core words in the Old English vocabulary: three were pronouns and one (*are*) was a form of our most commonly used verb, the verb *to be*. In addition, as we shall see below, contact with Old Norse may be one reason for the loss of inflections, a profound grammatical change which distinguishes Old English from Modern English.

> **Scandinavian influence on the vocabulary of English**
>
> Examples include:
>
> > place names ending in -*by* ('farm' or 'town'): *Derby, Grimsby, Rugby*
> >
> > surnames ending in -*son*: *Wilson, Robinson, Harrison*
> >
> > words with the hard -*sk* sound: *skirt, sky, whisk*
> >
> > pronouns: *they, their, them* (Old English used *hie, hiera, him*)
> >
> > many commonly used words: *both, same, to, sister, get, give, take.*
>
> Sometimes both the English and the Scandinavian words survive
> (the English word is given first): *hide/skin, sick/ill, rear/raise.*

Why did the grammar of Old English change?

The examples of Old English in Section 2.4 show how different Old English
was from Modern English. Not only have individual words changed in spelling
and pronunciation, but key features of grammar have altered too.

Indeed, the very *kind* of language has changed – from being an inflectional
language, with relatively free word order, to one with more characteristics of
an isolating language in which grammatical relations are signalled by word
order rather than inflections. For that reason, Modern English has a more fixed
word-order pattern than Old English. Sometimes non-linguistic (external)
factors can lead to language change; the effect of repeated invasions on the
vocabulary of English is one clear example. But there also exist *internal*
reasons for linguistic change. That is, the grammar of English may have had
some kind of built-in instability which made certain kinds of change likely. Or
there may be universal tendencies which make all languages evolve in similar
ways. Let's now look at various external and internal explanations for why the
inflectional system of Old English disappeared.

Internal causes of change

It has been suggested that over the centuries the stress in English speech has
tended to fall increasingly on the first syllable of words. A consequence of this
is that the inflected syllables at the end of words are more weakly stressed,
and their vowels are likely to be reduced to what linguists call a schwa sound
(represented phonetically as [ə] as in Modern English *sofa*). If the distinctive
vowel sounds of different inflectional endings are all reduced to [ə], then the
endings become redundant.

Also, you may remember that in certain of the noun paradigms mentioned
above, not all cases had distinctive endings. This has led some linguists to
argue that the Old English inflectional system was inefficient and was

therefore 'ripe for analogical re-modelling' (Lass, 1992, p. 104). This means that speakers themselves start to regularise the paradigms, and one way of doing this is simply to delete endings.

If you look back at the case endings for *drihten* (see 'Inflections') you'll notice that there is no distinction between nominative and accusative in either singular or plural. The case of a neuter noun such as *hus* ('house') is even more extreme. As the paradigm shows, not even the singular and plural forms for these cases are distinguished:

	Singular	Plural
Nominative	hus	hus
Accusative	hus	hus
Genitive	huses	husa
Dative	huse	husum

One problem with purely internal accounts of linguistic change such as these is that they are not explanatory enough. For instance, inflections have been retained in other Germanic languages even where stress is, in a similar way to that of English, on the initial syllable. And focusing on a language rather than its speakers begs the question as to how or why a change is adopted. Linguists generally agree that linguistic change cannot be brought about by an individual speaker alone. Although as individuals we are free to change whatever we like – as children and imaginative writers continue to demonstrate – such changes cannot be considered part of a language until they have passed into wider usage. So the question then arises: if one person starts using the language in a novel way – by pronouncing a word ending differently, or using a word in a new sense – why should other people start doing the same? Any answer to this question must take account of social relations among speakers, and this by definition forms part of the realm of the external.

External causes of change

In the later twentieth century, linguists with a special interest in language in relation to society – sociolinguists – showed that linguistic changes are often associated with particular groups in society, and that people tend to adopt changes introduced by more powerful or prestigious groups. (See Chapter 5, Section 5.9.) Any adequate account of linguistic change must make some reference to different groups within society, their relative status, and the patterns of contact existing among them.

The fact that inflectional breakdown seems to have begun in Northumbria has encouraged some sociolinguists to ask what existed in the external social context in that area to trigger the change. If you look back at Figure 2.8 you'll see that it's in the north-eastern half of England that the Vikings settled.

One vital aspect of this immigration from Scandinavia was that it went on long after Alfred's victory in 878 – in fact, until about the middle of the eleventh century. During that century it is likely that Scandinavian speech was quite prestigious, particularly as the king of England between 1016 and 1042 was actually Danish. It is not known how long the Scandinavian languages continued to be used in England. However, the linguistic historian Kastovsky (1992) argues that the large number of adoptions into English of Scandinavian vocabulary and grammatical forms evidenced by texts of the thirteenth and fourteenth centuries suggests that by then Scandinavian languages had been abandoned in favour of English.

It is also impossible to say whether the Anglo-Saxons and the Vikings found their respective languages mutually intelligible – Old Norse and Old English were, after all, related Germanic languages. It's therefore possible that numbers of speakers of both languages gradually became bilingual. Kastovsky (1992, p. 329) argues that at first there may have been greater pressure on the English to learn Scandinavian than vice versa, since the Vikings were invaders and because of the prestige factor mentioned earlier. If this was true, the English would have encountered many Scandinavian words which were similar to words in Old English. The Old English word for *summer*, for instance, was *sumer*, and the Scandinavian word was *sumar*. And although the Vikings used a similar range of inflections their actual forms were different: the dative singular of *sumer* was *sumera,* whereas the dative singular of *sumar* was *sumri*. Perhaps what happened between the two groups of people was that the inflectional differences between the languages were resolved largely by doing away with them altogether.

This explanation of why English changed is similar to that used to explain how pidgins arise in some language-contact situations. (We discuss English pidgins and how they arise in Chapter 4, Section 4.4.) In this view, the breakdown of inflections owes as much to processes of contact between speakers of different languages as it does to pressures of a purely internal kind. We have no direct evidence of this actually happening during this period, but we do know that such processes of inflectional simplification do happen, and are characteristic of contact situations in other places today. It may not be unreasonable, therefore, to apply them to the past.

Late Old English literary culture

After his defeat of the Vikings, King Alfred commissioned the translation into English of many Latin texts, including Bede's *Ecclesiastical History*. The reason he gave was a drastic decline in the knowledge of Latin and the wholesale destruction of Latin manuscripts by the invaders. It is also likely that Alfred commissioned the writing of *The Anglo-Saxon Chronicle*, which provides an account of Anglo-Saxon history from a Wessex point of view. And according to the *Oxford English Dictionary*, the word *Englisc*

('English') was first used to denote both people and language under his auspices.

In the tenth century there was another revival of learning and literary activity, this time associated with the influential Benedictine monasteries. The scriptorium of the monastery at Winchester, producing texts in the West Saxon dialect, seems to have made considerable efforts to regularise spellings and this has been seen as a move in the direction of standardisation in English. (See another book in this series, Graddol et al., 2007, for further discussion of this issue).

Most extant Old English manuscripts date from the late Old English period and they preserve, not only translations of learned Latin texts, but also an important body of vernacular literature in prose and poetry. Some of the poems are religious, following the example set by Caedmon, and others (such as *Beowulf*) stem from inherited Germanic traditions.

So far we've looked at Old English: where it came from, what it was like, how certain aspects of it changed, and how the process of change might be explained. We now move on to a different period of the English language, that known as 'Middle English'.

2.6 The transition to Middle English

We have seen that the English language was undergoing significant change during the early part of the tenth century. In 1066 an event occurred that was to have a profound effect on this process. In that year a French-speaking dynasty from the dukedom of Normandy was installed in England. This external event has long been seen as decisive, not only for the history of England (and consequently Britain) but for the English language as well. For scholars who have viewed the history of England and English as one of unbroken progress, the Conquest has often been a milestone on the road to 'civilisation', playing a key role in the development of Modern English. But another view, perhaps more widely held, sees the events of the Conquest in terms of (an at least temporary) decline: as the wrecking of a relatively sophisticated 'native' Anglo-Saxon culture by a 'foreign' and tyrannical French one, so that the continuity of English culture was ruptured and the continued existence of the English language threatened.

This latter view of events may be almost as old as the Conquest itself. It is the story known as the 'Norman yoke'. Versions of this were intermittently kept alive during the Middle Ages, probably because it was politically useful for certain groups within English society (including the monarchy itself). It again assumed importance during the English Civil War of the seventeenth century. By the late eighteenth century it seems to have become part of a common patriotic mythology that was anti-French. It was on these ideas that Sir Walter Scott drew in his novel *Ivanhoe*, first published in 1815:

> At court, and in the castles of the great nobles, where the pomp and state of a court were emulated, Norman-French was the only language employed; in courts of law, the pleadings and judgements were delivered in the same tongue. In short, French was the language of honour, of chivalry, and even of justice, while the far more manly and expressive Anglo-Saxon [Old English] was abandoned to the use of rustics and hinds [farm servants], who knew no other.
>
> (Scott, 1986 [1815], p. 9)

Whatever view of the Conquest is taken, we can be sure about one of its effects. It brought about a period of close contact and often bitter rivalry between the English and the French which in some respects has lasted into the present century. Ideas about 'Englishness' have often reflected whatever is considered to be 'not French', and these ideas have varied a great deal over this long span of history. In general, attitudes to French and France can be characterised as ambivalent: hostility mixed with admiration.

But these effects had less to do with the immediate aftermath of the Conquest than with later developments. For in comparison with the Vikings, the Norman invaders were few in number and were spread rather thinly across the country. Not only is there evidence to suggest that Scott's picture was too black and white, but it is arguable that the most important source of French influence was not the Norman French of the invaders but another dialect, the more prestigious central French of the French king's court in the area of Paris. Furthermore, it is less a matter of *spoken* French than of its written varieties.

The main reason for this is that in 1204 the dukedom of Normandy was gained by the king of France. The kings of England were therefore no longer also dukes of Normandy, and contacts with Normandy gave way to contact with the French court.

French in England after 1066

In this section we look at the evidence for the use of French in England in the period between the Norman Conquest and the fourteenth century, when the use of French began to die out. The picture is actually very complicated. We need to bear in mind: the geographical, social, institutional and temporal dimensions of French use; the possible extent of French–English bilingualism; and, within that last category, the *direction* of language learning – speakers of English learning French, speakers of French learning English.

Let's start by reminding ourselves of the contexts mentioned by Scott: the king's court, the nobles' castles, the courts of law in which Norman French was the language of 'honour', chivalry and justice. Starting with the king's court, it is certainly true that for 300 years after the Conquest all the kings of

England spoke French as their first language; indeed, some knew no English at all (although William the Conqueror himself is supposed to have tried to learn, and failed). The court patronised literature in French and in general was heavily influenced by French culture. However, by the fourteenth century, kings were usually bilingual.

A further linguistic consequence of the Conquest, as Scott suggests, concerned the language of law. But according to Clanchy (1993, p. 45), the Norman kings also greatly expanded the uses of writing for bureaucratic purposes in general. Some of this was in Latin, whereas in pre-Conquest times English would have been used. But a great deal of administrative writing was increasingly undertaken in French. This was so much the case that until the fourteenth century English was actually a minority written language within England.

As for the Norman landowning nobility, the picture is more complicated. The linguistic historian David Burnley found contemporary evidence suggesting that many people of this rank learnt English quite soon after the Conquest. But 'equal competence in both languages was rare' (Burnley, 1992, p. 424). One occupational group likely to be bilingual to a degree consisted of those known as *latimiers* ('interpreters'), who mediated between the Norman landowners and the labourers (Scott's 'rustics and hinds', who needed to know no language other than English).

One institution not mentioned by Scott was the church (where the senior positions at least were awarded to Normans). Here some bilingualism seems to have been essential, since it was the duty of the clergy to preach to an English-speaking congregation. And for a monolingual speaker of English to rise in the church hierarchy, becoming bilingual was also necessary, at least as far as written French was concerned.

Rather paradoxically, it seems that once the dynastic link with Normandy had been broken in 1204 and England had acquired greater autonomy, the influence of French in England grew stronger. If the nobility was to remain French-speaking, it had to learn central French with the help of tutors. French came to be associated with social aspiration, and could also be learnt by people who had previously known only English. We deal with French in educational institutions in Section 2.8. Meanwhile, let's see how French affected the English language.

The influence of French on English vocabulary

The most obvious effect of French on English is at the level of vocabulary. A great many French words were adopted into English and such words have often been seen in a negative light. If you look back at the Scott extract, you'll see that he characterises Anglo-Saxon as 'far more manly and expressive' than French. Elsewhere in *Ivanhoe* he presents the issue in terms of social stratification. In a famous conversation in the book, the jester Wamba discusses with a swineherd the naming of animals reared to be eaten.

A 'swine' (from the Old English word for 'pig') becomes, says Wamba, 'pork' (from the French) 'when she is carried to the castle hall to feast among the nobles' (Scott, 1986 [1815], pp. 14–15).

This conversation shows a further aspect of the process of adoption: English acquired a layer of French words to refer to things (in this case livestock) which already had names. The new French words were also associated with the new masters and the uses to which they put things. (In fact, adoptions from French rarely seem to refer to things or concepts unknown to the English.)

The earliest adoptions after the Conquest were from Norman French. Examples are *duc, cuntess, curt* ('duke', 'countess', 'court'), *messe, clerc* ('mass', 'scholar') and *werre, pais* ('war', 'peace'). They could be said to reflect the dominance of the Normans in powerful institutions such as the royal court and the church. These early adoptions in some cases coexisted with their central French counterparts adopted at a later date. So we have Norman French *warden, convey, gaol*, beside central French *guardian, convoy, jail*. Often the central French words belonged to the written medium, mainly of the fourteenth century (discussed in Section 2.7). It has been estimated that by this date about twenty-one per cent of the English vocabulary derived from French, in comparison with about nine per cent soon after the Conquest (Burnley, 1992, p. 432).

But most of these words were relatively 'exotic', belonging to the specialist discourses of church, law, chivalry (knightly behaviour) and the running of country estates. By far the most frequently occurring words were still of Germanic origin. Some of these points are illustrated in the extracts in the next section, where we see what English looked like in the so-called Middle English period.

2.7 Examples of Middle English

The first example we look at demonstrates the uneven effect of the Norman Conquest on the English language. It is an extract from a poem written about 130 years after the invasion, probably in a part of south-east England (perhaps what is now known as Surrey). It is evidence of one abrupt break with the past: the adoption of the French tradition of verse, which uses rhyme rather than stress and alliteration. The poem, which is known as *The Owl and the Nightingale*, shows how this tradition had been thoroughly assimilated by at least one poet writing in this variety of early Middle English.

You'll probably find this poem much easier to deal with than the Old English text about Caedmon. Notice that *æ* is replaced by *a* in *was* and *þat* and that a single letter ʒ (called '*yogh*'), as in *diʒele*, is used where we now use *gh*. Some of the word-order deviations from Modern English are dictated by the need to rhyme, though others still follow the needs of alliterative verse. For example,

> I   was in   a   summer valley
> Ich was in one sumere dale
>
> in   a   very hidden corner
> In one suþe diȝele hale
>
> heard I   held great debate
> Iherde ich holde grete tale
>
> an owl and a   nightingale
> An hule and one niȝtingale
>
> that pleading was stiff and firm and strong
> þat   plait was stif and starc an strong
>
> sometimes soft and loud in between
> Sumwile softe an lud   among

Figure 2.9 Extract from *The Owl and the Nightingale*. The intended punctuation is unknown – and modern editions of the poem punctuate it in different ways, so the punctuation has been omitted completely here. (quoted in Bennett and Smithers (eds), 1968)

where we would expect the word order *Ich iherde an hule and one niȝtingale holde grete tale*, we find *Iherde ich* stresses the *h* needed to alliterate with *holde*: and the positions of *tale* and *niȝtingale* result from the need to rhyme.

We can make out a case for saying that the language of this extract has been greatly affected by the Norman Conquest, but it's still possible to argue that it also shows a great deal of continuity with Old English. It's probable, for instance, that *lud* (*hlud* in Old English) was still pronounced as a long [uː] sound, much as in Old English. Look back at the Caedmon poem (Figure 2.7): does the alliteration in *stif an starc an strong* (in Figure 2.9) remind you of anything in Old English verse? Moreover, in this extract, the only word borrowed from French is *plait*, 'pleading', appropriately enough a legal term, reflecting the dominance of the Normans in the institution of law.

One final point of interest concerns the existence of two different forms for the indefinite article: *an* and *one*. The Old English form was *an*, with the vowel of *halig*. In the south of England this vowel tended to be rounded and spelt with an *o*, hence *one*. (In the north of England, however, it remained unrounded, as in the next extract.) Occasionally, it was also shortened, hence spelt *an*. So the quality of vowel in the older pronunciation is kept in the shortened form.

The next example is from about a century later, and from the north of England. It is a verse fragment from York. While it shows the influence of French versification, this fragment contains no adoptions from French. And unlike the previous extract, it shows that the Old English *a* (as in *haly*) has not been rounded in this part of England. In fact, it shows a different kind of influence – that of the Scandinavian languages spoken by the Vikings (York itself was a Viking centre).

alas who shall these horns blow
wel qwa sal thir hornes blau

holy cross (on) thy day
haly Rod thi day

now is he dead and lies low
nou is he dede and lies law

(who) was wont to blow them always
was wont to blaw thaim ay

Figure 2.10 Verse fragment, dated 1272 (quoted in Milroy, 1992)

The pronoun form *thaim* ('them'), for instance, comes from Old Norse *þeim* (see the box on 'Scandinavian influence on the vocabulary of English' at the beginning of Section 2.5). The form with *th* gradually spread southwards and westwards, replacing the older *h-* forms. A similar pattern occurs with the third-person singular verb inflection *-s*, as in *lies*. You may remember that in the West Saxon Caedmon text the ending was *-þ* (both this ending and the *h-* pronoun forms are preserved in *The Owl and the Nightingale*, though they do not occur in our extract). In the late Northumbrian Lindisfarne Gospels, however, the *-s* form was already being used. Like the *them* form, it has since gradually moved south and been adopted into the variety of English that is used today in print.

Two final points to make about this fragment illustrate important features of the language in the Middle English period. Two spelling conventions, *s* for *sh* (as in *sal*) and *q* for *wh* (as in *qwa*) are exclusively northern, and have remained in use today in texts written in Scots (see Chapter 4, Section 4.3). And notice that 'blow' has two spellings, *blau* and *blaw*. Consistent spelling wasn't seen as important at this time as it is today: this is one reason why scholars have often thought of Middle English as unstable. In fact, such inconsistency remained a feature of handwritten texts until well after the introduction of printing in 1476.

There is no evidence that regional differences in English (as exemplified above) were generally seen as a problem by contemporary observers. By the fourteenth century, though, a conscious interest was being taken in them. The diversity in English pronunciation, especially regarding the north and south, seemed 'a great wonder' to one contemporary observer, John Trevisa. In a famous passage from his translation (in 1384) of a text called *Polychronicon*, originally written in Latin in 1327, he characterises the speech north of the River Humber (especially at York) as *scharpe, slitting, frotynge and vnchape*, by which he meant that it was shapeless and grated like the sound of ripping cloth (Burnley, 1992). For southerners such as Trevisa this attitude to northern speech seems to have stemmed from a sense of cultural superiority. The north was less populous and poorer; parts of it even shared certain administrative arrangements and customs with Scotland (and until 1157 was actually claimed by that kingdom). To northerners, on the other hand, southern English was difficult to understand but was also an emblem of governmental power, for by the fourteenth century there was a new 'centre' in England – the south-east around London. Here the king held his court, and a commercial capital had emerged.

2.8   English in the later Middle Ages

Consider the following list of events:

1362	Statute of Pleading decrees lawsuits should be in English.
1380	Grammar-school masters advised to translate Latin into French as well as English.
1380s	New Testament translated into English.
	Chaucer writes *The Canterbury Tales*, in English.
1399	First king of England since 1066 (Henry IV) to speak English as a first language.

These events show that by the last half of the fourteenth century English was becoming increasingly used in those domains which had hitherto been dominated by French. How do we explain this process?

Histories of English have tended to explain it as an expression of English *national* identity. In this view, 'England' was a unity, a central aspect of that unity being the English language. As Baugh and Cable write in their widely used history of English (1978, p. 148), English was being restored 'to its rightful place as the language of the country'.

However, it might be safer to speak here of *patriotism*, based on hostility towards the French, rather than of nationalism in its fuller sense in which language is seen as the decisive component of a unified national identity. (Chapter 3 provides further discussion of nationalism and the English language.) It certainly seems difficult to find a general sense of unity throughout English society at this time and, as we found with the history of Old English, different interpretations are possible. Let's look at different institutions in turn, starting with the law.

In the preamble to the Statute of Pleading, widespread ignorance of French is mentioned as one justification for using English in law, yet the Statute also mentions the 'great mischiefs' that arise from ignorance of the law in general. So rather than seeing the Act as empowering all the realm's subjects by using the common language, we could see it as seeking to ensure that the government's laws were obeyed at a time of great social upheaval. The Statute followed shortly after a second outbreak of the plague known as the Black Death, which had so reduced the rural population that labour had become scarce. Landowners could no longer make the traditional demands on labourers, who in turn could now actually bargain with them for wages. One outcome of such changes in social relations was the so-called Peasants' Revolt in 1381.

Interesting light is cast on this change in the legal process by the recent discovery of records of a bigamy trial held at York in 1364. The judge dismissed the testimony of a witness on the grounds that the latter's language often shifted between northern English, southern English and Scots (the witness had spent his childhood in southern Scotland). The judge thought this a sign of dishonesty, suggesting that as far as the law was concerned, variation in English could be seen as a problem, at least for the accused (Bailey, 1992, p. 25).

The church was another institution facing acute divisions in the latter half of the fourteenth century. A group known as Lollards preached against what they saw as corrupt church practices and, to appeal to the lower classes where they had many supporters, they wrote largely in English. We could see the English translation of the New Testament in this more practical light, rather than as exemplifying 'national' pride in the English language.

English literature flourished at this time and the fourteenth-century poet Chaucer, author of the widely acclaimed *Canterbury Tales*, has often been celebrated as embodying the spirit of Englishness. But this privileging of imaginative writing as the supreme kind of language (and therefore the embodiment of the nation) was not that of Chaucer's own contemporaries. In fact, most imaginative writing was still produced anonymously (as in our two extracts discussed above). It was not until Caxton's promotion of Chaucer as someone who made English 'ornate and fayr' that our modern habit of naming imaginative writers and remembering their work began. (In Caxton's time the word *literature* – a fourteenth-century adoption from French – meant 'learned writing' in general; the specialisation in meaning to works of the imagination belongs to the nineteenth century.)

Although French was used at the royal court throughout the fourteenth century, most courtiers and the king himself seem to have been bilingual. The status of French at court was complicated by the fact that from 1337 England was at war with France for over a century (during the Hundred Years War). Any French or French-speaking favourites of the king might be targeted by jealous rivals, and language became an issue whenever anti-French patriotism was aroused. This feeling was most likely to be found among the emerging wealthy merchant class.

Turning to education we find that, although the study of Latin remained central to the curriculum, English replaced French as the medium of instruction in the course of the fourteenth century. A major source of evidence for this process is the *Polychronicon*, mentioned earlier. As well as translating this, John Trevisa added his own comments; he notes, for instance, that one year after the first occurrence of the Black Death an Oxford grammar-school master, John of Cornwall, first introduced English as the medium of education. That this was unpopular in some quarters is suggested by the concern about French recorded in 1380 (see the list of dates at the beginning of this section).

By the mid 1440s English was increasingly becoming the automatic choice for documents emanating from the crown. But it was a particular variety of English, essentially a London variety of the south-east Midlands dialect. A written form of this was developed by scribes working in that part of the royal administration known as Chancery.

This 'Chancery English' was less subject to the internal variation characteristic of earlier kinds of Middle English. It used the form *such* ('such', from Old English *swylc*), for instance, whereas earlier sub-varieties used in London had either *swic* or *sich* (rhymes with 'witch'). Many Chancery forms are the same as those used in print today and scholars, on the whole, regard this variety as the precursor of Standard English. Certainly Chancery scribes, such as the West Saxon scribes of the Winchester scriptorium, seem to have tried to eliminate variations in spelling, especially where these were based on local or individual pronunciations, and they respelt documents they copied according to their own conventions. The practice of regularising spellings is part of the process of standardisation: in fact, spellings are probably the easiest aspect of language to standardise. (We examine the process of standardisation in Chapter 3.)

ACTIVITY 2.6

<table>
<tr><td>Allow about
10 minutes</td><td>If you have any knowledge of written legal English, the following example of a Chancery document may seem familiar. (It entrusts Sir John Talbot with the post of Chancellor of Ireland, a territory claimed by the English crown since 1171.)</td></tr>
</table>

- Note any differences from Modern English spelling. Look particularly at the ends of words, at places where today we might use a different letter.
- Does Chancery use the same stock of letters as Modern English?

> The kyng by þadvise and assent of the lordes spirituell and temporell beying in this present parlement woll and grantith þat þe said Sir John Talbot haue and occupie the saide office of Chauncellor of Irelond by hym self or by his sufficient depute there after the fourme of the kynges lettres patentes to hym made þerof. The which letters patentes been thought gode and effectuell and to be approved after the tenure of the same. Also þat þe grete seal of þe saide lond belongyng to þe saide office, which þe said Thomas hath geton von to hym by delyuered to þe said Sir John Talbot or his sufficiente depute hauing power of hym to resceive hit.

Comment

You may have noted that final *e* (a relic of the old inflectional system) is retained in, for example, *fourme* ('form') and *saide* ('said') and that *-l* at the end of words is doubled (*spirituell*). The letter *y* is often used where today we would have *i*. But notice also that þ is retained initially alongside *th*. Some of these variations persisted into the printed literature of the fifteenth century.

2.9 Conclusion

This chapter has shown:

- How English has developed from complex patterns of contact between speakers of different languages.
- How there is continuity (and in the case of grammar, discontinuity) between Old English and Modern English.
- How from the earliest times English has varied, both regionally and stylistically (from poems to royal documents).
- How problems of evidence, its availability and interpretation, result in different narratives about the history of English.

Finally, throughout this chapter the focus has been on England. The English language in other parts of the British Isles has its own, complicated histories, which are dealt with in Chapter 4.

READING A: The Celtic language puzzle

David Crystal
(David Crystal is Honorary Professor of Linguistics at the University of Wales,
Bangor, and editor of the Cambridge Encyclopedia of English Language.)

Source: Crystal, D. (2004) *The Stories of English*, London, Penguin, pp. 24–33.

In fact there are two puzzles. First, why did the Anglo-Saxons not end up
speaking the Celtic languages of Britain? Arriving in such small numbers, we
might have expected them to adopt the language of the country, as can easily
happen after a period of settlement and intermarriage. This is what took place
at the time in Normandy, for example, where the Scandinavian invaders ended
up speaking French. It is also what took place in England after 1066, with the
Norman invaders eventually speaking English. But the Germanic invaders of
Britain retained their original language.

The second puzzle. When invaders arrive in a country and impose their own
language, they take in words from the indigenous language, often in large
numbers. To take a relatively recent example, there are thousands of words in
the *Dictionary of South African English* which have come from Afrikaans,
Xhosa, Zulu, and other African languages[1]. Although English arrived in South
Africa as a language of power, it quickly began to reflect local concerns by
assimilating new vocabulary. And we may generalise: even if an invading
group ends up adopting the conquered people's language, that language
leaves a sign of its presence. When the Vikings arrived in England in the late
eighth century, they introduced many Scandinavian loanwords and even
managed to exercise an influence on English grammar ... When the Normans
took over England, they introduced thousands of French loanwords into the
English they eventually adopted, as well as French conventions of spelling ...
Why, then, are there so few Celtic loanwords in Old English? How can the
Anglo-Saxons have failed to be influenced by the majority Celtic language
around them?

Apart from [certain] place-names ... the influence is indeed small, and many of
the words which are cited as of Celtic origin are of doubtful etymology. It is
sometimes difficult to tell whether a word entered Old English from Welsh,
after the Anglo-Saxons arrived, or whether it had been acquired on the
Continent from Latin, and was thus already in their language. For example, *bin*
'receptacle' might have derived from an early British word *benna* (compare
Welsh *ben* 'wagon') or from an even earlier Latin *benna*; *assen* 'ass' probably
came from an Old British word *assen*, but it might have been earlier from
Latin *asinus*. There are also cases of words which probably came from Celtic,
but because there are equivalent forms in some Germanic languages, the point
is not certain. These include *puck* 'malicious spirit' (Welsh *pwca*), which had
a similar form in Old Norse (*puki*), and *crock* 'pot' (Welsh *crochan*), also
found in several Scandinavian languages (such as Icelandic *krukka*).

Old English words which do seem to have a clear Celtic connection include *bannoc* 'piece of a loaf or cake', *broc* 'badger', *cammoc* 'cammock, a type of plant', *crag* (compare Welsh *craig* or *carreg*), *dunn* 'grey-brown' (compare Welsh *dwn*), and *wan* 'dark' (compare Welsh *gwan*). *Wan*, for instance, a word not otherwise known in Germanic, turns up in *Beowulf* (l. 702): *Com on wanre niht scriðan sceadugenga* 'The creature of the shadows came stalking in the dusky night' (John Clark Hall's translation). Three other Celtic words turn up in Northumbrian texts suggesting an ongoing British presence in the far north: *bratt* 'cloak', *carr* 'rock', and *luh* 'lake' (cf. modern *loch*). We must also add to the list a few words introduced by Irish missionaries, such as *ancor* 'anchorite', *clucge* 'bell', and *dry* 'sorcerer' (compare *druid*). There are several words of uncertain etymology with possible Celtic connections cited in the *Oxford English Dictionary*, but even if we included them all, we would only be talking of another twenty or so candidates. A number of other Celtic borrowings (such as *brogue*, *coracle*, and *plaid*) did come into English, but not until well after the Old English period.

There are various explanations, but all are speculation. Perhaps there was so little in common between the Celtic way of life as it had developed in Roman Britain, and the Anglo-Saxon way of life as it had developed on the Continent, that there was no motivation to borrow Celtic words. There might even have been a conscious avoidance of them. This could have happened if the Anglo-Saxons perceived themselves to be so socially superior to the 'barbarians' that Celtic words have been seen as 'gutter-speak'. Or there could have been avoidance for the opposite reason: because many Celts would have become highly Romanised (for the Romans were in the country for the best part of 400 years), perhaps the Anglo-Saxons perceived them as 'nouveau riche' and wished to distance themselves from such 'posh' speech. Either factor could have been relevant, in different times and places.

Then again, a completely different line of reasoning might have been involved. Perhaps the two ways of life were so similar that the Anglo-Saxons already had all the words they needed. Celtic words which the Anglo-Saxons might most usefully have adopted might already have come into their language from Latin because of the Roman presence in Europe. At the very least they would have been familiar with many Latin words, from encounters with Romans on the Continent. From this point of view, Latin – as the language of political power – would have been a more attractive source of words than Welsh; and this would have been consolidated when the Irish missionaries arrived in Britain, bringing Latin as the language of a different kind of power. The Celts, too, would have been familiar with Latin: there must have been many Latin-speaking Celts during the Romano-Celtic years. Latin certainly had an influence on early Celtic, as can be seen from such forms as Welsh *eglwys* 'church' from *ecclesia*, or *ysgol* 'school' from *schola*. Several early place-names show this influence, such as the many places whose names have a British form of *ecclesia* as their source: *Eccles, Eccleshall, Exhall, Eccleston*. ...

Genetic evidence is helping to throw some light on the situation. A study reported in 2002[2] showed a major difference in Y-chromosome markers between men from a selection of seven towns along an east–west transect from East Anglia to north Wales, suggesting a mass migration of Celts from England, with at least half the male indigenous Celtic population of England being displaced. The researchers, having also identified striking genetic similarities between English and Frisian men, concluded that the Welsh border was more of a genetic barrier than the North Sea. Such a significant population movement is suggestive of what we would today call 'ethnic cleansing' – and if this were so, one of the consequences would be a distaste for all things Celtic, especially the language. You do not borrow words from people you have just evicted.

But the linguistic evidence from personal names does not entirely support this scenario. There are not many Celtic names used by Anglo-Saxon personalities, but when they do occur they are of special interest. *Cædwalla, Ceadda, Cedd, Ceawlin, Cerdic*, and *Cumbra* are all Welsh names. *Cumbra*, for example, is very close to the Welsh word for 'Welshman', *Cymro*. But what is interesting is that these are all names of members of the Anglo-Saxon nobility. *Cædwalla*, for instance, was king of Wessex in 685, according to the *Anglo-Saxon Chronicle*, and his conversion to Christianity is described by Bede (Book V, Chapter 7). But *Cædwalla* is a distinctly Welsh name. Indeed, he has a namesake in the Welsh prince *Cadwallon* of Gwynedd – referred to as 'king of the Britons' by Bede (Book II, Chapter 20) – who killed the Northumbrian Kind Edwin in 633. What sort of society must it have been for Anglo-Saxon royalty to adopt Welsh names?

People are remarkably sensitive about choosing first names, as every parent knows. Great thought is devoted to the matter. No one would give their child the name of an enemy or of a person felt to be disreputable. When people are at war, they may even change their name to avoid being wrongly identified – as famously happened with the British royal family in 1917, when George V replaced Saxe-Coburg-Gotha by Windsor. On the other hand, choosing the name of a person whom one respects, or whom one wants to impress or thank, is a common practice – whether this be an older relative, a family friend, a business contact, or a political ally. People are also much influenced by social trends: some names become highly popular, and in modern times newspapers publish annual lists of the most fashionable choices. Religion exercises a strong influence, too, as with names of saints or biblical personalities. In older times – as still in many societies today – even greater significance was attached to the meanings of names, with children being deliberately called names which mean 'blessed', 'Christ-like', and so on.

So, if some Anglo-Saxon noblemen were giving their children British names, it must mean that, at the very least, there was respect for some members of Celtic society in some parts of the country. A likely scenario is that Anglo-Saxon chieftains would be living in accord with members of the Romano-Celtic nobility, and intermarrying with them. A child would be named for a senior member of one or other family, and this would just as easily be Celtic as Germanic. Some of these children would one day become nobility themselves and use of the name would spread. And if senior members of the household did such things, then junior members would also find it a fashionable thing to do. We do not know who were the parents of Cædmon – the seventh-century monastery stable-lad who, according to Bede (Book IV, Chapter 24), became England's first Christian poet – but they gave him a Welsh name. Why such intimate contact with Celtic tradition did not result in a greater influx of Celtic loanwords into Old English remains one of the great puzzles in the history of the language.

References for this reading

Bede. 1910. *The Ecclesiastical History of the English Nation*. London: Dent (Everyman's Library 479).

Branford, Jean and William Branford. 1991. *A Dictionary of South African English*, 4th edn. Oxford: Oxford University Press.

Weale, Michael E., Deborah A. Weiss, Rolf F. Jager, Neil Bradman, and Mark G. Thomas. 2002. Y Chromosome Evidence for Anglo-Saxon Mass Migration, *Molecular Biology and Evolution* 19, 1,008–21.

Notes
1 For South African English, see Branford and Branford (1991).
2 Weale, et al. (2002).

Modernity and English as a national language

Dick Leith and David Graddol with contributions by Liz Jackson

3.1 Introduction

This chapter describes some key developments in the English language from the end of the fifteenth century to the nineteenth century. It was during this period that English became standardised, and much of this chapter is taken up with consideration of how the idea of a 'standard' form of English, which could serve as a 'national' language of first England, then Britain, arose.

As in previous chapters, we examine here both changing linguistic characteristics and the wider social context within which English developed. That context was by any account remarkable. The sixteenth and seventeenth centuries form the period of English known as 'early modern'. It was the time in which Shakespeare, Dryden and Pepys lived, creating what many people today still regard as the 'great works' of English literature. It was also the era when Europe, as a whole, developed a radically new political and economic form, that of autonomous nation states each with a 'national' language.

During this period the English language was first taken overseas, to the new colonies in the Americas and Asia. In other words, just as it became a national language it became an international one as well. We focus in this chapter, however, on the development of English in England. Chapter 4 examines the expansion of English beyond England – to other parts of the British Isles and overseas.

3.2 Modernity and the rise of a national language

It was not only the language which became 'modern' during the period we discuss in this chapter, but the whole of European society. England, like many other parts of Europe, can in many ways be said to have made the transition from a medieval to a modern society during the sixteenth and seventeenth centuries, and that process was both complex and traumatic. For some – those who enjoyed the new wealth and intellectual liberation brought about by the growth of a market economy and the breaking away from the authoritarian dogmas of the Catholic church – it was a period of great excitement and opportunity. For many, such as the peasants who lost access to the land which provided them with a living, it was an oppressive period of poverty and social problems.

Modernity, in the sense that has come to be used by cultural theorists today, is both a state of mind and an economic and social condition. As a state of mind, it implies an intellectual outlook based on self-knowledge and rational argument rather than subservience to dogma or belief in magic. As a social condition, modernity implies particular forms of social relation based on forms of capitalism. Whether or not modernity is itself a transient condition is a moot point. In recent decades the political and economic structure of Europe has been undergoing another transformation, one which may prove to be as radical as that in the early modern period.

Modernity, as we use the term in this chapter, thus refers to ideas about social identity and language that are associated with wider intellectual, political and religious developments in Europe, particularly during the period 1500–1900. Modernity, in this sense, has also been experienced in other parts of the world where European culture was a major influence in social and economic development – most notably North America. In many ways, modernity can be regarded as a defining characteristic of 'the West'.

The Renaissance

The origins of this period of social upheaval lie in the intellectual movement that came to be known as the Renaissance or the 'revival of learning'. Starting in Italy in the fifteenth century and gradually spreading across Europe, the Renaissance was a time when scholars rediscovered the works of 'classical' scholars of Greek and Roman times. The invention of printing made it possible for these works to be distributed widely and read by a greater range of people than would otherwise have been possible, and one result was a rapid growth in translations of classics into local languages. The concept of a 'national language' originated in the European Renaissance. Contemporary attitudes to national languages were confused: it was *politically* necessary to defend them, but they were widely felt to be inferior to classical Greek and Latin. Also, language was seen by many Renaissance thinkers as an instrument to be shaped to suit the 'national' purpose.

The growth of capitalism

As international trade grew, so did banking and other financial services such as stock exchanges. For instance, Henry VIII of England (1509–1547) borrowed one million pounds on the Antwerp market in the last four years of his reign. With the growth of capitalism, new social class relations began to take shape. England, for example, was a major wool exporter but now began to manufacture and export cloth rather than the raw material. When the medieval 'guilds' controlled the supply of labour in the large towns, many merchants moved their operations to rural areas, where it was easy to find people willing to undertake spinning and weaving in their own cottages for low wages. Increasingly, merchants centralised production in 'manufactories' where workers could be supervised and where the complex division of labour could be managed. In the same way that the physical landscape of England was transformed when open land was enclosed by landlords for sheep rearing, so the social landscape took on a new shape as peasants increasingly became hired labourers and factory workers.

The growth of a market economy caused prices to rise throughout Europe. In Britain, basic commodities such as cereals and clothing are known to have quadrupled in price by 1600, while average wages only doubled. Entrepreneurs engaged in the new trade and industries became rich, but those on fixed incomes suffered and poverty emerged as a major social problem. Thus, one of the key features of the age was the restructuring of English society along lines of social class. As we discuss below, during the following centuries there arose new attitudes towards 'social correctness' and forms of English that indicated a speaker's social position.

The Reformation

The Reformation is the name given to the breaking away from the Roman Catholic faith and from the institutional authority of the Roman Catholic church in many parts of northern Europe. Throughout the period covered by Chapter 2, societies in western Europe owed allegiance to the Roman Catholic church, under the central authority of the Pope. By the sixteenth century, however, many of the tenets of the Catholic faith were being challenged by people who favoured a less elaborate form of worship based on individual faith, and who came to be called Protestants. Although originally a matter of religious doctrine, the challenge was championed by certain European leaders whose ambition was to set up states independent of the Pope's authority. In the early 1530s, Henry VIII declared himself (rather than the Pope) head of the English church.

The rise of humanist science

The Reformation led to a generally freer climate with regard to the pursuit of analytical studies involving the natural world. Scholars everywhere became more prepared to regard aspects of the human condition as the products of humans rather than of God. Language was one of many fields of scholarship which benefited from this 'humanist' enterprise, as scholars began to write treatises on language, construct grammars of English and compile dictionaries.

A remarkable expansion of knowledge occurred during the early modern period, partly as a result of European exploration of the world (most notably the Americas), and partly as a result of the sudden growth in scientific research. Indeed, the early modern period of English stretches from Copernicus's calculation in the early 1500s, that the sun rather than the earth was the centre of the solar system, to Isaac Newton's investigations into the properties of gravity and light. This was the period in which science in its modern sense emerged: the idea that knowledge resulted from the 'proof' of hypotheses based on careful experimentation and empirical observation. The discussion of such discoveries required a vast number of new words, and the new forms of reasoning and argument required innovation in the grammatical resources of English.

Puritanism

For some influential English people the reforms of the church instituted after Henry VIII's break with Roman Catholicism did not go far enough. These people favoured an even 'purer' form of worship, and they came to be known as Puritans. Their vested interest in the idea of an essentially 'English' church led some towards the study of Anglo-Saxon culture, which they celebrated as a golden age of freedom and equality disrupted by the 'Norman yoke' (see Chapter 2, Section 2.6). Many Puritans championed English over Latin, and favoured a 'plain' English purged of Latinate eloquence.

It is hardly surprising, then, that many Puritan scholars were involved in the study of Old English manuscripts. They also took an interest in English dialects. For example John Ray (Figure 3.1), a famous botanist, published in 1674 his collection of dialect words as an aspect of a locality's 'natural history'. Dialects were of interest to some Puritans because of their association with the Old English rather than Latinate component of the English vocabulary. But dialects have wider relevance too. In the course of the seventeenth century, several different Puritan sects emerged, drawing support from the entire social spectrum. Ordinary Puritans would have spoken regional dialects. So the Puritan perspective on language, with a grasp of history and a wide social base, created the possibility for an understanding of English as a 'national' language capable of uniting *all* English people in the eyes of God.

Many Puritans were drawn to the details of science, which in the seventeenth century were not opposed to those of religion, as they were later to become in the minds of many. Indeed, for Puritans, the scientist worked to the greater glory of God by helping to reveal to humanity the beauty and sophistication of the created universe – of which language was a part.

By the 1640s, Puritanism had become highly political. The growing power of the monarchy had been challenged by Parliament and, during the Civil War that followed, Puritans played an active role on the parliamentary side. Hostilities started in 1642 and, after numerous battles, Charles I was defeated in 1645. The king was executed in 1649 and a 'commonwealth' was declared. During this period, pamphlets circulated by certain Puritan sects argued not only that the king was a tyrant like the Norman conquerors, but that ownership of any kind of property, including land, was morally wrong. These radical arguments did not prevail among the wealthier parliamentarians, and although the arguments themselves survived (see Alexander, 1982), the sects which upheld them were increasingly marginalised. The monarchy was restored in 1660.

Figure 3.1   John Ray, English naturalist (1627–1705). His major three-volume work on botany, *Historia Plantarum*, covered 18,600 species and established taxonomic distinctions still drawn upon today. He also adopted a systematic approach to the study of language. (Science Photo Library)

The process of standardisation

The period in which Modern English arose was thus characterised by interconnected and fundamental changes in the structure of society. The key linguistic process associated with these social changes is **standardisation**: English was transformed from a vernacular language into one with a standardised variety that could be identified with England as a nation state.

A **standard language** is one that provides agreed norms of usage, usually codified in dictionaries and grammars, for a wide range of institutional purposes such as education, government and science. Sociolinguists tend to use the term '**Standard English**' to denote the primarily written, especially printed, usage of educated people.

In standardisation, there are four main processes (which may happen simultaneously):

- *Selection*: an existing language variety is identified as the basis. The variety selected is usually that of the most powerful or socially influential social or ethnic group.
- *Elaboration*: ensuring that the new language can be used for a wide range of functions. This may involve the extension of linguistic resources: for example, new specialised vocabulary or even new grammatical structures.

- *Codification*: reduction of internal variability in the selected variety, and the establishment of norms of grammatical usage and vocabulary. Since standard languages are rooted in written forms, standardisation often also involves the establishment of a standard spelling for words.
- *Implementation*: the standard language must be given currency by making texts available in it, by encouraging users to develop a loyalty and pride in it and by discouraging the use of alternative language varieties within official domains.

Standardisation thus has two main dimensions: as the sociolinguist Einar Haugen puts it, its goals are 'minimal variation in form, maximal variation in function' (Haugen, 1972, p. 107).

A number of languages have been turned into standard, national languages in the twentieth century as the result of deliberate policy and **language planning**: for example, Swahili in Tanzania and Tok Pisin in Papua New Guinea. Standardisation in English, however, was only partly a deliberate process. It resulted from a combination of social and economic conditions, though, as we will see, it was helped along by the activities of a large number of people. It is also important to note that standardisation in English has been only partly achieved. Indeed, Milroy and Milroy (1985, p. 24) suggest that no 'spoken language can ever be fully standardized'. Standard English remains something of an ideal, an imaginary form of English that is often rhetorically appealed to but never clearly identified. Standardisation is thus not simply a linguistic fact but an ongoing process and an ideological struggle.

Focusing

Sociolinguists have studied how reduction in variation in form (Haugen's first dimension) arises in speech communities without formal intervention by governments or language planners. Le Page and Tabouret-Keller (1985, p. 187) proposed a phenomenon that they call **focusing**. A focused linguistic community is one in which there is a strong sense of norms. There are four key 'agencies' of focusing:

1   Close daily interaction in the community.

2   The mechanisms of an education system.

3   A sense of common cause or group loyalty, perhaps due to the perception of a common threat.

4   The presence of a powerful model, such as the usage of a leader, a poet, a prestige group or a set of religious scriptures.

The concept of focusing is applied in the course of the discussion of standardisation in English that follows.

3.3 Selection: Caxton and the consequences of printing

Caxton did not invent printing but he was the first to bring the new technology to Britain (Figure 3.2), where it played a crucial role in the development of Standard English.

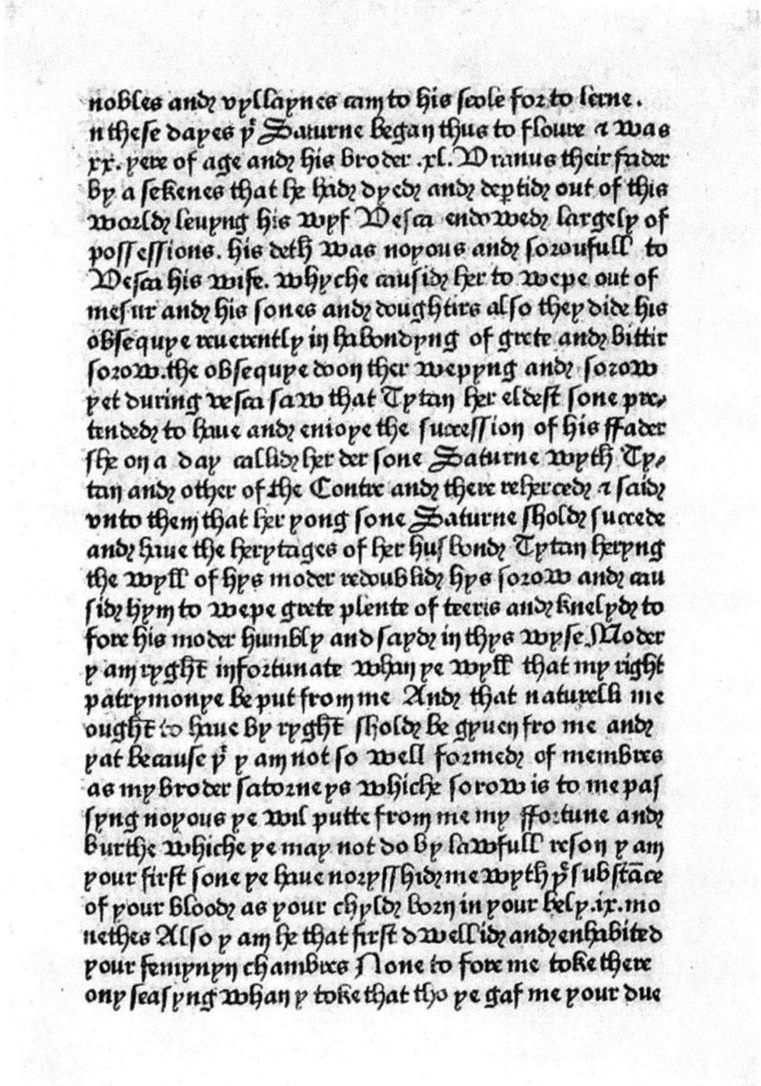

nobles and vyllaynes cam to his scole for to lerne.
n these dayes y^e Saturne began thus to floure & was
xx. yere of age and his broder .xl. Uranus their fader
by a sekenes that he had dyed and deptid out of this
world leuyng his wyf Vesca endowed largely of
possessions. his deth was noyous and sorowfull to
Vesca his wife. whyche causid her to wepe out of
mesur and his sones and doughtirs also they dide his
obseque reuerently in habondyng of grete and bittir
sorow. the obsequye doon ther weppyng and sorow
yet during vesca saw that Tytan her eldest sone pre-
tended to haue and enioye the succession of his ffader
she on a day callid her der sone Saturne wyth Tytan and other of the Contre and there reherced & said
vnto them that her yong sone Saturne shold succede
and haue the herytages of her husbond Tytan heryng
the wyll of hys moder redoublid hys sorow and cau
sid hym to wepe grete plente of teeris and knelyd to
fore his moder humbly and sayd in thys wyse. Moder
y am ryght infortunate whan ye wyll that my right
patrymonye be put from me And that naturelli me
ought to haue by ryght shold be gyuen fro me and
yat because y^t y am not so well formed of membres
as my broder satorne ys whiche sorow is to me pas
syng noyous ye wil putte from me my ffortune and
burthe whiche ye may not do by lawfull reson y am
your first sone ye haue norysshid me wyth ye substace
of your blood as your chyld born in your bely .ix. mo
nethes Also y am he that first dwellid and enhabited
your femynyn chambres None to fore me toke there
ony seasyng whan y toke that tho ye gaf me your due

Figure 3.2 The first book ever printed in English was *The History of Troy*, translated from the French and printed by Caxton in 1473. The black-letter typeface copied the style of gothic handwriting common in the Protestant countries of northern Europe. (John Rylands University Library of Manchester)

ACTIVITY 3.1

Reading A 'Caxton on dialects' is taken from a book by the linguists Roy Harris and Talbot Taylor called *Landmarks in Linguistic Thought* (which immediately gives you the authors' perspective on Caxton's significance).

Read this piece, then reread it, noting what the authors have to say about the problems posed by the lack of a fixed form for English and the solution Caxton adopted.

Comment

The problems facing all European printers including Caxton were that regional dialects proliferated, linguistic change was rapid, and there was a relative lack of conventionalised spellings and authoritative sources. Caxton solved this dilemma for England by default – by printing the dialect of the south-east Midlands.

You might have wondered about the authors' interpretation of Caxton's story reproduced at the beginning of the reading. Theirs is actually the most usual interpretation. The story is seen as authoritative evidence of linguistic disorder (and therefore justifying the argument that English was in need of standardisation). But you may have felt that too much fuss has been made about the eggs example. After all, aren't there plenty of similar examples of 'non-communication' in English today despite the process of standardisation that has since occurred?

One conclusion we could draw is that all Caxton is doing is highlighting the fact that language – *any* language – is variable, and that this at times causes problems for users. But we could also see Caxton as manipulating this example to suit his commercial interests. His argument that the English and their language were as variable as the effects of the moon makes a fanciful appeal, perhaps, to the idea of a readership united by a single characteristic. And the kinds of people able and interested enough to buy printed books were the newly literate middle class, who would be precisely the ones to identify with the mercer's sense of linguistic put-down.

There are also some points to add in relation to the introduction of printing technology and its cultural significance. Caxton certainly helped to familiarise people with the east Midlands dialect by establishing that dialect as the medium of print: using *I* rather than *ic(h)*, for instance, or *home* rather than *hame*. One consequence of this was that other dialects tended no longer to be printed. So a printed norm based on usage in only one part of the territory became the 'national' norm too. Caxton effectively accomplished the first stage of standardisation by selecting one variety.

By the way, Harris and Taylor refer to 'the dialect of London and the South-East' (in the last paragraph in Reading A), acknowledging changing notions of regional boundaries, whereas many sources refer to this same variety as the 'East Midlands' dialect taken as including London. Crystal (2004, pp. 201–2) explains that the earlier Mercian dialect area developed into two distinct regions; that termed 'East Midlands' can be viewed as particularly significant, including as it does a 'triangle' of special influence traceable between Oxford, Cambridge and London.

3.4 Elaboration

As Harris and Taylor say in Reading A, language during the Renaissance period generally became the object of attention and debate. There is plenty of evidence to show that, for the first time in its history, English was evaluated as a medium of serious communication, and its forms and structures scrutinised. There were many who considered English still unsuitable for literary or scholarly use, areas of life in which Latin and Greek were regarded as the perfect instruments. But there arose among a group of English authors the idea that the English language could be *made* more perfect, that it could be turned into as 'eloquent' a language as classical Latin. 'Eloquence' was a concept first associated with the ancient Greeks. Eloquence made a language more persuasive, and persuasion was central to the Greek ideal of the democratic city states such as Athens. The concept was important to the Romans too, who applied it to the writing of literature as well as public speaking.

One linguistic dimension of eloquence was *copiousness*: the language needed enough words to represent every idea. In fact, it needed more than this; in order to prevent repetition of the same word, a variety of synonyms were needed to provide stylistic variation. This could be achieved either by greatly increasing the word stock or by increasing what was called 'significancy' – the ability of words to mean more than one thing (**polysemy**). At the sentence level, eloquence also required the use of rhetorical structures, such as 'antithesis' in which oppositions are carefully balanced against each other. How, then, could English be made more eloquent so that it could take over from Latin in the writing of poetry and literature, and so that a 'national' literature could be created which expressed the emerging cultural identity of England? There were three principal solutions:

- The lexicon was extended. It is estimated that during the period 1500–1700 over 30,000 new words were added to the English vocabulary. The process reached its peak in the early 1600s when, on average, over 300 new words were recorded each year (see Figure 3.3).
- Existing words acquired more meanings (see Figure 3.4), thus increasing significancy.
- At the level of the sentence, eloquence was achieved by imitating the rhetorical structures of Latin. An example is the quotation from Ascham in Reading A, which illustrates the antithetical style.

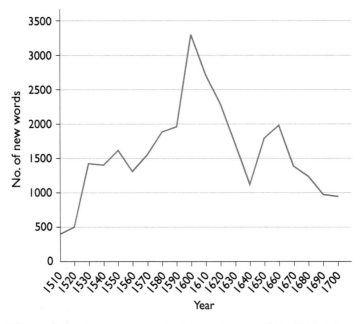

Figure 3.3   Changes in the English vocabulary 1500–1700 (adapted from Görlach, 1991, p. 137)

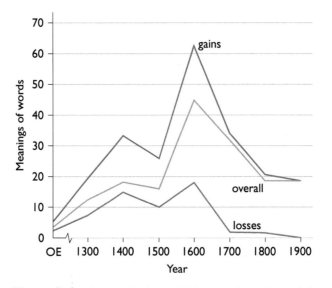

Figure 3.4   Growth in the multiple meanings of words in early modern English: the accretion and obsolescence of independent senses of eight polysemous words: *draught, form, sense, set, stock, trade, train, wit* (adapted from Görlach, 1991, p. 199)

By the end of the sixteenth century a new and flourishing English literary tradition had arisen and many literary men thought that English, through the works of writers such as Spenser and Shakespeare, had achieved literary greatness. In 1592 the writer Thomas Nashe, for instance, credited the 'Poets of our time' with having: cleansed our language from barbarisme and made the vulgar sort here in London ... to aspire to a richer puritie of speech' (quoted in Bailey, 1992, p. 37).

During the following century, however, the Protestant spirit of intellectual independence encouraged a rapid growth in scientific discovery and further elaboration of English was needed. Given the prominence of scientific English today it may seem surprising that no one really knew *how* to write science in English before the seventeenth century.

Why science came to be written in English

As was noted in Section 3.2, the European Renaissance is sometimes called the 'revival of learning', a time of renewed interest in the 'lost knowledge' of classical times. At the same time, however, scholars also began to test and extend this knowledge. The emergent nation states of Europe developed competitive interests in world exploration and the development of trade. Such expansion, which was to take the English language west to America and east to India, was supported by scientific developments such as the discovery of magnetism (and hence the invention of the compass), improvements in cartography and – perhaps the most important scientific revolution of them all – the new theories of astronomy and the movement of the earth in relation to the planets and stars developed by Copernicus (1473–1543).

A study of how Copernican theory gradually came to be accepted across Europe would illustrate how closely entwined were the various strands of the Renaissance process. Copernicus was one of the first generation of scholars who were able to publish and circulate their ideas to a wide audience by means of the printed book. The printing trade itself had an economic interest in translating such works into the national languages – in England there were many potential purchasers who did not understand Latin. But the spread of Copernican ideas was not welcomed by the Catholic church. Indeed, the whole project of humanist science – based on the intellectual independence of the scientists, free to test ideas empirically and by rational argument – was potentially subversive of the authority of the church, the transnational institution which had for so many centuries been the focus of learning in Europe. When Galileo dared to admit that he believed in Copernican theory, the Pope issued anti-Copernican edicts restraining Italian scientists from publishing or teaching theories which appeared to contradict the biblical account of the cosmos. The church effectively stifled the new science in Italy.

In England the eleven years of Puritan government which followed the Civil War may have helped to produce an intellectual climate of democracy, anti-authoritarianism and independence of mind, in which a distinctively British form of science – stressing the importance of empirical method, simplicity, utility and attention to detail – arose.

The Royal Society

England was one of the first countries where scientists adopted and publicised Copernican ideas with enthusiasm. Some of these scholars, including two with interests in language – John Wallis and John Wilkins – helped found the Royal Society in 1660 in order to promote empirical scientific research.

John Wallis

In 1653, one of the last of the Renaissance scholars, John Wallis (Figure 3.5), published a grammar of English, *Grammatica Linguae Anglicanae*, which is widely regarded as 'a very important landmark in the history of phonetics and English grammar' (Kemp, 1972, p. 1). The book was one of the last of the scholarly treatises to be written in Latin. Wallis was a controversial figure who became prominent in many fields. He was the inventor of the mathematical sign for infinity, developed a considerable reputation during the English Civil War for his ability to decipher secret messages, and was involved in a system for teaching the deaf. His contemporary, John Aubrey, said:

> To give him his due prayse he hath exceedingly well deserved of the commonwealth of learning, perhaps no mathematical writer so much. Tis certain that he is a person of real worth, and may stand with much glory upon his own basis, needing not to be beholding to any man for fame, of which he is so extremely greedy, that he steals flowers from others to adorn his own cap.

(quoted in Kemp, 1972, p. 15)

Figure 3.5   John Wallis (1616–1703)

In his preface to the 1699 edition of his grammar, Wallis (1699, pp. xxiv–vi) wrote:

> ... many people want to learn our language, but foreigners often complain that it is so difficult that they cannot easily acquire it. Even some of our own countrymen, surprising though it may seem, have the foolish notion that the structure of our language is somehow complex and over-involved, and scarcely obeys any grammatical laws. Would-be learners and would-be teachers usually approach it in such a muddled way that the inevitable result is a great deal of boredom and difficulty. My purpose in taking it upon myself to write this book is to remedy this unfortunate situation. I aim to describe the language, which is very simple in essence, in brief rules, so that it will be easier for foreigners to learn, and English people will get a better insight into the true structure of their native tongue.
>
> I am well aware that others before me have made the attempt at one time or another and have produced worth-while contributions ... None of them, however, in my opinion, used the method which is best suited to the task. They all forced English too rigidly into the mould of Latin (a mistake which nearly everyone makes in descriptions of other modern languages too), giving many useless rules about the cases, genders and declensions of nouns, the tenses, moods and conjugations of verbs, the government of nouns and verbs, and other things of that kind, which have no bearing on our language, and which confuse and obscure matters instead of elucidating them.
>
> (Wallis, 1699, pp. xxiv–vi, in Kemp, 1972, pp. 107, 109, 111).

Across Europe, similar academies and societies arose, creating new national traditions of science. The scholars of many of these countries, such as France, Italy and Spain, published in their national languages. But those countries which found themselves on the periphery of the great expansion in scientific learning were faced with a difficult choice: if they wished to ensure that their own scholarly institutions were able to exchange knowledge internationally, then they were forced to adopt one of the international languages of science. This helps to explain why Latin persisted as a lingua franca alongside national languages for some time. The use of an international language, however, cut off the fledgling scientific institutions from their own national audiences, inhibiting the diffusion of the new learning among their populations. Some countries, such as Sweden, adopted a bilingual policy: two scientific academies were founded at the start of the eighteenth century, one of which used Latin as its official language, the other Swedish. The language dilemmas that faced such countries then continue to face them today, but now English stands in the place of Latin.

In the initial stages of the scientific revolution most publications in the national languages were popular works, encyclopedias, educational textbooks and translations. Original science was not done in English until the second half of the seventeenth century. For example, Newton published his mathematical treatise known as the *Principia* in Latin, but published his later work on the property of light – *Opticks* – in English (Figure 3.6).

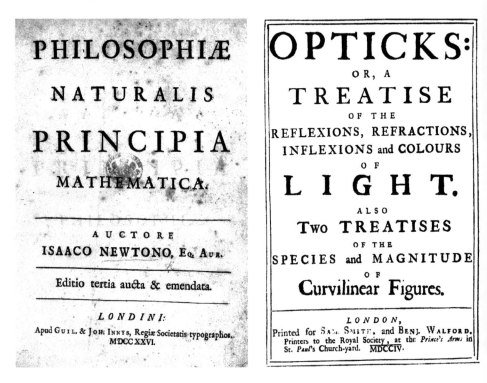

Figure 3.6   In the interval between the publication of Newton's *Principia Mathematica* (first published 1667; the title page from the third amended edition of 1726 is shown here) and his *Opticks* (1704), original science came to be written in English. (*left:* British Library)

There were several reasons why original science continued to be written in Latin. The first was simply a matter of audience. Latin was suitable for an international audience of scholars, whereas English reached a socially wider but more local audience. Hence popular science was written in English.

A second reason for writing in Latin may, perversely, have been a concern for secrecy. Open publication had dangers in that it put into the public domain preliminary ideas which had not yet been fully exploited by their 'author'. This growing concern about intellectual property rights was a feature of the period – it reflected both the humanist notion of the individual, rational scientist who invents and discovers through private intellectual labour, and the growing connection between original science and commercial exploitation. There was something of a social distinction between 'scholars and gentlemen' who understood Latin, and men of trade who lacked a classical education.

And in the mid seventeenth century it was common practice for mathematicians to keep their discoveries and proofs secret by writing them in cipher, or in obscure languages, or in private messages deposited in a sealed box with the Royal Society. Some scientists might have felt more comfortable with Latin precisely because its audience, though international, was becoming increasingly socially restricted. Medicine and surgery clung the most keenly to Latin as an 'insider language'.

But a third reason why the writing of original science in English was delayed may have been to do with the linguistic inadequacy of English in the early modern period. English was not well equipped to deal with scientific argument. First, it lacked the necessary technical vocabulary. Second, and in some ways more interestingly, it lacked the grammatical resources required to represent the world in an objective and impersonal way, and to discuss the relations, such as cause and effect, that might hold between complex and hypothetical entities.

Fortunately, several members of the Royal Society possessed an interest in language and became engaged in various linguistic projects. One, the most ambitious, was to create a new, universal language which would incorporate the new scientific taxonomies in its vocabulary structure, permit logical argument, and be politically and religiously neutral. Perhaps the best known of these enterprises was the 'Real Character' of John Wilkins.

The Royal Society played with the idea of forming a committee which would act as a lead body in establishing new forms of English, like the language academies of other European countries. In 1664 the society voted that there be a committee for improving the English language. Although this proposal came to little, the society's members did a great deal to foster the publication of science in English and to encourage the development of a suitable writing style. Many members of the Royal Society also published monographs in English. One of the first was by Robert Hooke, the society's first curator of experiments, who described experiments with microscopes in *Micrographia* (Hooke, 1961 [1665]; see Figure 3.7). This work is largely narrative in style, based on a transcript of oral demonstrations and lectures.

In 1665 a new scientific journal, *Philosophical Transactions*, was inaugurated (Figure 3.8). This was perhaps the first international English language scientific journal and it encouraged the development of a new genre of scientific writing, that of short, focused accounts of particular experiments. One historian suggests that foreign scholars frequently complained about the use of English for the *Philosophical Transactions*, 'being clumsy in the English language' (Hunter, 1989, p. 250).

The seventeenth century was thus a formative period in the establishment of scientific English. In the following century much of this momentum was lost as German established itself as the leading European language of science. It is estimated that by the end of the eighteenth century, 401 German scientific journals had been established as opposed to 96 in France and 50 in England

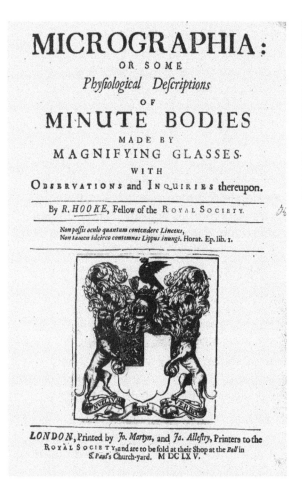

Figure 3.7 Hooke's *Micrographia* was one of the first scientific treatises written in English. (British Library)

Figure 3.8 *Philosophical Transactions*, volume 1, number 1, was possibly the first international journal written in English. (Cambridge University Library)

(Houghton, 1975, p. 19). However, in the nineteenth century, scientific English again enjoyed substantial lexical growth as the Industrial Revolution created the need for new technical vocabulary and new, specialised, professional societies were instituted to promote and publish in the new disciplines.

The creation of scientific English

We have claimed that the English language had to be made capable for scientific discourse, a project which was to take at least 300 years. The creation of scientific English was a part of a wider Renaissance project of elaborating the English language so that it could be used in a wide range of communicative domains. One of the first arenas to benefit had been literary language. However, the highly ornate style that had become common in literary discourse was not regarded as suitable for precise, unambiguous description

and clear logical argument. An early history by one of the founding members
of the Royal Society, Thomas Sprat, indicates something of the Puritan aversion
to the 'eloquence' of the times. '*Eloquence*,' he said, 'ought to be banish'd out
of all *civil Societies*, as a thing fatal to Peace and good Manners' (Sprat, 1959
[1667], p. 111, original emphasis). He suggested that the society had:

> ... been most vigorous in putting in execution, the only remedy that can be
> found for this *extravagance:* and that has been, a constant Resolution to
> reject all amplifications, digressions, and swellings of style: to return back
> to the primitive purity, and shortness, when men deliver'd so many *things,*
> almost in an equal number of *words.* They have exacted from all their
> members, a close, naked, natural way of speaking; positive expressions;
> clear senses; a native easiness: bringing all things as near the Mathematical
> plainness, as they can: and preferring the language of Artizans,
> Countrymen, and Merchants, before that, of Wits, or Scholars.

> (Sprat, 1959 [1667], p. 113, original emphasis)

It is worth noting that the motivation for neologising (coining new words or
expressions) in science was rather different from that in literary genres.
Whereas literary English sought synonyms in order to provide alternative
forms of expression (eloquence), science required a precise and standardised
language in which, ideally, there were only as many words as referents
(i.e. things, processes, etc. referred to).

Terminology

One of the pressing linguistic needs of the new scientific community lay in
terminology. This lack was felt keenly by the early translators of classical
works. In this situation any translator is faced with several choices:

- The Latin term can be 'borrowed' in its entirety into English, adapted to
  English morphology.
- The Latin word can be translated element for element into English (what is
  technically known as a '*calque*').
- A new English word can be invented.
- An existing word can have its meaning extended so that it acquires
  a specialised, technical, as well as everyday sense.

All these techniques were used to develop scientific English, but by far the
commonest was the first: the simple adoption of the Latin term. One of the
earliest attempts to render a technical discussion into the English language is
a Middle English work by Chaucer drawing on a Latin work, *Compositio et
Operatio Astrolabii,* by the eighth-century Arabian astronomer, Meeahala. In
many ways it was no more than an instruction manual, though one written for
a young boy – possibly Chaucer's own son – who had not yet learnt Latin. In
the first part of this treatise on the *Astrolabe (I.1),* Chaucer takes care to
introduce a number of terms taken from Latin, such as 'altitude': 'Thyn
astrolabie hath a ring to putten on the thombe of the right hond in taking the

height of thinges. And tak kep, for from henes forthward I wol clepen [call] the heighte of any thing that is taken by the rewle 'the altitude', withoute moo wordes' (Chaucer, *c.*1391, in Robinson, 1966, p. 546).

Chaucer's willingness to borrow from Latin was in contrast to the Old English period, when the vocabulary of English was still almost entirely Germanic in origin and the calque was a more popular strategy. For example, the Old English scholar Aelfric translated the grammatical term *praepositio* as *foresetnys*, a term which was later replaced by a Latin loan: the *Oxford English Dictionary* (OED) attributes *prepisicion* to Wycliffe in 1388.

Not all the science that was translated into English originated from European scholars. As Chaucer's work shows, both Muslim science and the science of ancient Greece were important in the medieval world. Several of the words to be translated from Latin were thus already loans from Arabic or Greek. Examples of Arabic terms from astronomy include *azimuth, zenith, nadir*; from mathematics, *algebra, cipher, zero* and – from the name of a Muslim mathematician, al-Khwarizmi – *algorithm*; from alchemy, *alcohol, alkali*. From Greek came many terms in geometry, such as *diagonal, hypotenuse, pentagon, polynomial*.

In the second half of the seventeenth century, English scientists were themselves increasingly responsible for discoveries and inventions. As the horizons of knowledge expanded, particularly in botany, geography and chemistry, new forms of classification and nomenclature arose. There were so many new things to be described and new concepts to be communicated that the vocabulary of English again needed to be enhanced in a systematic manner.

Latin, for several reasons, remained an important resource for neologisms in this period. One was that new concepts were invented by the discoverers and theorists – the leading-edge scholars who were familiar with Latin and found in its inflectional system a production morphology for the creation of adjectives and nouns (particularly those based on the name of the discoverer). But the use of Latinate neologisms also provided something close to shared vocabulary among scientists in different countries. The national languages thus provided a matrix into which a common technical vocabulary could be inserted, just as today many languages have adopted a common technical vocabulary based on English.

The liberal incorporation of Latin words into English texts, however, was not without its problems. One of the purposes of publishing works in English was to make them available, for both educational and commercial reasons, to a wider national audience. But the use of so many strange and foreign words could have the effect of making them inaccessible.

Grammar

One form of neologism is the extension in the use of an existing word to a new word class. For example, a noun can be used as a verb, or a verb as a noun. Shakespeare frequently made nouns behave as verbs. For example, in

Shakespeare's play, King Lear describes his daughter Cordelia (Act 1, Scene 1) as 'Unfriended, new-adopted to our hate, /Dower'd with our curse, and stranger'd with our oath'. Renaissance science seems to have encouraged the transformation of verbs to nouns. Such changes are not just stylistic: whether an idea is presented in language as a 'process' (verb) or a 'thing' (noun) may be important. Shakespeare was a dramatist and no doubt wished to portray the world as consisting of happenings. The project of humanist science can, at one level, be regarded as one which imposed order on the fluid experience of the world: a reconceptualisation of the world as consisting of 'things', of objects of study. The language of Shakespeare and the language of science thus provide alternative modes of construing the world.

In a study of scientific language from Newton's *Opticks* to the present day, Halliday (1993) schematically describes the evolution of scientific discourse and its mode of representing the world in the following way. He suggests that the preferred grammatical format for describing physical phenomena was originally in the form of:

a happens; so x happens

Gradually, through the centuries, there is a movement towards the form:

happening a is the cause of happening x

In the first grammatical structure, events are described by means of a verb in a conventional narrative form. In the later structure these events have become expressed through nominal (i.e. noun) forms. These noun phrases grow in length and complexity, whereas verbal forms become fewer.

The linguistic sleight of hand by which events and processes are represented in language as states or things (i.e. as nouns or noun phrases), Halliday calls 'grammatical metaphor'. Such language not only allows the natural world to be objectified but also enables the scientist to develop a complex, and at times abstract, argument. It allows, for example, a complex phenomenon to be 'packaged' linguistically as one element in a clause so that the whole can be positioned within an unfolding argument. It is a feature of English grammar that noun phrases can be extended in this way whereas verb phrases cannot. In the following extract from *Electricity and Magnetisim* (1675), by Robert Boyle (a founding member of the Royal Society), the author uses four noun phrases in the second sentence: 'the modification of motion in the internal parts', 'the Emanations of the Amber', 'the degree of it', and 'the Attraction':

[I]t has been observ'd, that Amber, & c. warm'd by the fire, does not attract so vigorously, as if it acquire an equal degree of heat by being chaf'd or rub'd: So that the modification of motion in the internal parts, and in the Emanations of the Amber, may, as well as the degree of it, contribute to the Attraction.

(Boyle, 1927 [1675], pp. 8–9)

In such constructions the verb does not describe a process in the world but rather proposes a relationship *between* such processes, either causative or logical. Thus scientific discourse typically uses verbs to express logical relations and argument, and nouns to represent entities and processes in the world. Halliday suggests that this is how Renaissance scientists came to be able to conduct the new science, which brought together experimental method with theoretical interpretation, in English, since 'up to that point, doing and thinking remain as separate moments in the cultural dynamic: in "science" the two are brought together' (Halliday, 1993, p. 67).

It was not until the late nineteenth century that realist scientific discourse could be said to have been perfected. By then it had become common for scientists to avoid the use of the first person (*I*) even when describing experimental method. Newton, in contrast, began his account of Experiment 1 in the *Opticks*: 'I took a black oblong stiff paper ... this paper I view'd through a prism of solid glass'. The world as construed by scientific English had, by the start of the twentieth century, achieved complete objectivity: it existed 'out there' independently of the agency or examination of the scientist.

There are, however, linguistic costs attached to such grammatical structures, as Halliday points out. In English the verb phrase provides the richest mechanism for describing relationships between entities. Hence the use of long nominal expressions means that the precise relations between entities *within the phrase* cannot be made explicit. Halliday identifies some of the ambiguities in one text as follows:

> What is *lung cancer death rates*: how quickly lungs die from cancer, how many people die from cancer of the lung, or how quickly people die if they have it? What is *increased smoking*: more people smoke, or people smoke more? What is *are associated with*: caused by (you die because you smoke), or cause (you smoke because you are – perhaps afraid of – dying)? We may have rejected all but the 'right' interpretation without thinking – but only because we know what it is on about already.
>
> (Halliday, 1993, p. 68)

Hence scientific English often requires a certain knowledge and understanding of the subject matter: it may be better at high-level, abstract argument than at low-level, explicit description.

3.5 Codification

During the sixteenth century, English became the object of serious academic study by people with practical interests who were responding to the political, cultural and religious controversies of their times (as seen in the previous section). One such practical interest arose because English had now become a language taught in school (see item 2 in the list of focusing agencies in Section 3.2).

One of the first grammars in English was William Lily's *A Shorte Introduction of Grammar*. Although known as 'Lily's Grammar', the book was actually compiled from various sources after his death in 1523 (see Figure 3.9). This was one of the first books in English to become 'authorised' by King Henry VIII – it remained the 'national grammar' for several centuries and versions of it were used in English schools until the nineteenth century. Although written in English it was essentially a grammar of Latin, but it provided the basic introduction to grammar that all the English writers of the early modern period, including Shakespeare, Spenser and Ben Jonson, were brought up on. As one editor has commented, 'This was the introduction to the classics of Rome for those who were to create the classics of England' (Flynn, in Lily, 1945 [1542], p. xi).

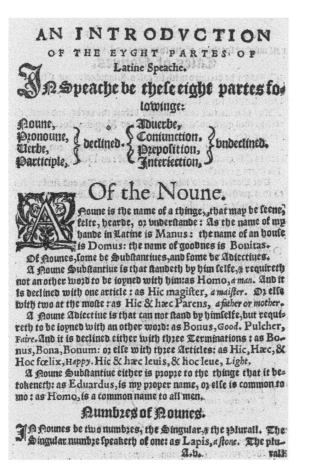

Figure 3.9 A page from Lily's *A Shorte Introduction of Grammar*, published in 1542, which established grammatical terminology in English. The book is also interesting typographically: black-letter type, which had largely been replaced in English books by roman type, is retained here for English. Latin words are set in roman type and English translations in italic. (Folger Shakespeare Library)

The grammatical analysis described by Lily was already an ancient one. The earliest Greek grammar, written by Dionysius Thrax in approximately 100 BC, identified eight 'parts of speech'. Since grammar was considered a universal structure which, like rhetoric, could be applied to any language, this number of parts of speech was sought in other languages, such as Latin (by Donatus in the fourth century AD) and then later in English. Lily therefore established not only an English terminology for grammatical ideas but also a grammatical analysis of English, closely modelled on that of Latin. Thus began a tradition of writing grammars of English that followed Latin models, a tradition that was not entirely broken until the nineteenth century.

The first grammar to attempt a description of the English language in English was Bullokar's *Bref Grammar for English*, published in 1586. One of its purposes, like those of Lily's Grammar, was educational – to 'rationalise' English spelling, vocabulary and grammar. In this respect, its conception of grammar differed from that of modern linguistics. In fact, *grammar* for Bullokar meant the 'art of writing', its meaning in ancient Greek (Bullokar, 1977 [1586]). This conception dominated European thinking about grammar until well past Bullokar's time, and has had vital implications for education and the processes of standardisation, as we will see. Such a grammar served more than an educational purpose, however: it could be seen as symbolic of the dignity of English by other Europeans. The writing of grammars for European languages had become politically expedient by Bullokar's time and any European state desiring autonomy needed to have its own grammar of the so-called national language.

During the eighteenth century a hierarchical view of language was developed by many observers in the social and cultural context of a literate middle class, based partly in the London coffee houses (Figure 3.10). Here language, politics and the history of literature were discussed, and essays on these subjects were published in several newly established periodicals. It was in this context that the word 'standard' seems first to have been applied to issues of language. Significantly, however, its most common meaning seems to have been 'level of excellence'. The OED (Simpson and Weiner, 1989) quoted a writer from 1711 asserting that the Greeks 'brought their beautiful and comprehensive Language to a just Standard'. Also significant is the continued association of the word with the classical languages, and the fact that it denoted a standard of *literary* correctness or excellence. In the following year, however, the clergyman and writer Jonathan Swift applied the term to English. He wanted to refine the language 'to a certain standard' (Crowley, 1989, p. 93).

Swift and other commentators like him were very concerned to protect English against the charge of 'barbarism'. The way to do this was to 'fix' the language so that it no longer varied and changed. One mechanism was to emulate states such as France and Italy and set up an academy to regulate usage. But the idea, most famously proposed by Swift himself in 1712, came

Figure 3.10   An eighteenth-century coffee house (Mary Evans Picture Library)

to nothing. Another course was to write a definitive dictionary, of the kind attempted by Dr Samuel Johnson in 1755, which we discuss below.

The desire for linguistic order did not arise simply from a desire to emulate the classical languages. Writers such as Swift were anxious to preserve the *political* order: for these writers the fixing of the language was to help safeguard what Swift called the 'civil or religious constitution'. As Dr Johnson wrote some forty years later: 'tongues, like governments, have a natural tendency to degenerate: we have long preserved our constitution, let us make some struggles for our languages' (2006 [1755], paragraph 91).

Let's now consider these points in relation to one of the most influential books in the history of English, Johnson's *A Dictionary of the English Language* (see Figure 3.11).

ACTIVITY 3.2

Allow about
30 minutes

Bearing in mind Johnson's words about the struggle for the language, read the five extracts from the 'Preface' to his *Dictionary* given in Figure 3.11. As you read, consider the questions below.

- What are the problems Johnson sees in writing a dictionary of English? What help, if any, was available to him?
- What kind of English usage does he include, and what does he exclude?
- What 'story' of language seems to guide him? And what does he have to say about change in language?
- What are his views on translation and academies?

1   When I took the firſt ſurvey of my undertaking, I found our ſpeech copious without order, and energetick without rules: wherever I turned my view, there was perplexity to be diſentangled, and confuſion to be regulated; choice was to be made out of boundleſs variety, without any eſtabliſhed principle of ſelection; adulterations were to be detected, without a ſettled teſt of purity; and modes of expreſſion to be rejected or received, without the ſuffrages of any writers of claſſical reputation or acknowledged authority.

Having therefore no aſſiſtance but from general grammar, I applied myſelf to the peruſal of our writers; and noting whatever might be of uſe to aſcertain or illuſtrate any word or phraſe, accumulated in time the materials of a dictionary, which, by degrees, I reduced to method, eſtabliſhing to myſelf, in the progreſs of the work, ſuch rules as experience and analogy ſuggeſted to me; experience, which practice and obſervation were continually increaſing; and analogy, which, though in ſome words obſcure, was evident in others.

2   So far have I been from any care to grace my pages with modern decorations, that I have ſtudiouſly endeavoured to collect examples and authorities from the writers before the reſtoration, whoſe works I regard as *the wells of Engliſh undefiled*, as the pure ſources of genuine diction. Our language, for almoſt a century, has, by the concurrence of many cauſes, been gradually departing from its original *Teutonick* character, and deviating towards a *Gallick* ſtructure and phraſeology, from which it ought to be our endeavour to recal it, by making our ancient volumes the ground-work of ſtile, admitting among the additions of later times, only ſuch as may ſupply real deficiencies, ſuch as are readily adopted by the genius of our tongue, and incorporate eaſily with our native idioms.

But as every language has a time of rudeneſs antecedent to perfection, as well as of falſe refinement and declenſion, I have been cautious leſt my zeal for antiquity might drive me into times too remote, and croud my book with words now no longer underſtood. I have fixed *Sidney's* work for the boundary, beyond which I make few excurſions. From the authours which roſe in the time of *Elizabeth*, a ſpeech might be formed adequate to all the purpoſes of uſe and elegance. If the language of theology were extracted from *Hooker* and the tranſlation of the Bible; the terms of natural knowledge from *Bacon*; the phraſes of policy, war, and navigation from *Raleigh*; the dialect of poetry and fiction from *Spenſer* and *Sidney*; and the diction of common life from *Shakeſpeare*, few ideas would be loſt to mankind, for want of *Engliſh* words, in which they might be expreſſed.

3   Nor are all words which are not found in the vocabulary, to be lamented as omiſſions. Of the laborious and mercantile part of the people, the diction is in a great meaſure caſual and mutable; many of their terms are formed for ſome temporary or local convenience, and though current at certain times and places, are in others utterly unknown. This fugitive cant, which is always in a ſtate of increaſe or decay, cannot be regarded as any part of the durable materials of a language, and therefore muſt be ſuffered to periſh with other things unworthy of preſervation.

4   Total and ſudden transformations of a language ſeldom happen; conqueſts and migrations are now very rare: but there are other cauſes of change, which, though ſlow in their operation, and inviſible in their progreſs, are perhaps as much ſuperiour to human reſiſtance, as the revolutions of the ſky, or intumeſcence of the tide. Commerce, however neceſſary, however lucrative, as it depraves the manners, corrupts the language; they that have frequent intercourſe with ſtrangers, to whom they endeavour to accommodate themſelves, muſt in time learn a mingled dialect, like the jargon which ſerves the traffickers on the *Mediterranean* and *Indian* coaſts. This will not always be confined to the exchange, the warehouſe, or the port, but will be communicated by degrees to other ranks of the people, and be at laſt incorporated with the current ſpeech.

5   The great peſt of ſpeech is frequency of tranſlation. No book was ever turned from one language into another, without imparting ſomething of its native idiom; this is the moſt miſchievous and comprehenſive innovation; ſingle words may enter by thouſands, and the fabrick of the tongue continue the ſame, but new phraſeology changes much at once; it alters not the ſingle ſtones of the building, but the order of the columns. If an academy ſhould be eſtabliſhed for the cultivation of our ſtile, which I, who can never wiſh to ſee dependance multiplied, hope the ſpirit of *Engliſh* liberty will hinder or deſtroy, let them, inſtead of compiling grammars and dictionaries, endeavour, with all their influence, to ſtop the licence of tranſlatours, whoſe idleneſs and ignorance, if it be ſuffered to proceed, will reduce us to babble a dialect of *France*.

Figure 3.11   Extracts from the 'Preface' to Dr Johnson's *Dictionary*, taken from the fourth edition of 1773

Comment

From the first extract we get a glimpse of Johnson's classicising desire for perfection in language: English has no 'settled test of purity'. To make matters worse, there was nothing except 'general grammar' to help him. Almost all the dictionaries available to Johnson were specialist ones: lists of so-called hard words (adoptions from Latin and Greek), bilingual dictionaries and so on. So he had to scrutinise the work of writers. The second extract tells us that he favours the writing, not of the present but of the past, notably of the late sixteenth or seventeenth centuries. This was a golden age for Johnson, from which the language had degenerated, partly because of influence from French ('Gallick'); but note that his remark about a 'time of rudeness antecedent to perfection' suggests yet another linguistic story: that a language may first gestate and then blossom. We can call this a *cyclical* view of language. But we find that Johnson refers only to writing of a certain kind: *literature*, by which he meant writing such as theology (Hooker) and scripture (the Bible), or scientific and governmental works (Bacon and Raleigh), as well as literature in the narrower sense more commonly used today. The third extract shows that he excludes the (presumably spoken) usage of the 'laborious [working] and mercantile part of the people' on the grounds that this usage does not last. Mercantile matters are also singled out in the fourth extract: it is 'commerce', rather than 'conquests and migrations', that 'corrupts' English; and in the final extract he also blames translation. His opposition to an academy is based on a notion of 'liberty' that he sees as essentially English (as opposed to the fanatical adherence to tyrannical laws, seen as an attribute of the French).

The doctrine of correctness

Johnson's *Dictionary* was followed by several 'grammars' of English which recommended certain grammatical usages as 'correct'. For instance, the cumulative negative construction such as the one in the Caedmon text (in Chapter 2, Section 2.4) – *Ne con ic noht singan* ('Not know I not (how) to sing') – was deemed illogical, therefore incorrect. It contained two negative particles, *ne* and *noht*, which in accordance with the laws of algebra must cancel each other out. So, according to this logic, the correct (modern) form ought to be *I don't know how to sing*, with just one negative particle (*n't*).

These arguments, a further aspect of the eighteenth-century discourse of standardisation, were sometimes given a divine justification. In an earlier section we discussed the idea that everything in nature was an expression of God's order. If the way a society is organised – its 'constitution', to use Johnson's word – can be claimed as part of nature, then it, too, reflects God's will. The 'genius' of English – to quote Johnson again (2006 [1755], paragraph 61) – reflected the English way of life, and part of this genius was its grammar. To deviate from correct grammar, then, was to displease God. The grammarian Robert Lowth, who was to become a bishop, and for whom the English translation of the Bible was the 'best standard of our language', thought that correct grammar was next to godliness. His grammar, first published in 1762, ran to twenty-two editions in thirty years (Lowth, 1968 [1762]).

The doctrine of correctness was also applied to pronunciation in the form of pronouncing dictionaries. A very famous one was John Walker's *A Critical Pronouncing Dictionary* of 1791, which prefixed word meanings by the 'Rules of Pronouncing' (Walker, 1968 [1791], titlepage). Walker acknowledged the range of dialectal pronunciations throughout England and gave 'rules to be observed by the natives of Scotland, Ireland and London, for avoiding their respective peculiarities' (1968 [1791], titlepage). He gave particular attention to Londoners, 'who, as they are the models of pronunciation to the distant provinces, ought to be the more scrupulously correct (1968 [1791], p. xii)'. His 'Fourth Fault' of Cockney, the lower class dialect of London, was 'Not sounding *h* where it ought to be sounded, and inversely. Thus we not infrequently hear, especially among children, *heart* pronounced *art*, and *arm*, *harm*. (p. xiii)' He ends this discussion by saying that 'the vulgar pronunciation of London, though not half so erroneous as that of Scotland, Ireland or any of the provinces, is, to a person of correct taste, a thousand times more offensive and disgusting' (p. xiv).

Modern linguists would characterise Walker's tone here as **prescriptive**: he is telling people how he feels they should speak. It seems likely, however, that pronouncing words like *arm* with initial /h/ arise precisely because some speakers have been made to feel anxious about 'correct' pronunciation. If they do not customarily pronounce initial /h/ (there is evidence for /h/-less pronunciation as far back as the Middles Ages; see Milroy, 1992), they will not know which words (e.g. *heart*) are supposed to have it, and which do not (e.g. *hour*). So they hypercorrect, by adding initial /h/ to any word that starts with a vowel.

The *Oxford English Dictionary*

In the nineteenth century the codification of English was continued by those scholars involved in compiling the OED, widely seen as the finest achievement of the philological method and as a work of the greatest authority. One of their concerns was the issue of what constituted the national language: questions about what to include and how to present information were considered in great detail by members of the Philological Society who prompted the dictionary. In a Proposal of 1858 there were five main points:

It should be exhaustive.

All English books should be admitted as authorities.

There should be a chronological limit as to the earliest texts from which quotations would be drawn.

It should chart the history of each word, its form and senses.

It should show the origins of each word and its relationships with words in other (related) languages.

The criterion of exhaustiveness (the first point) was, in the end, sacrificed by decisions such as to exclude much technical vocabulary and to make dialect vocabulary a separate project. In 1873 the English Dialect Society was set up specifically to compile a dialect dictionary, which was published in 1898. The final decision to focus on one variety of English at the expense of the others – an issue central to this chapter – is summed up in this sentence from the Proposal: 'As soon as a standard language has been formed, which in England was the case after the Reformation, the lexicographer is bound to deal with that alone'. For the compilers of the dictionary this meant in practice the 'standard literary' language. Why this limitation? Why such a forceful word as 'bound'?

During the nineteenth century, English literature had become the object of academic study. There were political reasons for this. By appealing to a shared literary past, so the argument went, the growing gulf between the urbanised working class and the social groups above them could be bridged. Tony Crowley argues that the OED reflected the era's preoccupation with nationalism and he quotes one contemporary commentator who wrote that the study of 'native literature' from past to present was the 'true ground and foundation of patriotism' (Crowley, 1989, p. 123). One problem, however, was that the records demonstrating this literary past were scattered and incompletely understood. It was necessary for scholars to find the texts in the first place, explicate their language and then publish them. The dictionary depended on this research, which was helped by the formation of the Early English Text Society in 1864 and by numerous other specialist societies such as the New Shakespeare Society, established in 1873.

As regards the third point of the Proposal, it was originally intended to go no further back than the emergence of an 'English type of language', which was supposed to date from about 1250. Some language scholars at this time argued that since Old English was 'unintelligible' to the modern reader, the new dictionary should avoid quoting words from the Anglo-Saxon period. On the other hand, there was to be no chronological limit as far as the *origins* of words were concerned (the fifth point). The idea was to take a word back as far as it could go, even to the reconstructed 'Old Teutonic' originally spoken by the Germanic ancestors of the Anglo-Saxons. In this respect the historical boundaries between English and other languages were blurred.

So the new dictionary was to be primarily historical: it was to show where the English vocabulary came from, how it had changed over the centuries and how the meanings of words had changed. One of the problems with seeing words from the perspective of origins is that we tend to assume that a word has an 'essence' located in its oldest meaning and form. So the history of any word's meaning is in danger of becoming a story of *decline* from a golden age.

3.6 Implementation

In the sixteenth century the new technology of printing played a central role in making texts available in the dialect of the south-east Midlands, the variety Caxton had selected. Printing made it possible for books to be distributed widely and read by a greater range of people than would otherwise have been possible, the first process of implementation introduced earlier in the context of the Renaissance. It also made it possible for identical material to be read *simultaneously* by people throughout an entire territory. This became especially true when newspapers were first introduced during the eighteenth century. Print therefore assisted the first of the focusing agencies listed in Section 3.2: 'daily interaction'. Print can therefore be seen as instrumental in *creating* images of a 'national' community. Without it, it is difficult to imagine the existence of distinct nations in the modern sense.

Among the wider readership available to Caxton and his successors were the new merchant classes who had money to buy books but, by and large, did not have the kind of education which enabled them to read Latin. This is one reason why the development of printing stimulated a rapid growth in translations of important texts into English and specifically into the variety of English selected for print. Probably the most influential translation was that of the Bible into English, first carried out in 1526. A slightly later translation, together with the Book of Common Prayer in 1549, became the focus of the service in the new Church of England, breaking the long association between Christianity and Latin. The English Bible – which could now be widely disseminated in print – became an important focusing agency in itself (see item 4 in the list in Section 3.2) and its publication has often been regarded as a decisive moment in the creation of Standard English. The Authorized Version of the Bible published in 1611 was, by the eighteenth century, regarded by some as a kind of 'classical' variety of English, representing a golden age of usage.

The political significance of translation seems to have been grasped by the post-Reformation monarchy as a means of asserting its authority. The Catholic church had its own body of laws in Latin, a language that was incomprehensible to most people in England. To translate these laws into English could be a symbolic challenge to papal authority and Henry VIII was probably behind the translation of many legal texts. Ancient governmental statutes in Latin (such as the Magna Carta of 1215) were also translated, helping to give the impression of a distinctively English, as opposed to international, law. The effects of the Reformation, then, were to focus on English as opposed to Latin and other European languages, and to establish the selected variety in the official domains of religion and the law, making possible the second process of implementation which we noted earlier owed much to the influence of Puritanism.

It was also after the Reformation that English writers developed a stronger loyalty and pride in the English language. Two important results of Henry VIII's action in declaring himself head of the English church were a radical change in the status of the clergy and an enormous growth in the power of the monarchy. A third result was religious conflict and persecution that lasted for generations, giving rise to a definition of 'Englishness' that was Protestant, upright, industrious and defensive towards the outside world. In terms of the agencies of focusing, this defensiveness can be related to the sense of an external threat which stimulates feelings of a common cause (see item 3 in the list of focusing agencies in Section 3.2). The language of England, with its regional diversity and Anglo-Saxon past, became the object of antiquarian study. This was helped in the late 1530s by Henry's closure of the (Catholic) monasteries – institutions that housed many of the manuscripts on which our knowledge of Old English depends and which then became more generally available.

A later example of growth in loyalty and pride occurred in the nineteenth century, particularly in its second half, when many British people felt a sense of national identity and confidence as never before: the British colonies in India and elsewhere became incorporated into the British empire under Queen Victoria; British technological invention led the world; and private enterprises and corporations were creating wealth which might benefit all sectors of society. During this period a large number of national institutions and societies were established (i.e. public bodies outside the control of central government) which helped to consolidate and regulate national culture and science in a manner that was, by now, typically British. One such society was the Philological Society which, as we noted earlier, initiated the compilation of the OED.

The third aspect of implementation is discouraging the use of alternative language varieties in official domains. We have seen how the translation of Latin texts established the selected variety in the domains of religion and the law, but what of the growing number of texts that were being written in English? Which variety was suitable for them? Activity 3.3 looks at part of the debate about the variety to be used, and the varieties to be discouraged, in another domain: literature.

ACTIVITY 3.3

Allow 15–20
minutes

Read the following extract through fairly quickly.

But after a fpeach is fully fafhioned to the common vnder-
ftanding, & accepted by confent of a whole countrey &
natiō, it is called a language, & receaueth none allowed
alteration, but by extraordinary occafions by little &
little, as it were infenfibly bringing in of many corruptiōs
that creepe along with the time: ... Then when I fay
language, I meane the fpeach wherein the Poet or
maker writeth be it Greek or Latine, or as our cafe
is the vulgar Englifh, & when it is peculiar vnto a
countrey it is called the mother fpeach of that people:
... fo is ours at this day the Norman Englifh. Before the
Conqueft of the Normans it was the Anglefaxon, and
before that the Britifh, which as fome will, is at this
day, the Walfh, or as others affirme the Cornifh. ...
This part in our maker or Poet muft be heedyly looked
vnto, that it be naturall, pure, and the moft vfuall of all
his countrey: and for the fame purpofe rather that
which is fpoken in the kings Court, or in the good townes
and Cities within the land, then in the marches and
frontiers, or in port townes, where ftraungers haunt for
traffike fake, or yet in Vniuerfities where Schollers vfe
much peeuifh affectation of words out of the primatiue
languages, or finally, in any vplandifh village or corner
of a Realme, where is no refort but of poore rufticall or
vnciuill people: neither fhall he follow the fpeach of a
craftes man or carter, or other of the inferiour fort,
though he be inhabitant or bred in the beft towne and
Citie in this Realme, for fuch perfons doe abufe good
fpeaches by ftrange accents or ill fhapen foundes, and
falfe ortographie. But he fhall follow generally the
better brought vp fort, ... men ciuill and gracioufly
behauoured and bred ... neither fhall he take the termes
of Northern-men, fuch as they vfe in dayly talke,
whether they be noble men or gentlemen, or of their
beft clarkes all is a matter: nor in effect any fpeach vfed
beyond the/riuer of Trent, though no man can deny
but that theirs is the purer Englifh Saxon at this day,
yet it is not fo Courtly nor fo currant as our Southerne
Englifh is, no more is the far Wefterne mās fpeach: ye
fhall therfore take the vfuall fpeach of the Court, and
that of London and the fhires lying about London
within lx. myles, and not much aboue.

Figure 3.12   An extract from *The Arte of English Poesie*, published in 1858 and
attributed to George Puttenham (1936 [1589], pp. 144–5)

The extract in Figure 3.12 comes from *The Arte of English Poesie*, first published in 1589. It discusses the variety of English to be used by poets (or 'makers'). You probably found the language of this extract easier than any of the texts so far, but you may have had problems recognising certain words because many spelling conventions (the use of *u* and *v*, for instance, as in *vnciuill* (uncivil) are similar to those mentioned at the end of Chapter 2. And in three words – *natiō, corruptiō* and *mās* (man's) – the *n* is indicated by a line above the preceding vowel.

Now reread the extract. We don't expect you to understand every word, but we do expect that you'll find it a lot easier the second time. As you reread it, think about the following questions.

- What are the main points that Puttenham makes in this section?
- Puttenham uses the words 'language' and 'speech'. What does he seem to mean by them? Can you think of a modern word to characterise what Puttenham calls 'language'?

Puttenham is discussing which *kind* of English is appropriate for poets (or 'makers') to use. The most eloquent variety, he argues, will not be found in ports or remote villages, nor on the northern or western peripheries, but within a radius of sixty miles ('lx.myles') around London. But this geographical dimension is complicated by other factors, both occupational (avoid the 'affectation' of university scholars and the speech of craftsmen) and social (look at the usage of the gentry at court).

Historians of English have generally argued that this extract is evidence for the existence of a Standard English when Puttenham was writing. The passage shows clearly that dialect speech is a sign of social status, and that the upper-class usage of the London area was considered prestigious. But there are problems with using the term Standard English here. The *written* norm that Puttenham says even non-Londoners use is not the same as a spoken one, and a spoken norm may be a matter of vocabulary, grammar or (perhaps) pronunciation. Puttenham lumps these together: at one point he is discussing accent, 'ill shapen soundes', at another, vocabulary. And what are we to make of his description of south-eastern courtly language as 'naturall, pure, and the most vsuall'? As the usage of a tiny minority, it can hardly be the most 'usual' of the country.

These apparent confusions are not so surprising if we remember that Puttenham was not writing a sociolinguistic description of sixteenth-century English but a manual for *poets*. He was seeking favour at the royal court by recommending that poets should use the language of courtiers. In so doing, he introduced a crucial association between ideas about the 'best' English usage and social exclusiveness. As we shall see, this association has remained an issue ever since. He was also clearly discouraging the use of any variety other than one corresponding closely to the one selected by Caxton.

Finally, we look briefly at a fourth domain of implementation: education. In the eighteenth century, a distinction was made between polite and vulgar which effectively disparaged all popular, dialectal speech. Words such as 'offensive' and 'disgusting' (as used by Walker to describe Cockney speech; see above, 'The doctrine of correctness') were commonplace at this time. Such views were reinforced by the increase in educational provision during the nineteenth century. The wealthy were able to send their sons to the new fee-paying 'public schools' which promoted a highly focused form of pronunciation later known as Received Pronunciation (RP) – discussed in depth in Chapter 5. Linguistic correctness became a most important mark of education and it was at this time that the term 'Standard English' first came to be used, increasingly so in connection with spoken as well as written English. When compulsory state education was introduced in the 1870s, one of its aims was the teaching of 'Standard English' at the expense of local dialects, which were severely discouraged. This 'national' education policy was applied in all parts of Britain; the local speech of Scotland, for example, was regarded as a dialect of English (an alternative view of its status is explored in Chapter 4).

3.7 Dialect speech and the discourse of democracy

Most of this chapter has been concerned with the development of a standard variety of English. In this last section we want to look at some of the social and intellectual movements which helped to create an opposing force – towards regional rather than national pride and the celebration of dialect rather than standard speech.

There was an opposing attitude towards English dialects which saw them as the authentic source of English culture and language, unadulterated by the social effects of industrialisation and urban living. During the 1760s, writers had drawn attention to the 'popular' traditions of verse that had existed in medieval times, or that had since coexisted with the literature of the 'polite'. This stimulated interest in the idea of literature of, and for, the common people, an interest culminating in the poet Wordworth's famous preface to his *Lyrical Ballads* in 1802. These poems were not aimed at satisfying the taste of the 'polite' reader; instead they celebrated the 'rustic life' of ordinary people, whose feelings were supposedly untainted by social vanity. Above all, though not written in the dialect of Wordworth's Cumberland home, they purported to use the very language of ordinary people. Wordworth's sentiments were possible because a reaction to the discourse of standardisation had taken place.

From the 1840s onwards, there emerged a flourishing literature in dialect in various parts of industrialised northern England (Joyce, 1991). Significantly, this literature was both printed and sold by local publishers. Many of the dialect writers were workers and they were often self-educated in the new textile factories of Lancashire and Yorkshire. By the 1850s, industrial cities such as Manchester had their own local newspapers, and were fiercely proud of their manufacturing traditions. Much of the literature reflects a regional 'patriotism', with a strong antipathy towards the south-east of England.

This tradition of writing lasted well into the twentieth century. Below is an extract from a poem, *In Praise o' Lancashire*, published in 1923. It celebrates the working people of Lancashire who, unlike the *chirpin* cockneys of London, have made their county the *engine-heause* ('house') of Britain. As well as fighting for their country they have also fought for 'freedom', by agitating for representation in Parliament and by building trade unions. The poem embodies a working-class conception of manliness and ends with a celebration of the dialect as an expression of solidarity.

So give us th' good owd dialect,	[old]
That warms eaur hearts an' whums,	[our, homes]
That sawders us together,	[solders]
An' that cheeans us to eaur chums.	[chains]
It may be rough-and-ready stuff,	
An' noan so fal-lal smart,	[not, highfalutin]
But it's full o' good an' gumption,	[vigour]
And it's gradely good at th' heart!	[properly]

(Clark, 1923, quoted in Joyce, 1991, pp. 291–2)

Dialects were now being seen by some scholars as making a significant contribution to the language. Max Müller, Professor of Comparative Philology at Oxford University in the mid nineteenth century had advocated paying them proper attention, but this was generally seen in terms of what they preserved from the archaic past. Systematic dialect scholars such as A.J. Ellis (1890) and Walter Skeat (1962 [1912]) perceived that traditional dialects could be fading in the light of more widespread education and better communications. However, Skeat was particularly enlightened in realising that this could mean, not the absolute extinction of dialect but rather the emergence of new varieties: 'it is no more possible to do away with them than it is possible to suppress the waves of the sea' (Skeat, 1962 [1912], p. 2).

A final point about dialect in the nineteenth and beginning of the twentieth centuries is that it was understood to be essentially rural. But one reason for rural depopulation was the rise of manufacturing industry – the so-called Industrial Revolution – which forced people to move from the countryside to work in factories in towns and cities. This 'working class', as these people had come to be called, were often seen by the class above them as a threat. In fact, some observers even saw them as barbarians, with all the accumulated meanings of that term: outsiders, destroyers of 'culture', cruel, little better than savages. This was especially the case with the poor of London. In 1902 the sociologist C.F.G. Masterman, in a book appropriately entitled *From the Abyss*, wrote of their 'bizarre and barbaric revelry' (quoted in Crowley, 1989, p. 217). The London poor were regarded by many middle-class people as 'inarticulate', so the term 'dialect' was considered too good for them. Even today, urban working-class speech – often regarded simply as 'bad English' – continues to be the image of unacceptability for many people. It was only from about the middle of the twentieth century that the term 'dialect' came to be used by language scholars to include the local speech of towns and cities. This was a significant innovation, making it more difficult to dismiss dialect as merely obsolescent.

3.8 Conclusion

We have tried to show that during the so-called 'modern' period, English has been developed as the language of an autonomous state, and that it has been seen as expressive of English nationality. But we have also tried to show that the concept of the national language is problematic. On the one hand, it can be seen as *inclusive*, although this raises the issue of where the boundaries of the language actually are (as in the case of Scots, discussed in Chapter 4); on the other hand, it can be seen as *exclusive,* based on the usage of an elite located in the south-east of England. It is the second meaning that is associated with the term 'Standard English'.

We have examined the sociolinguistic processes that have led to standardisation and we have suggested that the history of English during the entire modern period may be explored in relation to the concept of *focusing*. We have looked at the way the introduction of printing promoted close interaction in the national community, at the growth of national pride and a sense of a common cause, at the effects of the introduction of universal education and at different 'powerful models' (classical, literary, biblical, the usage of a prestigious social grouping) which influenced thinking about English at various times. Some of these models, as in the debates about the meaning of Standard English, appear to pull in different directions. Finally, we have shown that there were opposing tendencies, such as regional pride and interest in local dialects. The existence of such competing forces – which some scholars have called 'centripetal' (pulling in to the centre) and 'centrifugal' (tending to pull away from the centre and fragment) – is one reason why a single, homogeneous variety of English will never be achieved.

READING A: Caxton on dialects

R. Harris and T.J. Taylor
(Roy Harris is Emeritus Professor of General Linguistics at the University of
Oxford and Talbot J. Taylor is L.G.T. Cooley Professor of English and
Linguistics, College of William and Mary, Virginia.)

Source: Harris, R. and Taylor, T.J. (1989) *Landmarks in Linguistic Thought:*
The Western Tradition from Socrates to Saussure, Vol. 1, London, Routledge,
pp. 86–90.

> And certaynly our language now vsed varyeth ferre from that whiche was
> vsed and spoken whan I was borne. For we Englysshe men ben borne
> vnder the domynacyon of the mone, whiche is neuer stedfaste but euer
> wauerynge, wexynge one season, and waneth and dyscreaseth another
> season. And that comyn Englysshe that is spoken in one shyre varyeth
> from a nother. In so moche that in my dayes happened that certayn
> marchauntes ... wente to lande for to refreshe them; And one of theym. ...
> axed for mete; and specyally he axyd after eggys: And the goode wyf
> answerde, that she coude not speke no Frenshe. And the marchaunt was
> angry, for he also coude speke no Frenshe, but wolde haue hadde egges,
> and she vnderstode hym not. And thenne at laste a nother sayd that he
> wolde haue eyren: then the good wyf sayd that she vnderstod hym wel.
> Loo, what sholde a man in thyse dayes now wryte, egges or eyren.
> Certaynly it is harde to playse eueryman by cause of dyuersite and
> chaunge of langage.

> ([Prologue to *Eneydos*], William Caxton, 1490)

The linguistic mentality of modern Europe is one in which English, French,
German, Spanish, Portuguese, Italian, Dutch, etc. are all recognized as
established national languages. Each has its own literature, history and
grammar. Each is backed by the authority of an independent state. Each is the
official medium of communication for all legal and constitutional purposes
within certain political frontiers. This state of affairs, which Europeans
nowadays take for granted, and which leads them to treat languages as
national badges of affiliation, came into being only at the Renaissance.
Throughout the Middle Ages, linguistic thought in Europe had been moulded
by the intellectual predominance of the two great languages of antiquity.
Greek, although few could read it and even fewer speak it, was identified with
the primary sources of European culture: it was the language of Homer, of
Plato, of Aristotle, of Demosthenes. Latin, on the other hand, was the
international working language of European education and administration:
it was the language of law, of government, of the universities and of the
Church. The eventual end of the long reign of Greek and Latin, together with

the accompanying rise in status of the local European vernaculars, marked a most important watershed in the history of the Western linguistic tradition.

William Caxton (c. 1422–1491), the first English printer, translated and published a number of French works, including the *Eneydos*, from his Prologue to which the above excerpt is taken. The fact that Latin is a moribund language and European culture no longer has a genuine *lingua franca* presents Caxton, as printer and publisher, with an opportunity but at the same time with a difficult linguistic choice.

For any writer of the 15th and 16th centuries, the only viable alternative to writing in Latin was to write in one or other of the current European vernaculars. But half a century after Caxton English writers were still apologizing for writing in English. For example, Roger Ascham, in his treatise on archery (1545) thinks it necessary to explain as follows:

> ... And as for ye Latin or Greke tonge, euery thyng is so excellently done in them, that none can do better. In the Englysh tonge contrary, euery thinge in a maner so meanly, both for the matter and handelynge, that no man can do worse.

> (*Toxophilus* Dedication)

The question of the 'inferiority' of the vernacular languages was a much laboured Renaissance debating point. But a much more mundane, practical problem was foremost in the mind of the first English printer. What most worried Caxton was the fact that English, unlike Latin, had no recognized common usage. It varied considerably from one part of the country to another, causing practical difficulties of everyday communication, as Caxton's anecdote about the merchant who wanted eggs illustrates. To put this problem in its historical perspective one must remember that when Chaucer, whose works were among those which Caxton printed, wrote *The Canterbury Tales* a hundred years earlier, the language of government in London was still officially French. ... the century in which Caxton set up the first printing press in Westminster (c. 1476) was the first century in which the English language in England was no longer in competition with French.

Although Caxton specifically addresses the problem of linguistic variation in English, and offers the quaint explanation that the English are destined to linguistic vacillation because they are born under the sign of the moon, he would have been unobservant not to notice in the course of his long residence on the Continent that 15th-century French was no more uniform than 15th-century English. Every country in Europe was a linguistic patchwork of dialects, and would remain so for many generations after Caxton's death. But Caxton's observation is of historical significance because, for the first time this is seen as a problem.

The lack of uniformity in English usage posed in fact more than one problem for Caxton. In a country where some people say *egges* but others say *eyren*, and those who say one do not understand those who say the other, it is a problem for any publisher who wishes to sell books to as many people as possible to know which among the conflicting dialects will be most widely understood. But even if that problem is soluble, there is a further question to be faced; namely, how to spell the dialect you have chosen to print, given that there is no accepted assignment of letters of the alphabet to the various competing dialectal pronunciations. These difficulties are further complicated if, as Caxton recognizes, the dialects themselves are caught up in a process of change. ...

He ... observes that English had undergone considerable modifications during his own lifetime. Perhaps his awareness of those changes was enhanced by the fact that he had spent much of his earlier career as a merchant and diplomat abroad and was struck by the disparity when he eventually returned to the country of his birth. Finally, it must be borne in mind that the problems relating to English usage which Caxton faced could not be solved by consulting dictionaries or grammars of the English language, because in Caxton's day English, unlike Latin, had no dictionaries or grammars.

The uncertainties of linguistic usage which Caxton found himself wrestling with were in certain respects by no means new. From antiquity onwards, scholars had recognized that vacillations might arise because of linguistic clashes between (i) different *dialects*, (ii) different *orthographies*, and (iii) different *generations*. The dialect problem, the orthographical problem, and the problem of linguistic change arise from conditions which are endemic in every literate society once it reaches a certain size and phase of development. What was novel about Caxton's dilemma (although not unique to Caxton's particular case) was that these old problems were brought into much sharper focus than ever before by the invention of printing.

Printing was the technological foundation of the European Renaissance, and the most radical innovation in human communication since the invention of writing. Caxton is a man caught at the crossroads of history in more senses than one. He is trying to introduce and popularize a new technology which is destined to revolutionize the availability of information in civilized society. The political and educational consequences of this new technology will be profound. But this profoundly important initiative is being undertaken in the most linguistically adverse circumstances possible. For what has just broken down is the universal linguistic viability of Latin; and in England there is no comparably stable language to take its place. Printing is a communications technology which demands uniformity: and in Caxton's England, to say nothing of the rest of Europe, there was none.

Printing is the classic case of a technical innovation which necessitates rethinking basic assumptions about society; and in this particular instance about society's linguistic organization. Caxton's historical problem as England's first printer arose from the fact that he was committed to a technology which did not make it possible, as it had been when every readable document was laboriously hand-copied, to make individual alterations to individual copies. Printing means mass replication. It also means replication at great speed (relative to the speed of producing hand-written copies). These two factors – exact mechanical replication and speed of production – combine to afford unprecedented marketing possibilities for the product. They also combine to expand potential readership out of all (previous) recognition. But these possibilities are thwarted if the linguistic condition of society is such that linguistic fragmentation (for whatever reason) is valued above uniformity. One of the paradoxes of the Renaissance is that 'Caxton's problem' would never have arisen if printing had been invented two hundred years earlier. For then Latin would still have reigned unchallenged as the official language of Europe.

In Caxton's remarks we see no indication of a realization that he himself, and the technology he was introducing, were to play a key role in solving the problem of linguistic diversity which he so clearly perceived. By deciding, for better or for worse, to adopt the dialect of London and the South-East as the English for his books, Caxton took a decisive step forward in establishing that particular variety as 'the English language'. In retrospect, Caxton seems to have forged history's answer to his own question.

Notes

The Prologue to Caxton's translation of *Eneydos* is reprinted in W.A. Craigie, *The critique of pure English from Caxton to Smollett* (Oxford: Clarendon Press, Society for Pure English Tract LXV, 1946), and also in W.F.Bolton, *The English language* (Cambridge: Cambridge University Press, 1966).

English – colonial to postcolonial

Dick Leith

4.1 Introduction

The previous two chapters have described the history of English within England, from the first arrival of Germanic immigrants on British shores in the fifth century AD through to the present day. This chapter describes the 'expansion' of English: how it became established as the first language – or one of the languages – of many communities outside England, starting first with the other countries of the British Isles. Later, it spread to many other parts of the world as colonies of English speakers were established in places such as the Americas, Africa, India and Australia.

An important theme of this chapter is language contact. As we have seen from earlier chapters, English within England was shaped by repeated contact with other languages – particularly Latin, Scandinavian languages and French. During the process of expansion, English again came into contact with other languages (such as Celtic within Britain, or native American languages in America). Furthermore, in several of the overseas colonies, people speaking different varieties of English settled together. Here, I describe some of the linguistic consequences of such contact, and how new varieties of English, with distinctive grammar, pronunciation and vocabulary, have emerged in different parts of the world.

As in previous chapters, I provide a social and cultural analysis of the spread of English and of the political contexts in which it occurred. Central to the process of expansion, over several centuries, was the experience of colonisation: the sometimes forcible establishment of communities of English speakers, who maintained economic and cultural links with England and who positioned themselves in a relation of power with pre-existing inhabitants.

A second theme in this chapter, then, relates to the varying experience of colonisation in different parts of the world, the complex issue of cultural identity and divided language loyalties associated with colonisation and the different symbolic roles that English has subsequently played in the emergence of new national identities.

4.2 The colonial experience

David Crystal (1988, p. 1) estimated that between the end of the reign of Elizabeth I (1603) and the beginning of the reign of Elizabeth II (1952) the number of mother-tongue English speakers in the world increased from

5–7 million to about 250 million, of whom four-fifths lived outside the British Isles. This growth was largely due to the colonial expansion of England which began in the sixteenth century.

However, I suggest that the process of colonisation began even earlier within the British Isles themselves, when English first became established as the main language of the Celtic-speaking territories of Ireland, Scotland and Wales. The spread of English has been closely associated, therefore, with a colonial process from the twelfth to the twentieth centuries.

There was no single, universal colonial experience. Each colony provided a unique context politically, socially and linguistically. Nevertheless, it is possible to discern a common sequence of events in many of those colonies where English emerged as a main language:

- First, an original settlement was made by English speakers.
- Second, there was political incorporation.
- Third, a nationalist reaction which sometimes, but not always, led to independence.

Each stage had linguistic implications, which I deal with in turn.

Colonisation

In three areas of the British Isles – Ireland, Scotland and Wales – Celtic languages continued to be widely spoken long after the Germanic invasions of the fifth century which established English in England. Although the spread of English within Britain can be seen as part of a colonial process, it was not a simple matter of one nation state – 'England' – setting up a colony in another. As Chapter 3 explained, it was only during the Renaissance that nation states took form in Europe. How, then, can the spread of English in the twelfth century be regarded as a colonial process?

According to the historian Robert Bartlett (1993) the peripheral areas in Europe – which include the Celtic territories of Britain – were colonised during the Middle Ages from what he calls the 'centre', formed by Latin Christendom (Figure 4.1). This 'centre' included four key areas: Rome (more significant for Christian authority); France (centralised political power and intellectual life); the coastal cities of northern Italy and northern Europe (finance); and Flanders (manufacturing). From these centres the culture of towns, stone castles and armoured, mounted knights seeking landed estates with their armed followers, was gradually imposed on the European periphery. In the north-western periphery, this process of colonisation affected all the Celtic territories of the British Isles. The motives were political and religious, involving both the subjugation of the population and the reinforcement of Christianity as defined by the Pope. In the British Isles, after 1066, the Norman monarchs encouraged the colonisation of first Wales and then Ireland by awarding land to knights in return for subduing the local population (the situation in Scotland was slightly different, as we discuss below). These knights and their followers were of mixed origins but they shared a commitment to Roman Christianity. The linguistic consequence was the introduction of varieties of English into these territories.

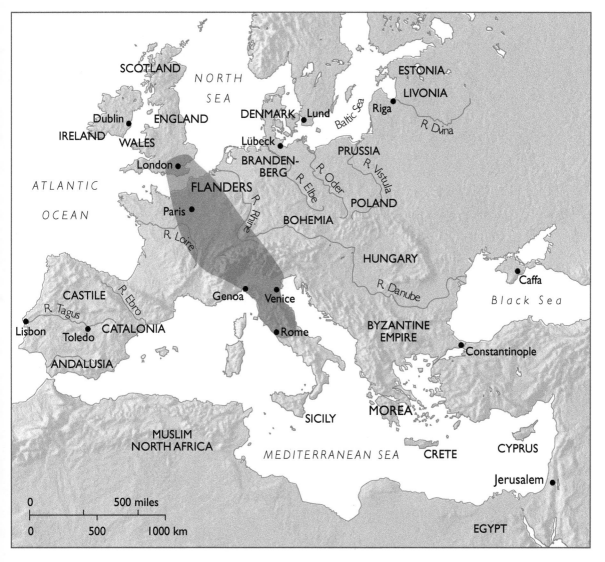

Figure 4.1 The 'centre' in medieval Europe (adapted from Bartlett, 1993, p. xvi)

Colonies were first established beyond the British Isles at the end of the sixteenth century. The motives here were threefold:

- *Economic*: companies run by capitalist entrepreneurs were granted a monopoly over a certain commodity by the monarch, who gained by taxing the profit made in trading it.
- *Social*: in England, economic problems such as unemployment and inflation combined with population growth to create a large class of

dispossessed 'vagrants' and political dissidents; these could help solve the problem of providing labour in colonies overseas.

- *Political*: rivalries developed among European states, especially the Portuguese, Spanish, and Dutch in the seventeenth century; the French in the eighteenth; and, by the end of the nineteenth, the Germans.

We shall see below how the history of English in the colonies needs to be understood against this background.

Since the process of colonisation beyond the British Isles lasted more than 300 years and affected four continents, it is very difficult to make generalisations about its character. In this chapter I identify and illustrate three types of English colonisation, each with its own linguistic consequences.

- *Displacement*: substantial settlement by first-language speakers of English displaced the precolonial population (example: North America).
- *Subjection*: sparser colonial settlements maintained the precolonial population in subjection, allowing some of them access to learning English as a second, or additional, language (example: Nigeria).
- *Replacement*: a precolonial population was replaced by new labour from elsewhere, principally West Africa (examples: Barbados and Jamaica).

We will look at these types in more detail, but first we look in more general terms at processes involved in colonisation.

Political incorporation

As colonies developed and became of greater strategic importance to England, the English government took greater responsibility for their administration. The Celtic territories were the first to experience such political incorporation; for instance, consider these dates and events:

1536	'England' as the name of the state also included Wales. In dealing with Scotland, however, the English government revived the old term 'Britain'.
1707	England (including Wales) and Scotland were formally joined as 'Great Britain'.
1800	Ireland was formally incorporated as part of what had come to be called 'the United Kingdom'.

For the greater part of the nineteenth century all these territories were officially 'British', and many individuals from Ireland, Scotland and Wales played an active part in forming the British empire overseas. And in all of them, broadly speaking, English came to be identified as the language of the state.

Originally, colonists were subjects of the English monarchy, economically dependent on, and controlled by, 'the mother country'. Linguistically, this meant that the usage of England remained a powerful model. But political incorporation beyond the British Isles took a looser form than in the case of the Celtic territories described above. It was not until the nineteenth century that the British government rather than the various trading companies assumed the administration of the remaining colonies, creating the 'British empire'. And by that time the issue of political incorporation had been complicated by nationalist reaction.

Nationalist reaction

The political incorporation of communities that feel they have a distinct cultural identity provides fertile ground for the emergence of nationalist reaction. From the late eighteenth century onwards, different forms of nationalist activity characterised political life in many of the areas colonised by the English. Language figured prominently in such nationalist reaction: in some cases, the precolonial language provided a focus for the assertion of a separatist identity, in others this role was played by English itself.

For example, by the end of the nineteenth century the newly emerging nationalisms in Ireland, Scotland and Wales were beginning to fear for the survival of the Celtic languages, and campaigns were mounted to promote them. One consequence of this is that they became taught languages, learnt by many people who otherwise knew only English. Another consequence was that they became increasingly sentimentalised, as much by the English as by the Celts themselves. The Victorian educationalist and literary scholar Matthew Arnold, for instance, spoke of the 'lively Celtic nature' expressed by Irish and Welsh writing. Overseas, too, nationalist reaction was being felt:

1776   Nationalist reaction began in North America, when political independence was achieved by armed force and the new state declared itself a republic.

1867   Fearing that the North American experience may set a precedent, the British government offered a form of self-government (known as dominion status) to the US's neighbour, Canada.

In later years, more recent British colonies were granted dominion status, with substantial settlement from the British Isles:

1901   Australia (Commonwealth)

1907   New Zealand (Dominion)

1910   South Africa (Union; but this was complicated by the presence of a large Dutch settlement)

And a few decades later:

1931   Statute of Westminster confirms independence of the Dominions, which continue to be linked to Britain in the 'Commonwealth of Nations'.

In the dominions, nationalist sentiment has tended to take a cultural rather than political form. It is most clearly seen, perhaps, in debates about literature. National and linguistic identities are often created in relation to other, more powerful ex-colonies: Canada in relation to the USA; New Zealand to Australia.

On the other hand, movements that emerged in India and many of the new African colonies during the twentieth century were for political independence. The language of these movements was also English, even though this was a second (or at least additional) language for most of the inhabitants.

Some linguistic consequences of colonisation

One of the more striking linguistic consequences of colonisation has been the appearance of new varieties of English worldwide. Some of these remain local languages of relatively low social status, while others have become codified, standardised and adopted by newly independent states as an official or main language. Let's look briefly at some of the linguistic processes that have been associated with colonisation.

The colonial process brought English into contact with a variety of other languages and it did so within particular relations of power. Indeed, an important part of any definition of colonisation must relate to the pattern of social, economic and political inequalities which privileged the English language and those who spoke it. The colonial conditions of language contact played an important role in shaping the new varieties of English that emerged.

In North America and Australia, where Europeans largely displaced the precolonial populations, the influence of the original local languages on English was slight – usually restricted to the adoption of words relating to phenomena new to the Europeans, such as local cultural practices, animals and geographical features. It was rare, in this kind of colony, for phonological or grammatical features of precolonial languages to be adopted into English.

ACTIVITY 4.1

Allow about
5 minutes

Why do you think that in colonies where English speakers displaced indigenous populations, elements of vocabulary, but not syntactical or phonological features, sometimes entered into local English usage?

Comment

Where colonising populations encountered new natural phenomena they often borrowed words from native populations. However, contact between the languages was not in some cases sufficiently sustained to impact upon the language at a deeper level. You will read about this in Section 4.4 below, with regard to the specific example of English in North America.

ACTIVITY 4.2

Allow about
10 minutes

One example of a borrowing into English (quoted in Carver, 1992, p. 134) was the small, furry, cat-sized animal called a 'raccoon', which came from the Algonquin *ara 'kunem*, which means 'he scratches with his hands'. What has happened to the Algonquin phrase to turn it into an English word?

Comment

First, the phrase (of two words) has become a single word, and that word has taken on a recognisable English spelling so that it can become fully assimilated into the English language.

The social conditions in such colonies did, nevertheless, give rise to forms of linguistic change, including dialect levelling and the creation of new varieties.

Dialect levelling

In all the colonies – from the first established in Ireland in the twelfth century to much later ones, such as Australia, where settlement was first established in the late eighteenth century – English-speaking settlers formed a diverse group of people. Many came from lowly social positions in England but found themselves in a position of power in relation to the original, precolonial populations. Some were economic migrants from rural communities (the outstanding case of this is probably the migration from Ireland to North America during the Irish famines of the nineteenth century). Others were political or religious refugees (such as the Protestants who created some of the first North American colonies in the seventeenth century). The restructuring of social identity is a typical colonial process and applies to both the incoming community (in this case European) and to members of the precolonial population who become incorporated into the colonial system. Ambivalent cultural and linguistic loyalties commonly arise.

The mixed demographic background of early settlers suggests that the varieties of English taken to the colonies were diverse and often non-standard. When speakers of different varieties of English are brought together in a new community, either as a result of resettlement or because patterns of communication are restructured, a process of **dialect levelling** often occurs. That is, differences between speakers tend over time to become eroded and a more uniform variety emerges.

In Chapter 3 we applied the concept of focusing to the development of a standard variety of English within England. The same concept can also be applied to the emergence of new varieties of English in the colonies. For example, the tendency towards dialect levelling is encouraged by the same focusing agencies (see Section 3.2) that we saw at work in England itself: close daily interaction, education, group loyalty and the presence of a powerful and high-status model. In those colonies which retained close trading links with England, for instance, the prestigious English of London and the south-east of England often formed such a model. When political incorporation occurred, this model was reinforced by the high-status English speakers sent out as representatives of the British government.

Nationalist reaction, and the seeking of independent political and cultural identity, sometimes had the opposite effect by encouraging the identification and codification (particularly in spelling books and dictionaries) of a local variety of English. This sometimes created a cultural and political tension over the legitimacy of any local variety of English. Ambivalent attitudes to local forms of English are still evident in many of the former colonies.

The creation of new varieties

The processes I have described are ones which tend to produce uniformity from a pattern of difference. There were, however, other tendencies that led to internal differentiation. As colonies expanded and became more established, different areas usually developed a sense of local cultural and linguistic identity. This might be reinforced by contact with local languages, by new kinds of social hierarchies (often positioning precolonial people as low status), or by different forms of continuing relationship with Britain. Further discussion of the formation of new varieties appears in Chapter 6, Section 6.8.

The most complex linguistic situation was found in those colonies where bilingual communities were created. This was the case in India and West Africa, where a relatively small number of Europeans imposed political and economic control over precolonial populations. Here, the English language came into the most intimate contact with other languages and new, sometimes radically divergent, forms of English arose. When a language is imposed on a community as part of a colonial process, speakers tend to incorporate many linguistic features from their first language when speaking the new, imposed one. Such a widespread influence, which might include the adoption of a phonological system or set of grammatical patterns, is sometimes described as a **substrate**.

At first, this might occur simply because local people learn English as a second or additional language, and knowledge of their first language interferes in a systematic way with their English. However, as time goes on, a new variety of English establishes itself, acquires a stability and coherence, and becomes the target language learnt by young people. At that point, we can describe the emergent variety of English as possessing a distinct identity and, typically, as having a generally understood social status within the community.

A good example of a linguistic substrate is provided by Hiberno-English (also called Irish English), the variety that arose in Ireland as a consequence of contact between English and Irish. In this, several grammatical structures and features of accent seem to be the result of an Irish substrate, even though very few speakers of Hiberno-English learn Irish as their first language.

Perhaps the extreme consequence of language contact, where only the vocabulary appears to be English and the grammar is derived from elsewhere, can be found in the English pidgins and creoles which have appeared in many parts of the world since the seventeenth century. Many of these are a linguistic legacy of the slave trade which brought speakers of African languages to the American colonies, and speakers of Oceanic languages to Australia. We examine these more closely later in the chapter.

4.3 The spread of English within the British Isles

I have argued that the global spread of English began within the British Isles, towards the end of the twelfth century. Figure 4.2 gives you a snapshot of the historical background to what we cover in this section. It includes some

The Gaelic-speaking Scottish monarchy offered sanctuary to English refugees from William the Conqueror and, in the 12th century, land to Anglo-Norman families. New burghs (towns) became centres of English usage. The English attempt to conquer the Scots, begun by Edward I, failed at Bannockburn in 1314.

Norse hegemony over the west and north of Scotland was ended in 1263. The present border with England was contested until the 16th century.

- Kingdom of Scotland
- Principality of Wales
- Norman castles of the 11th century
- Castles established under Henry I (1100–1135)
- Castles established under Henry II (1154–1189)
- Castles established under Edward I (1272–1307)
- Boroughs/burghs

KINGDOM OF SCOTLAND

Bannockburn

Ulster

IRELAND

Connaught

Meath

ENGLAND

Leinster

Munster

PRINCIPALITY OF WALES

Anglo-Norman influence in Ireland began in 1167 under Henry II. Dublin was occupied and by 1250 only the north-west remained in Irish hands. English was established in the boroughs. But during the next 200 years the Irish reasserted control, leaving only the Pale – a small area around Dublin – in English hands.

The process of castle-building along the Welsh border was begun by William the Conqueror. Under Henry I, English- and Flemish-speaking settlers were planted in the south-west. Edward I overcame Welsh resistance in the north-west and in 1284 established the Principality of Wales. The rest of the territory was divided into earldoms and lordships subject to the English crown.

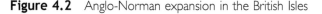

Figure 4.2   Anglo-Norman expansion in the British Isles

details on the situation in Wales which we have mentioned briefly earlier in the chapter, and you may find it useful to refer back to this figure as you read the cases of Ireland and Scotland in this section. I take Ireland and Scotland as case studies, arguing that many aspects of the growth of English usage in these formerly Celtic-speaking areas can be seen as an early colonial process which in some ways provided a model for later English colonisation overseas. The new varieties of English which arose in these areas have also been influential in the development of English beyond the British Isles, since Irish and Scottish emigrants formed a substantial proportion of some English colonies.

I outline the stages of colonisation, political incorporation and nationalist reaction experienced in each territory, and then discuss some of the linguistic consequences for English.

The colonisation of Ireland

The first colonies were established in the south-east of Ireland towards the end of the twelfth century. English law was introduced to protect the colonists and disadvantage the Irish. New towns or boroughs – which were a distinctive form of Anglo-Saxon settlement that contrasted with local dispersed habitations – were built and became centres of Anglo-Norman influence (records from the late twelfth century show immigration to Dublin, Ireland's capital, from towns in the south-west of England and Wales). A century later, two-thirds of Ireland had been conquered after military campaigns against the Irish earls (princes).

It is a feature of colonial activity that personal identities and loyalties change. By the fourteenth century, it seems, many of the colonists had married among the Irish and adopted the 'manners, fashion' and, significantly, 'the language of the Irish enemies', in the words of a Statute of 1366. This process continued, so that by the late fifteenth century English control was limited to a small area around Dublin known as 'the Pale'.

English control, however, was reasserted during the sixteenth century, reflecting the monarchy's preoccupation with territorial boundaries. Henry VIII's Proclamation of 1541 urged that 'the king's true subjects' in Ireland 'shall use and speak commonly the English tongue'. The Protestant Reformation (discussed in Chapter 3, Section 3.2) gave a new twist to Anglo-Irish relations, since the Irish continued to practise Roman Catholicism. Under Elizabeth I (1558–1603) England was at war with Catholic Spain and Irish Catholicism was seen as treachery. An English army was sent to overcome the resurgent Irish chieftains. In the course of long and bitter fighting, the invading English defined the enemy as the opposite of all those qualities claimed for the Protestant English. According to the attorney general for Ireland, Sir John

Davies, in 1610 the 'wild' Irish did not 'build houses, make townships ... or improve the land as it ought to be' (Stallybrass, 1988, p. 206). They were also described as filthy, long-haired and promiscuous. The Irish were eventually defeated, and their land confiscated and awarded to fresh colonisers. Many of these colonisers in the north-east of Ireland were Scots (see Figure 4.2), who gave rise to the linguistic area known today as Ulster Scots. Among the other colonisers were the poorest sections of the English population in London, encouraged to go to Ireland because the government feared they would be 'seditious' if they stayed in England (Stallybrass, 1988).

Political incorporation

The new colonists of the seventeenth century clung to their Protestant, non-Irish identities, while the Irish were resettled in the poorer west of the country. Anti-English sentiment among the Irish was strong enough to support any cause that threatened the British state, especially if a Catholic power were involved in that cause. But by the end of the eighteenth century the new democratic and nationalist ideas discussed in Chapter 3 had fuelled a movement for independence from English rule which also took root among sections of the Protestant population. It was after an uprising in 1798 that Ireland was incorporated into the United Kingdom by the Act of Union of 1800.

Nationalist reaction

It has been estimated that by 1800, English was the first language of half the population of Ireland. In the course of the nineteenth century Irish was increasingly abandoned. Three reasons have been suggested for this (Harris, 1991, p. 38). One of these was depopulation. Famines in the 1840s greatly reduced the Irish-speaking population, either by death or emigration (principally to America). Another reason was the introduction of universal English language education. The final one is significant in the context of ideas linking nationalism and language. English, not Irish, became the language of the two institutions which claimed to speak on behalf of the Irish population: the Catholic church and the independence movement. The latter gathered pace in the course of the century, culminating in the establishment of the Irish Free State (Irish Republic) in 1921, whereby twenty-six counties in southern Ireland gained independence from the UK. Northern Ireland remained part of the UK.

Before the seventeenth century, Irish was the first language of the whole population. Today it is used as a first language by only about two per cent of the population of the Irish Republic (see Figure 4.3), although it remains the 'national' and 'first official language'. As such, it is a compulsory subject in secondary schools and is cultivated as the language of literature, broadcasting and government publications. English is recognised in the Irish constitution as a 'second official language', but in practice is used alongside Irish. Despite the fact that an overwhelming proportion of Irish people have chosen to speak English in their daily lives, they often explicitly express loyalty to the idea of Irish as part of their 'national' identity.

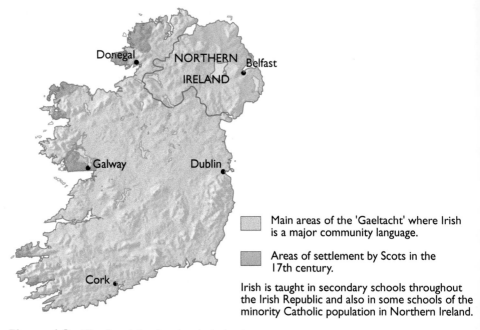

Figure 4.3   The linguistic situation in Ireland

This language loyalty, and the role of Irish in the Irish Republic today, can both be seen as the result of nineteenth-century language nationalism. By 1893 three organisations had been set up to revive the Irish language (which, like regional dialects in England, was seen by some as obsolescent). They were largely led by literary figures and intellectuals, often from the upper class, for whom the Irish language was linked to the images of both an ancient literary culture and the non-literate usage of the peasantry in the west. For these movements, language was at the heart of Celtic culture: remove the language, and everything else dies.

Some features of Irish English

In time, there emerged a distinctive form of English spoken in Ireland, now known as Hiberno-English or Irish English. This was influenced in various ways by the Irish language which was the first language of many of its original speakers. Irish English gradually became the form of English learned by monolingual English speakers in Ireland.

According to the linguistic historian Bliss (1984), Hiberno-English is relatively uniform throughout much of the west and in the area colonised by the English. He explains this uniformity as resulting from the original pattern of contact, but adds that over the centuries the influence from Irish has actually increased, rather than diminished. This influence can be felt primarily at the level of pronunciation. For example, Irish speakers tend to pronounce /t/ (as in *tin*) with the tip of the tongue placed against the top front teeth, rather than against the ridge behind the teeth, as in most varieties of English spoken in England. One consequence of this 'dental' pronunciation of /t/ is that the contrast with /θ/ (as in *thin*) tends to be lost, so that *tin* and *thin* sound the same. The influence of Irish on the grammar of Hiberno-English is more controversial. One grammatical construction characteristic of Hiberno-English is exemplified by the following expression, recorded in Wicklow near Dublin (Filppula, 1991, p. 55): 'It's looking for more land a lot of them are'. This structure is technically known as 'clefting'. In Standard British English it might be translated as 'A lot of them are looking for more land'.

Many commentators have claimed that this construction reflects a similar one in Irish. However, Irish has not been spoken in Wicklow for more than 200 years, so if this is a consequence of language contact it suggests there is a uniformity in Hiberno-English based on Irish substrate. There may be another explanation. Many grammatical patterns in Hiberno-English may derive not from contact with Irish, but from the many different regional varieties of seventeenth-century English which were taken to Ireland by colonists and have become obsolete (or at least very scarce).

Recent research on Hiberno-English suggests that it may be less uniform than was originally thought. And the problems of deciding the source of specific characteristics are instructive for a number of reasons. First, it may be that no single explanation for a linguistic feature is possible: a source in Irish, say, may be reinforced by a similar construction in a variety of English. Second, how are we to evaluate such features – as 'mistakes', or simply local variants? Both these issues are ones we shall encounter again in connection with new varieties of English in other parts of the world.

Colonisation in Scotland

So far I have described Scotland as a Celtic territory, and this is true in several respects. When the Romans left Britain, much of the area now known as Scotland was inhabited and controlled by Celts closely related to those encountered by the Anglo-Saxons (see Chapter 2). The language they spoke was Brythonic Celtic, an ancestor of modern Welsh (they are sometimes referred to as 'Strathclyde Welsh'). In the northern and eastern area were the Picts – another Celtic group about whom little is known.

A major reason why the Romans abandoned Britain was the large-scale migrations of peoples from northern Europe, such as the Anglo-Saxons who invaded England. During AD 400–800, Scotland experienced invasion and settlement from three sides. The first people to arrive (in the fifth century, at the time the Anglo-Saxons were first landing in eastern England) were yet another group of Celts from Ireland, who settled in the western area.

They spoke a Goidelic Celtic language closely related to Irish, which became the ancestor of Scottish Gaelic.

By the seventh century, the Anglo-Saxons of Northumbria had expanded northwards into southern Scotland, gradually spreading westwards to southwest Scotland. The fact that *The Dream of the Rood* was inscribed on the Ruthwell Cross near Dumfries is testimony to the fact that a variety of English has been spoken in southern Scotland for almost as long as in England.

The third wave of invasions came later, from Scandinavia in the eighth century. The northern islands of Shetland and Orkney, together with part of the Scottish mainland, became a central part of the Viking world, linking Norway with Iceland. The people in this area remained Norse-speaking until about the sixteenth century and the regional dialects in this area today possess a Scandinavian substrate seen most clearly in vocabulary and pronunciation.

By the tenth century there were thus five linguistic groups in Scotland:
* the (newer) Scottish Gaelic people
* the Anglo-Saxons of Northumbria who settled in southern Scotland
* the Norse-speaking people in the far north
* the remainder of the original Pictish people, and
* a residue of Brythonic (later Welsh) people.

The argument that Scotland experienced colonisation is thus more complex than in the case of Ireland. Of the five tenth-century linguistic groups, the dominant one was Scottish Gaelic. They had by then developed a centralised Gaelic-speaking monarchy which controlled even the south-eastern, Northumbrian-speaking area. In fact, in contemporary accounts these Gaelic people and their language were referred to as 'Scots' or 'Scottish'.

The next development, as in Ireland, was Anglo-Norman colonisation, but unlike the Irish case, this came about because of an invitation rather than by conquest. The Scottish kings welcomed refugees from the Norman conquest after 1066 and were so attracted by what they saw as the superior military technology of the Anglo-Normans that they gave lands to individual knights (partly in the hope of strengthening the power of the monarchy). Another aspect of Anglo-Norman culture – town-building – was also adopted. New towns were established and populated with English-speaking merchants. As in Ireland, towns came to be associated with 'Inglis' (the name given to English by the Scots) and by the thirteenth century the royal court itself spoke Inglis.

An attempt at military conquest was made by the English at the end of the thirteenth century when Edward I pursued a claim to the throne of Scotland. However, the English forces were finally defeated at the battle of Bannockburn in 1314, stimulating a fierce patriotism – based on hostility to England – among sections of the Scottish nobility. After Bannockburn, Scotland can be described as a 'state' independent of England for nearly 300 years, with its own educational, administrative and legal institutions.

During this period, Inglis was cultivated as the language of the Scottish state, based at Edinburgh. From 1494, in fact, Inglis came to be referred to as 'Scottis' or 'Scots', reflecting the fact that it, rather than Gaelic, was now regarded as the state language. A flourishing literature in this language developed. Both Scots and English, however, seem to have been understood in Scotland. In the sixteenth century, English influence was also associated with the Reformation. Protestantism was received enthusiastically in Scotland, but the Bible used there was printed in English, not Scots.

Political incorporation, nationalist reaction and the status of Scots

The process of political incorporation began when Elizabeth I of England died childless in 1603. James VI of Scotland was invited to become King James I of England. The two territories were united formally as the state of Great Britain in 1707. Gaelic culture remained strongest in the mountainous and peripheral areas of Scotland known as the Highlands and Islands. In this area a Gaelic culture similar to that of Ireland survived until the defeat of the highland chieftains during a rebellion of 1745. In the following 100 or so years the highlands were forcibly depopulated, the number of Gaelic speakers fell dramatically and a Gaelic revivalist movement similar to that in Ireland was created. Today, it is only in the Hebridean Isles, especially the outer ones, that Gaelic is still a majority language (see Figure 4.4).

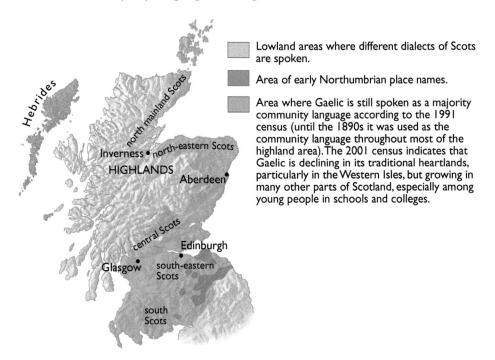

Lowland areas where different dialects of Scots are spoken.

Area of early Northumbrian place names.

Area where Gaelic is still spoken as a majority community language according to the 1991 census (until the 1890s it was used as the community language throughout most of the highland area). The 2001 census indicates that Gaelic is declining in its traditional heartlands, particularly in the Western Isles, but growing in many other parts of Scotland, especially among young people in schools and colleges.

Figure 4.4 The linguistic situation in Scotland

The process described above, which produced widespread Gaelic/English bilingualism, can be seen as Anglicisation. In many respects it paralleled the situation in Ireland: the destruction of the Gaelic culture was accompanied by a supremacist attitude which saw the Gaelic-speaking highlanders as savages. This attitude did not only come from the government in London, however. It was most vigorously held among the urban Scots in the lowlands. More Scots actually fought on the government side in the 1745 rebellion than on the side of the rebels.

Lowland nationalism looks to the Scots language as a symbol of cultural identity. But how far is it appropriate to see this as a language distinct from English, and a possible candidate for being Scotland's 'national' language? In the process of political incorporation in the eighteenth century, whereby Scotland retained distinctive educational, administrative and legal practices, it was English rather than Scots that came to be prestigious in Scotland. During the eighteenth century the idea of educated speech in Scotland was based on the 'polite' usage of London and the south-east of England, while Scots continued to be used among the working class, especially in rural areas. However sections of the Scottish intelligentsia maintained it as a literary medium expressing a cultural identity distinct from that of England. Other kinds of writing in Scots were also maintained, such as by certain Scottish newspapers, especially in the north-east (Donaldson, 1986).

Scottish 'national' identity can be associated with either highland (Gaelic) or lowland (formerly known as Inglis) culture. Transcending this difference, however, is a widespread sense that to be Scottish is to be not English, although some Scots are also proud to be both Scottish and British and, of course, there is also the European impact of membership of the European Union.

A key case for the presentation of Scots as Scotland's contemporary national language was eloquently presented in a pamphlet entitled *Why Scots Matters* by the Scottish language scholar Derrick McClure (1988). McClure argued that although Scots was originally a variety of Northumbrian English, it became the language of an independent state in the late Middle Ages. Its relationship with English at this time can be seen as similar to that of Portuguese and Spanish today: closely related linguistically, but each identified with a separate state. Like English and the other languages mentioned, Scots has its own range of dialects, each with its own spelling conventions. Assuming that a state represents the whole people (the 'nation'), the language of that state deserves to be distinct from that of other nations; the best way of symbolising Scottish distinctiveness is thus through Scots. Since Scottish devolution in 1999, Scots has increased its official status, with more emphasis in the educational curriculum and representation in the workings of the Scottish Parliament.

4.4 The spread of English beyond the British Isles

The establishment of English-speaking colonies in North America at the beginning of the seventeenth century was the first decisive stage in the colonial expansion of England that made English an international language. The first English settlers, however, were by no means the first Europeans to set up colonies. South America was the first to be 'discovered' by Europe – by the Portuguese and Spanish – in the late fifteenth century. This is a useful reminder that other European languages often came into contact with English in the colonies and influenced its development. The much later colonisation of Australia in many ways followed a pattern similar to that in North America. In both cases, large-scale immigration of English speakers and other Europeans displaced existing populations.

English in North America: an example of displacement

Although Newfoundland was discovered and had a small settlement earlier, in 1607 an expedition established the colony of Jamestown in Virginia. A group which became known as the 'Pilgrim Fathers' was among those who followed, landing from the 'Mayflower' to settle in Plymouth, Massachusetts, in 1620. Their colony was perhaps the most successful at attracting settlers: within twenty years a further 25,000 Europeans had migrated to the area.

The pilgrims, like many of the early English settlers, sought religious freedom (one effect of the Reformation, discussed in Chapter 3, was the persecution of Puritans as well as Catholics). Pennsylvania, further south, was settled originally by a Quaker colony, but attracted English and Welsh settlers of various religious denominations too. In each direction, there were colonists from other European states, French to the north and north-west, and Dutch to the west.

The pattern of colonisation in the southern areas differed slightly from that of the north. Huge plantations and estates developed in the south – in contrast to the northern smallholdings – growing rice at first and later cotton. These colonies were settled by a high proportion of people from the south and west of England (many of them deportees and political refugees). Labour for the plantation was supplied by slaves who were transported from Africa. In South Carolina by 1724 slaves outnumbered free people by three to one. These estates formed the nucleus of what has come to be known as the American South.

The complex relationship between North American settlement and the slave trade is illustrated in Figure 4.5, which shows some of the main West African languages which were to influence the new forms of English that became spoken by slaves in North America and the Caribbean. This map also shows the major precolonial languages spoken in North America. You may like to refer back to this map during the discussion of West Africa and the development of English pidgins and creoles (later in this section).

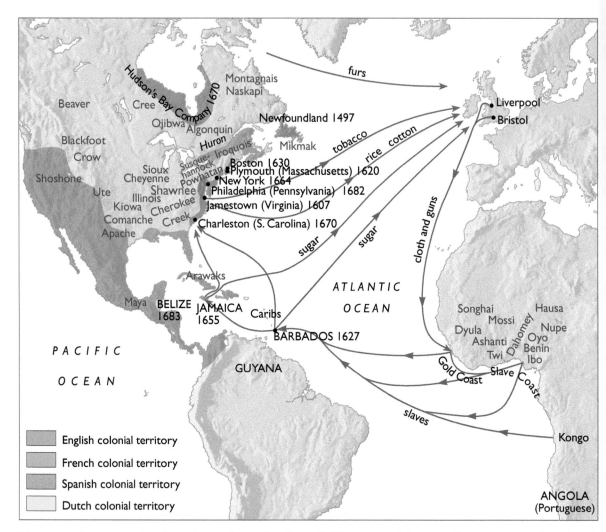

The names of some precolonial peoples are shown thus: Crow. In Africa, many of these peoples were organised in relatively centralised kingdoms. Unlike the French and Spanish, English-speaking colonists in America settled in dense numbers and tended eventually to displace precolonial inhabitants. In the Caribbean, however, the Arawaks were virtually wiped out by the earliest Spanish colonists.

Figure 4.5   The Atlantic slave trade and colonisation in America and the Caribbean

Any linguist examining the early period of settlement is faced with two main questions. First, how and when did American English become differentiated from British English and recognised as an independent variety? Second, how did internal dialect differences in American English arise? These two questions are similar to ones which were asked in Chapter 2 in relation to the first Anglo-Saxon settlement of England and the emergence of Old English.

The variety of English which was implanted in North America was that of the early modern period, described in Chapter 3. It has sometimes been claimed that many of the differences between American and British English can be explained in terms of a 'colonial lag': the language of colonial settlers is more 'conservative' than that of the country they left. Thus, some features of American English, such as the widespread pronunciation of /r/ in words like *cart* and *far* (known technically as 'non-prevocalic /r/') might be attributed to the fact that /r/ in such words was generally pronounced in Elizabethan English. Although the speech of Londoners later became /r/-less, this was too late to influence the speech of those who had already left.

The problem with this explanation is that in some areas on the east coast – the oldest settlements among them – there has long been an /r/-less tendency. This area seems to have maintained close cultural and trade links with England and the British model of speech remained a powerful model of social correctness. Other, more inland communities seem not to have maintained such close ties with England. Hence this feature, at least, of modern dialect variation is better explained by different patterns of contact with England after the first settlement.

You will recall that this is the same explanation put forward by David DeCamp (1958) for the pattern of Old English dialects (see Chapter 2, Section 2.3). The original Germanic settlers of England came from different locations and the question arose as to whether the dialect areas which emerged in England derived from the patterns of first settlement (i.e. speakers of different language varieties settling in different areas). DeCamp argues that English dialect variation was 'made in Britain' after the first settlement and reflected differences in the extent of continuing links with continental Europe.

It might be supposed that in North America some dialect variation arose from contact with different indigenous languages. The influence of precolonial languages on American English, however, has been surprisingly slight. Different settlements had various motives for contact with the precolonial population; some tribes had more interest in it than others. Some Puritan colonists wanted to convert the local people, or to enlist their help as household servants, so schooling was arranged for them (see also Figure 4.6 showing an example of a Puritan publication on laws for the colony) and parts of the Bible were translated into their languages. But the native Americans were reluctant to have their identities changed in this way, and as the colonies expanded westward, they were pushed in the same direction.

Sociolinguists, such as Carver (1992; see box on 'Indian words in American English'), use the same assumption to explain the limited influence of precolonial languages on American English as was discussed in relation to the lack of Celtic influence on Old English: that the language of a conquered people has little effect on that of the conquerors. (Note that Carver uses 'Indian' for Native Americans.)

Figure 4.6 A Puritan North American publication

Indian words in American English

About half of all the 300 or so American Indian loanwords current today entered the language in the seventeenth century, including ... *skunk*, *squash*, *squaw*, *terrapin*, *tomahawk*, *totem*, *wigwam* and *woodchuck* ...

A colonial Indian from the colonial era would probably not recognize any of these words because they were radically changed in the course of being adopted into American speech ... Often the words were abbreviated or clipped (... *squash* from *asquutasquash*, *hichory* from *pawcohiccora*). Sometimes the Indian word was changed by folk etymology, an attempt to make sense of a new and unusual-sounding word by analysing it (incorrectly) in terms of known words. For example, the Indian word *muskwessu* or *muscassus* became *muskrat*, a musky-smelling rodent ...

The influence of the Indian culture was not negligible when we take into account the numerous combinations in which these loanwords occur (e.g. *skunk*-cabbage, ... *skunk* weed), not to mention the couple hundred or so combinations made with *Indian* (e.g. *Indian pony*, *Indian mallow*). In addition, there are many expressions derived from features of Indian life: *on the warpath, peace pipe, to bury the hatchet,* ... *medicine man, war paint, war dance* ...

In the larger picture, however, given that the Americans Indians were reduced to a conquered people, it is not surprising that their languages had a relatively slight influence on American English, aside from the large number of place names that are of Indian origin (over half of American state names, for example, are Indian loanwords). Moreover, all the American Indian loanwords are nouns, which indicates a casual rather than a true mingling of the two cultures.

(Carver, 1992, pp. 134–5)

Another phenomenon which may have affected both Old English and the English of the American colonies is that of dialect levelling (see Section 4.2). This process seems to occur whenever a new community is formed containing speakers of many closely related language varieties. British English, because of its continued prestige, seems to have acted as a focusing agent in America. Hence American speech tended to level out in the direction of the educated usage of London and south-east England, even though the speech of the majority of the early settlers was non-standard.

As English settlements in North America became more established, there arose another tendency towards internal differentiation. The different economy of the southern area, for example, gradually pulled its culture and speech habits in a different direction from that of the north. So emerged one of the major modern dialect boundaries of the USA: that between northern and southern speech. For instance, the English dialect forms of *see* in the past tense were not levelled. *Seed*, as in *I **seed*** (derived from adding a 'weak' ending *-d*), is common in the south, whereas *seen*, as in *I **seen*** (originally a 'strong' past tense form co-occurring with *saw*), is used in the north. As these local economies developed, and conflicts of economic interest with England grew, the colonists became increasingly aware of the linguistic differences among themselves. Once the colonies were independent of England in 1783, this became a burning issue for some of the founders of the new republic such as Noah Webster.

For Webster, America in 1783 was no longer a colony but it was not yet a nation. A written constitution defined it politically as a republican state (more precisely, a federation of individual states), but national unity had to be worked for, and a crucial arena for this was language. Even if American speech was diverse, linguistic uniformity could follow from the achievement of a distinctive visual identity through spelling, which in turn could influence speech over the generations. In wanting to make American English look different from the English of England, Webster drew on some of the ideas about language, especially Puritan ones, which were discussed in Chapter 3, Section 3.2.

The nationalist ideal of linguistic uniformity in American English has, however, not been completely achieved. One reason is that the processes of internal differentiation mentioned above have not diminished. The economic and cultural division between north and south led to the Civil War of the 1860s, which ended with the north victorious. In part, the war was a confrontation between the forces of political centralisation, represented by the north, and those of regional autonomy. Ever since, the south has often been represented as a bastion of older, agricultural, hierarchical values outside those of mainstream America. Its dialect has also been vigorously defended. In a book of his published lectures, one of the most influential of twentieth-century literary critics, Cleanth Brooks, asks whether the language of the South had any future. Its 'most dangerous enemy', he says, 'is not education properly understood, but miseducation: foolishly incorrect theories of what constitutes good English, an insistence on spelling pronunciations, and the propagation of bureaucratese, sociologese, and psychologese, which American business, politics and academies seem to exude as a matter of course' (Brooks, 1985, p. 53).

Another source of differentiation is the sheer diversity in the American population since the late eighteenth century. Figure 4.7 shows the progress of settlement west of the early colonies. By the mid nineteenth century, settlers had advanced as far west as the Mississippi, their numbers swelled by thousands of land-hungry Scots Irish from Ulster. By the end of that century the west too had been settled, partly by millions of immigrants from various parts of Europe. A levelled form of pronunciation, known as 'general American', is associated with these states. Theoretically, the newcomers were to form what is often called the 'melting pot' of American society, in which ethnic origin is subsumed by a common American citizenship; in practice, however, new composite identities such as 'Irish American' and 'Italian American' have been created, and European cultural practices maintained.

In the course of the twentieth century, some observers came to see this ethnic diversity as a threat to the nation. Recent Spanish-speaking immigrants from Mexico have confronted the states of Texas and California with the language of the earliest European colonists in America and reminded them that the USA has no official 'national' language in the legal sense (federal legislation on this issue has actually been called for). And, despite civil rights legislation, a substantial proportion of the black population, the descendants of slaves, still feel less than full American citizens. African American English shares many features with the American South, but also with many creoles. The latter association has often been stressed by blacks themselves, as a means of claiming a separate, 'African' identity through language, an issue discussed in the next section.

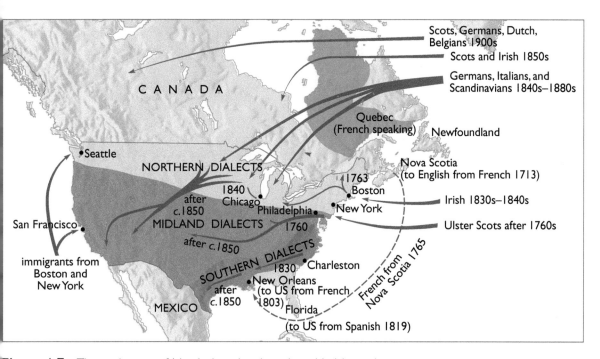

Figure 4.7 The settlement of North America since the mid eighteenth century

English in West Africa: an example of subjection

Earlier I identified three types of English colony (see Section 4.2). America represented the first group I mentioned: the wholesale immigration of native-speaking English settlers who displaced the local, precolonial population. I want now to move on to an example of the second type of colony, where sparser colonial settlements maintained the precolonial population in subjection.

Sierra Leone, where the first European slaving expedition occurred in the sixteenth century, was settled by escaped and (after 1807) freed slaves. A little later, Liberia was established by the USA for ex-slaves. The significance of these ventures was the association of slaves with an African 'homeland', an association based on the notion of 'descent' from African tribes. One eventual outcome of this development was the sense of common cause between black people in both America and Africa. This commonality was aided in the British colonies by the existence of a shared language, English.

New British colonies were established in Africa after 1880. Between that date and the end of the century virtually the entire continent was seized and shared out among the European powers. In West Africa, however, there was no substantial settlement by people from the British Isles. Instead, the new colonies were administered by a small number of British officials. The population remained overwhelmingly African, with a small number receiving education in English from missionaries, and a larger number using English-based pidgins in addition to the languages they already spoke.

During the nineteenth century, Britain came to see the role of colonies such as those in Africa as that of producing raw materials, while Britain remained the source of manufacturing. The precolonial populations were not given any rights as far as the vote and compulsory education were concerned, despite the fact that these had been granted to the working class in Britain. These economic and political arrangements were justified by appealing to contemporary theories of racial difference. The precolonial populations were classified as dark-skinned, and considered to be at a lower stage of cultural and intellectual development than white Europeans. Colonial service could therefore be conceived as a duty and as a way of demonstrating 'manliness', a key aspect of nineteenth-century Englishness.

The system described above is often referred to by the word **colonialism**. First used in the nineteenth century, it reflects changes in the relationship between Britain and its colonies as they were incorporated into what was called the British empire. The term is more loaded than 'colonisation', partly because it has been used most frequently by those who were opposed to it, on the grounds that it amounted to exploitation of the weak by the powerful. In one respect, it names the process from the point of view of the less powerful, and has often been used pejoratively. In fact, the *Oxford English Dictionary* (Simpson and Weiner, 1989) has a citation for the word in 1957 as 'the commonest term of abuse nowadays throughout half the world'.

According to the African linguist Ali Mazrui, British colonialism, with its emphasis on the difference between the subject black population and its white rulers, set the tone for colonialism in Africa in general (Mazrui, 1973). And according to him, it was in the British colonies that Africans led the struggle for independence. This was partly because they felt a solidarity with the black ex-slaves in the USA, involved in their own struggles for full citizenship. A movement known as pan-Negroism emerged, based on what was seen as a shared ethnic identity. This gave way to pan-Africanism, an anti-colonial struggle for blacks in Africa alone. Mazrui argues that the language of both of these movements was English, and that this may have led Africans in French colonies to feel somewhat excluded from them.

Why was it that English was so bound up with the anti-colonial struggle? For Mazrui, the fact that the African elite could enjoy higher education in (English speaking) North America as well as Britain meant that their attitudes were partly shaped by the issue of black emancipation there. But he also discusses the possibility that, in the French colonies, Africans – at least in theory – were considered citizens of France itself. Accordingly, they viewed the French language with affection. In the British colonies, on the other hand, attitudes to English seem to have been more pragmatic (as perhaps was also the case in nineteenth-century Ireland).

But there are other ways in which the movement for African independence and the English language have been linked. These have to do with supposed properties of the language itself. Edward Blyden (Figure 4.8), who was born in 1832 in the Caribbean and later became a professor of languages in Liberia, argued that English was best suited to unify Africans because it 'is a composite language, not the product of any one people. It is made up of contributions by Celts, Danes, Normans, Saxons, Greeks, and Romans, gathering to itself elements ... from the Ganges to the Atlantic' (Blyden, 1888, quoted in Mazrui, 1973, p. 62). In other words, it is the very impurity and hybridity of English that makes it so useful. In addition, the diversity of African society, symbolised by the huge numbers of different languages spoken (often many by one individual), is seen as a problem for the cause of independence.

Figure 4.8 Edward Blyden (1832–1912), politician, diplomat and intellectual; sometimes called 'the father of Pan-Africanism'

Observers have often explained this diversity as produced by 'tribalism'. For promoters of independence, this tribalism needs to be replaced by a different, European concept: that of nationalism, which involves a state with fixed territorial boundaries that represents the interests of, and has legitimate control over, its people.

In this view, learning English helps Africans to recreate their identities as members of nations rather than tribes. It has sometimes been claimed that British colonialism has helped Africans to 'modernise' themselves by introducing them to the English language and, in so doing, to a new culture with concepts such as 'freedom' and 'national identity'.

This view raises a number of problems. For example, it claims that a particular language encodes particular ways of thinking. Many Africans have themselves expressed it, often in debates about the role of English in postcolonial society.

Many writers of literature have argued that English is an inadequate medium for the expression of an authentically 'African' experience. Others, however, have argued that the postcolonial African identity is a hybrid one, and that an African exposed to the English language and to concepts derived from European experience is no less 'African' than any other. So it is the task of the writer to create a kind of English capable of expressing the 'authenticity' of Africa. We see an instance of this below in relation to English in Nigeria, an area of West Africa colonised after 1884, which achieved independence in 1960.

ACTIVITY 4.3

Reading A, 'Identifying Nigerian usages in Nigerian English' by Ayọ Bamgboṣe, discusses some of the problems of identifying and describing characteristics of one of the 'New Englishes' which have arisen in English colonies where many speakers of precolonial languages acquired English as a` second or additional language. Please read it now. What differences and similarities are there between this and the patterns of linguistic contact described earlier in this chapter?

Comment

One issue the author discusses has already been raised in this chapter: the question of to what extent language varieties being compared may be termed 'the same', 'similar' or 'different'. This may be termed a problem of delineation. Another is the question of 'interference' from substratum languages which I discussed earlier in relation to Ireland. But this question is more complicated in Nigeria, since at least 390 African languages are spoken there.

Bamgboṣe's reference to the Nigerian novelist Amos Tutuọla perhaps needs some comment. He quotes Tutuọla's phrase 'born and die babies' as an example of 'substandard' English. But in a footnote to the original paper he explains this as referring to African beliefs about babies which 'die and return, usually to the same parents'. In this respect, Tutuọla is trying to use English to represent concepts for which he feels there is no English expression. Does this mean that English is capable of representing African experience 'authentically'? Many of Tutuọla's readers have found these usages poetic rather than substandard. To use Bamgboṣe's terms, what is 'deviant' from one perspective may be 'creative' from another.

English in Jamaica: an example of replacement

I now return to the role of the slave trade which brought Africans to America and elsewhere to supply cheap labour for the developing colonies. The long-term effect of the slave trade on the development of the English language is immense. It gave rise not only to black English in the USA and the Caribbean, which has been an important influence on the speech of young English speakers worldwide, but also provided the extraordinary context of language contact which led to the formation of English pidgins and creoles. Here then I shall look at the third type of English colony that I've identified: where a precolonial population is replaced by new labour from elsewhere, principally West Africa.

The origins of the slave trade belong to the earliest stages of colonial activity. In 1562 an Elizabethan Englishman called Sir John Hawkins sailed with three ships and 100 men to the coast of West Africa and captured 300 Africans 'partly by the sworde, and partly by other meanes' (in the words of a contemporary account). He sold them in the Caribbean, filled his ships with local hides, ginger, sugar and pearls, and returned to England 'with prosperous success and much gaine to himself and the aforesayed adventurers [London merchants]'. This venture marked the beginnings of the British slave trade (Walvin, 1993, p. 25).

The Africans Hawkins took were from a place that is known today as Sierra Leone. It is possible that they had already had contact with the Portuguese, who had been trading in the area for about a century (Le Page and Tabouret-Keller, 1985, p. 23). We don't know what languages they spoke, or even whether they had any language in common (in Sierra Leone today eighteen languages are spoken), but it is possible that they had some knowledge of a simplified language used between Africans and the Portuguese for the purposes of trade – a pidgin. As you may recall, pidgins typically have a small vocabulary and little grammatical complexity, and often depend heavily on context for understanding. They occur when limited communication is required (often for reasons of trade) between speakers who have no language in common.

One trade controlled by the Portuguese was the shipment of slaves from Africa to the islands of the Caribbean colonised by the Spanish. They used their pidgin in dealing with African middle-men, who traded slaves (captured from other tribes) in return for other goods. In selling his slaves to the Spanish colonists of Hispaniola (later Haiti) Hawkins was taking trade from the Portuguese; but it seems that the Portuguese-based pidgin was used widely enough to survive the successful attempts by both the English and Dutch to capture the slave trade (Le Page and Tabouret-Keller, 1985, pp. 29–30).

It is possible that on Hispaniola, Hawkins's slaves substituted Spanish words for the Portuguese ones in their pidgin, and thus created a Spanish-based pidgin. Or perhaps they were resold, as often happened, to another set of colonists in a different Caribbean territory. Lack of evidence makes it very difficult to keep track of every shipment of slaves. What we do have, from such contemporary accounts as Ligon's *A True and Exact History of the Island of Barbados* (1647) is a description of slaving practice and estimates of numbers in one of the earliest of the British colonies in the Caribbean, Barbados. According to Ligon, shipments of slaves were 'fetch'd from several parts of Africa, who speak severall languages, and by that means, one of them understands not another' (Ligon, 1647, p. 46).

Perhaps it is this statement that has encouraged linguists to take the view that the 'policy of the slave traders was to bring people of different language backgrounds together in the ships, to make it difficult to plot rebellion' (Crystal, 1988, p. 235). If this view is accepted then pidgin would have been the only form of communication available to slaves on the new plantations, and over the generations the African languages they spoke would have been abandoned. But since pidgin had only been used for very simple kinds of interaction, its vocabulary and grammar would have been limited. So it would have needed extending and adapting. As a pidgin develops into a fully functioning language it becomes a creole.

Creoles

As a pidgin is passed on to the children of a community, and used by them as a first language, it becomes a creole. The first stage of creole development is typically indigenisation. However, the distinction between a pidgin and a creole is not always clear. For example, Bislama is often referred to as a pidgin, although it is an official language of Vanuatu and seems to be creolised in urban areas.

In many parts of the world, particularly the Caribbean, continued contact with standard forms of English results in decreolisation – a convergence with the 'lexifier' language (i.e. the language on which the vocabulary is primarily based). This typically produces a creole continuum – a diversity of language usage from a near-standard form of English, known as the acrolect, to the most divergent forms, known as the basilect, with intermediate varieties being termed the mesolect.

Creoles have emerged in many parts of the world and linguists have long been puzzled why so many of them seem to share many grammatical characteristics. One theory is that they all had a common root in some unknown trade language. This idea, partly through lack of evidence, has lost favour in recent years. An alternative explanation has been put forward: that similarities among creoles are due to an innate 'bio-programme' for language. According to this view, creoles provide a unique insight into the basic nature of human language capacity.

An English creole possesses a very different grammar from other varieties of English – at the syntactic level it has more in common with creoles of other languages than with Standard English. It is called an English creole because English is the lexifier language.

Figure 4.9 shows some of the places where English-based pidgins and creole languges are found.

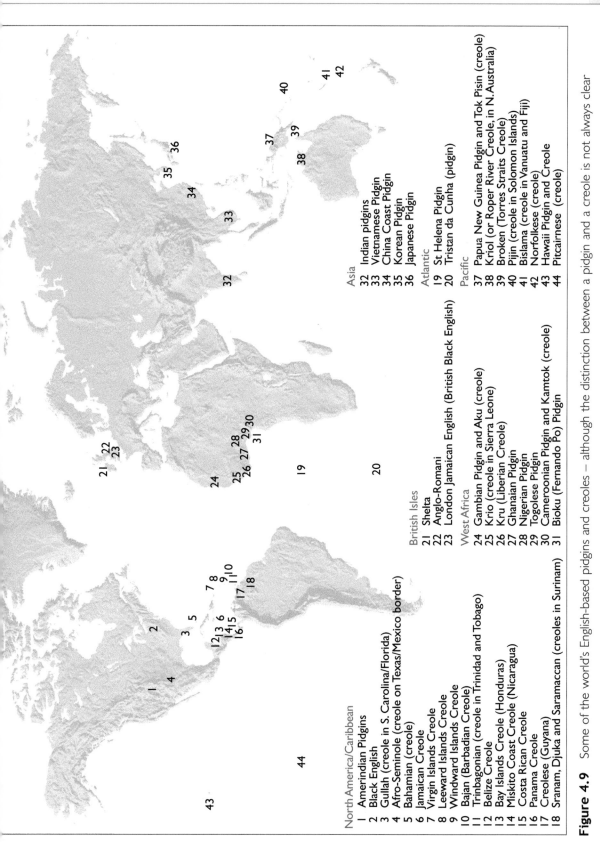

North America/Caribbean
1 Amerindian Pidgins
2 Black English
3 Gullah (creole in S. Carolina/Florida)
4 Afro-Seminole (creole on Texas/Mexico border)
5 Bahamian (creole)
6 Jamaican Creole
7 Virgin Islands Creole
8 Leeward Islands Creole
9 Windward Islands Creole
10 Bajan (Barbadian Creole)
11 Trinbagonian (creole in Trinidad and Tobago)
12 Belize Creole
13 Bay Islands Creole (Honduras)
14 Miskito Coast Creole (Nicaragua)
15 Costa Rican Creole
16 Panama Creole
17 Creolese (Guyana)
18 Sranam, Djuka and Saramaccan (creoles in Surinam)

British Isles
21 Shelta
22 Anglo-Romani
23 London Jamaican English (British Black English)

West Africa
24 Gambian Pidgin and Aku (creole)
25 Krio (creole in Sierra Leone)
26 Kru (Liberian Creole)
27 Ghanaian Pidgin
28 Nigerian Pidgin
29 Togolese Pidgin
30 Cameroonian Pidgin and Kamtok (creole)
31 Bioku (Fernando Po) Pidgin

Asia
32 Indian pidgins
33 Vietnamese Pidgin
34 China Coast Pidgin
35 Korean Pidgin
36 Japanese Pidgin

Atlantic
19 St Helena Pidgin
20 Tristan da Cunha (pidgin)

Pacific
37 Papua New Guinea Pidgin and Tok Pisin (creole)
38 Kriol (or Roper River Creole, in N.Australia)
39 Broken (Torres Straits Creole)
40 Pijin (creole in Solomon Islands)
41 Bislama (creole in Vanuatu and Fiji)
42 Norfolkese (creole)
43 Hawaii Pidgin and Creole
44 Pitcairnese (creole)

Figure 4.9   Some of the world's English-based pidgins and creoles – although the distinction between a pidgin and a creole is not always clear

Creolisation happened in many parts of the English-speaking Caribbean, including Jamaica. This island was captured from the Spanish in 1655, rapidly turned over to sugar production, and settled by English speakers from Barbados and other Caribbean islands such as St Kitts and Nevis (settled in the 1620s), and by convicts from Britain. By 1673 these seem to have been matched in number by African slaves, but by 1746 the latter outnumbered the former by over ten to one, and the owners of the plantations (which were often very large) lived in perpetual fear of slave revolt. Even if the slaves were kept separate linguistically, this did not prevent them from rebelling, despite the severest punishments.

In what language did the slaves plot their revolts? Did they develop their creoles to create meanings unavailable to the slave owners? Or did they retain their African languages? It is noteworthy that if they did abandon the latter, they did so while still retaining their culture of religious, medical and artistic practices. They also often hung on to their names, despite the fact that they were renamed by the planters as a mark of ownership (Walvin, 1993, p. 63). On the other hand, Wolof, an African language spoken today in Senegal and Gambia, is said to have been quite widely spoken in the slave-owning southern states of America during the eighteenth century (McCrum et al., 1992, p. 226), where conditions seem to have been much less conducive to its retention than in Jamaica. This is because in America, plantations were generally smaller than in Jamaica, slaves were often resold or moved from one plantation to another and, above all, owners soon preferred to produce new slaves from within the existing slave community, rather than continue to import them from Africa (so contact with African languages from freshly imported slaves would have been lost).

Whether or not the African languages were abandoned, it seems that their influence can be traced in creoles. Words such as *adru* (a medicinal herb) from Twi, *himba* (an edible wild yam) from Ibo, and *dingki* (a funeral ceremony) from Kongo have all been found in Jamaican Creole.

ACTIVITY 4.4

Allow 5–10 minutes

Reread the last sentence in the paragraph above. In the light of the discussion of slave culture and language, do you think there is anything especially appropriate about these Africanisms? Now look at Figure 4.5 to find out where Kongo, Twi, Ibo and Jamaican Creole are spoken. What does this suggest about the source of slaves?

Comment

The Africanisms refer to knowledge and practices the slaves brought with them to Jamaica. They also show the vast 'catchment area' for the slave trade. The English at first preferred slaves from the Gold Coast (now Ghana), but by the second half of the eighteenth century most of the slaves came from further east and as far south as Angola. When it is known that in Ghana today at least forty-six languages are spoken, it is possible to infer that the slave traders hardly needed to ensure that slaves speaking the same language were kept separate.

Jamaican Creole also has words from Portuguese (*pikni*, 'a small child'), Spanish (*bobo*, 'a fool'), French (*leginz*, 'a bunch of vegetables for a stew'), Hindi (*roti*, 'a kind of bread'), Chinese (*ho senny ho*, 'how's business?') and even Arawak, the language of the precolonial population who had been exterminated by the time English was first spoken in Jamaica (*hicatee*, 'a land turtle', adopted via Spanish). The English element includes dialect words now scarcely heard in England (for example, *higgler*, 'a market woman'). An eighteenth-century account of Jamaican speech also notes the presence of nautical terms such as *berth* ('office'), *store* ('warehouse'), *jacket* ('waistcoat'), *windward* ('east') and *leeward* ('west'), suggesting that the 'maritime' speech of English seamen (drawn from a mix of dialects of British English) may have influenced the formation of an English-based pidgin (Bailey, 1992, p. 126).

Since the nineteenth century, formal education, officially based on the teaching of Standard English, has been available in Jamaica. But, as in the case of Ireland, access to the prescribed linguistic model, especially in relation to speech, has been limited. New varieties of Jamaican speech that can be described as more standardised, however, have been evolved alongside Jamaican Creole. This is the process that linguists call decreolisation. Individual Jamaicans are said to move along a continuum with creole at one end and more standardised English at the other. As in many other parts of the Caribbean, use of creole is firmly linked to a sense of local identity.

4.5 Conclusion

In this chapter we have examined the spread of English from England, first to other parts of the British Isles and then to other areas of the world. The processes of colonisation, political incorporation and nationalist reaction suggest that these take different forms in different contexts and have different linguistic consequences. By way of illustration, we looked at various case studies: Ireland and Scotland in the British Isles; the USA as an example of a country in which English speakers largely displaced the precolonial population; Nigeria as an instance of a country that was more sparsely settled by English speakers, but where a proportion of the precolonial population had access to English as an additional language; and Jamaica, where a displaced population was replaced by people who spoke different languages, brought in initially as slaves, and where communication between these people and English speakers resulted in the development of a pidgin language that subsequently creolised. Each case showed the changing role of English in emerging national identities.

The varieties of English that have arisen in these different places have been shaped by contact: contact with other languages, as well as between the varieties of English used by settlers. Some of the linguistic characteristics of these varieties, and their possible origins, focusing mainly on vocabulary, grammar and pronunciation, are discussed in later chapters.

If you bear in mind the discussion in Chapter 2 of the different kinds of story that have been told about the history of English, you probably won't be surprised to learn that the worldwide spread of English has often been told as a progressive, even triumphalist story, reflecting the glory and international superiority of England and Englishness. But just as the Welsh took a different view of the 'triumph' of the Anglo-Saxons (see Gildas's account in Chapter 2, Section 2.3), so it is possible to regard the global success of English as the result of centuries of exploitation and oppression. For many users of English today, the story might feel more like one of imposition.

But, before the end of the twentieth century, it was also possible to see English as having become a genuinely 'world' language, transcending all differences of culture, race and belief. It is worth noting that it was North America, with far more speakers of English than the British Isles, that had probably played the major role in spreading the language. While some people might regard the influence of the USA as a new form of cultural imperialism, there is also a sense in which 'ownership' of English had finally passed out of the hands of the 'native-speaking' countries: it had become a resource to be exploited, culturally and commercially, by many countries across the world.

Because of the huge scope of the subject dealt with in this chapter, it has only been possible to include a limited number of case studies that illustrate the main developments in the global spread of English. But I have tried to emphasise the range of meanings English has for its speakers and for those who come into contact with it. Such meanings will not always be clearly delineated, and individuals may have rather ambivalent attitudes towards English – a theme that runs throughout the book.

READING A: Identifying Nigerian usages in Nigerian English

Ayọ Bamgboṣe
(Ayọ Bamgboṣe is Emeritus Professor, Department of Linguistics and African Languages, University of Ibadan, Nigeria.)

Source: Bamgboṣe, A. (1982) 'Standard Nigerian English: issues of identification' in Kachru, B.B. (ed.) *The Other Tongue: English across Cultures*, Urbana & Chicago, University of Illinois Press, pp. 102–7.

An inevitable point of departure in describing usage in a second-language situation is a conscious or unconscious comparison with a native variety of the language concerned. This is precisely what has been done in the description of Nigerian English. Labels such as 'same', 'different', or 'similar' must be justified in terms of observed usages in the varieties to which they are applied. Three approaches may be identified: the interference approach, the deviation approach, and the creativity approach.

The interference approach attempts to trace Nigerian usages to the influences of the Nigerian languages. This approach is certainly most relevant as far as the phonetics of Nigerian English is concerned. But as I have pointed out elsewhere, even at this level there are 'features which are typical of the pronunciation of most Nigerian speakers of English' (Bamgboṣe) 1971, p. 42) irrespective of their first-language background. Besides, a typical pronunciation may result from a factor other than interference. For example, most speakers of English from the eastern part of Nigeria pronounce the possessive 'your' as [jua] or [ja], even though all the languages in that area have the sound [ɔ]. The prevalence of this pronunciation is no doubt due to its widespread use by teachers and generations of pupils who have passed through the same schools.

The interference approach is even less justifiable in lexis and syntax. Adekunle (1974) attributes all of standard Nigerian English's Nigerian usages in lexis and syntax to interference from the mother tongue. It is quite easy to show that while some usages can be so attributed, the vast majority, at least in Educated Nigerian English, arise from the normal process of language development involving a narrowing or extension of meaning or the creation of new idioms. And most such usages cut across all first-language backgrounds. For example, when 'travel' is used in the sense 'to be away', as in *My father have travelled* (= My father is away), it is not a transfer of a first-language expression into English, but a modification of the meaning of the verb 'to travel'.

One final objection to the interference approach is that not all cases of interference can validly be considered Nigerian usages. Some clearly belong to the level of pidgin English. For instance, the absence of a gender distinction in third-person pronominal reference may result from first-language interference, e.g. *He talk say* (= He/She says that ...), but it is unlikely that this will be considered a feature of any variety of Nigerian English.

The deviation approach involves a comparison of observed Nigerian usage with Native English, and the labelling of all differences as 'deviant'. Such deviance may result from interference, or from an imperfect attempt to reproduce the target expressions. For example, *Borrow me your pen* (= Lend me your pen) is clearly a case of interference from a first language which makes no lexical distinction between 'lend' and 'borrow'. On the other hand, the pluralization of 'equipment' in *We bought the equipments* indicates a failure to grasp the distinction between countable and mass nouns.

There are two main weaknesses in the deviation approach. First, it tends to suggest that the observed usage is 'imperfect' or 'non-standard' English. The fact that some so-called deviations have now achieved the status of identifying markers of a standard Nigerian English tends to be overlooked in a description that lumps all divergences together as deviant usage. Second, the deviation approach ignores the fact that certain characteristic Nigerian usages in English result from the creativity of the users.

The creativity approach tends to focus on the exploitation of the resources of Nigerian languages as well as English to create new idioms and expressions. According to this approach, a usage which might otherwise have been classified as resulting from interference or deviation is seen as a legitimate second-language creation. Thus, from the expression *She has been to Britain* a noun, *been-to*, has been created to describe anyone who has travelled overseas, particularly to Britain.

The main advantage of the creativity approach is that it recognizes the development of Nigerian English as a type in its own right. But not all cases o usage in Nigerian English can properly be regarded as arising from creativity. Besides, certain usages motivated by creativity are, at best, substandard English. Amos Tutuola's novel, *My Life in the Bush of Ghosts*, is a good example of this. The incidents in the novel take place 'in those days of unknown year' when 'slave wars were causing dead luck to both young and old'; and the hero visits 'Deads'-town' and sees 'born and die babies' as well as 'triplet ghosts and ghostesses' [see Tutuola 1954, pp. 17, 18, 62 and 63].

The above discussion shows that while each approach throws some light on the nature of Nigerian English, none is by itself adequate to characterize the whole spectrum of Nigerian English. Besides, not every feature thrown up by each approach necessarily exemplifies Nigerian English. A combination of all approaches is therefore required, and a certain amount of subjective judgement regarding acceptability will be required in determining what falls within or outside the scope of Nigerian English.

...

Some typical features of standard Nigerian English

In order to illustrate such features as I consider typical, I provide (below) examples based on my general observation of the use of English by [educated Nigerian] speakers. I believe these features cut across different first-language backgrounds, and no amount of drilling or stigmatization is going to lead to their abandonment.

...

Morphology and syntax

These are generally the same as in standard English, except for features such as the following: 1) Peculiar word formation may occur with plurals (e.g. *equipments, aircrafts, deadwoods*), antonyms *(indisciplined)*, and adverbials *(singlehandedly)*. 2) Dropping of 'to' from the infinitive after certain verbs; e.g. *enable him do it*. 3) A preposition may be employed where Native English will avoid or will use a different preposition; e.g. *voice out* instead of 'voice' (I am going to voice out my opinion), *discuss about* instead of 'discuss' (We shall discuss about that later), *congratulate for* instead of 'congratulate on' (I congratulate you for your brilliant performance). 4) A focus construction is often used, involving the subject of the sentence as focus and an anaphoric pronoun subject, e.g. *The politicians and their supporters, they don't often listen to advice. A person who has no experience, can he be a good leader?*

Lexis and semantics

As has often been observed, most differences between Nigerian English and other forms of English are to be found in the innovations in lexical items and idioms and their meanings. Following are some of the features concerned. 1) New lexical items may either be coined from existing lexical items or borrowed from the local languages or from pidgin, either directly or in translation. For examples of coinage, consider *barb* (to cut [hair]) from 'barber', *invitee* (guest) from 'invite', *head-tie* (woman's headdress), and *go-slow* (traffic jam). Loan words and loan translations are generally drawn from different aspects of the cultural background, including food, dress, and customs for which there are quite often no exact equivalent lexical items in English; e.g. *akara balls* (bean cakes), *juju music* (a type of dance music), *bush meat* (game), *tie-dye cloth* (cloth into which patterns are made up by tying up parts of it before dyeing), and *white-cap chiefs* (senior chiefs in Lagos whose rank is shown by the white caps they wear). 2) Some lexical items acquire new meanings; e.g. a *corner* becomes a 'bend in a road', *globe* is an 'electric bulb', *wet* means 'to water (flowers)', and a *launcher* is someone called upon to declare open a fund-raising function. *Locate* means 'to assign to a school or town' and is used when speaking of newly qualified teachers. *Land* is 'to finish one's intervention or speech', *environment* is a 'neighborhood', and *bluff* means 'to give an air of importance'. 3) Other lexical items have retained older meanings no longer current in Native English. *Dress*, 'move at the end of a row so as to create room for additional persons', is a retention of the earlier meaning recorded by the *Shorter Oxford English Dictionary*: 'to form in proper alignment'. *Station*, 'the town or city in which a person works', is a retention of the earlier meaning recorded by the same source: 'the locality to which an official is appointed for the exercise of his functions'. 4) Certain idioms acquire new forms or meanings. To *eat one's cake and have it* is an inversion of 'to have one's cake and eat it' (Example: You can't eat your cake and have it). *As at now* replaces 'as of now' (Example: As at now, there are only two men available). 5) Some totally new idioms are developed; e.g. *to take in* for 'to become pregnant'. (Example: She has just taken in). *Off-head*, 'from memory', is similar to standard English *offhand* (Example: I can't tell you the number off-head). To *take the light* means to make a power cut (Example: Has the National Electrical Power Authority (N.E.P.A.) taken the light again?). And *social wake-keeping* refers to feasting, drumming, and dancing after a burial (Example: There will be social wake-keeping from 10 p.m. till dawn).

Context

Even when lexical items or idioms have roughly the same meanings as in Native English, they may be used in completely different contexts. Examples which have been given in the literature include the use of *sorry* as an expression of sympathy, for example, to someone who sneezes or stumbles, or *wonderful* as an exclamation of surprise. To these may be added the use of *please* as an indication of politeness (for example, in a formal or official letter), *Dear Sir* for opening a personal letter to someone older than oneself, and *my dear* for addressing practically anyone, including strangers.

References for this reading

Adekunle, M. A. (1974) 'The standard Nigerian English', *Journal of the Nigeria English Studies Association*, vol. 6, no. 1, pp. 24–37.

Bamgboṣe, A. (1971) 'The English language in Nigeria' in Spencer, J. (ed.) *The English Language in West Africa*, Longman, pp. 35–48.

[Tutuọla, A. (1954) *My Life in the Bush of Ghosts*, London, Faber & Faber.]

5 Accent as social symbol

Lynda Mugglestone

5.1 Introduction

> It is impossible for an Englishman to open his mouth without making some other Englishman despise him.
>
> (George Bernard Shaw, 1972, [1910], Preface to *Pygmalion*)

In *Pygmalion*, by the Irish playwright George Bernard Shaw, a cockney flower girl is transformed into a society lady by little more than a gruelling series of elocution lessons. The play was first produced in 1916. As its author, Shaw no doubt felt authorised to speak on a subject of some controversy which continues to be controversial today. The subject was accent – the way we pronounce and intone the words we speak – and the extremely strong feelings that different accents can arouse in listeners.

These strong feelings may vary, like the accents themselves, from region to region wherever English is spoken. An Australian may react quite neutrally to a Louisiana accent which could have a US listener making all sorts of (unfounded) judgements about the speaker's intelligence, sophistication and political views. Similarly, a Californian watching a TV sitcom imported from Australia could be impervious to the ways in which the accents of the suburban Sydney characters are positioning an Australian audience to make judgements about those characters.

In other words, reactions to a particular accent are generally culture specific. An accent may carry for a particular group of listeners implications to do with a whole range of qualities attributable to the speaker, from intelligence and trustworthiness to idleness and even potential criminality. But those implications – call them prejudices if you like – will only be shared and understood by those who are able to place the accent within its social and regional context. The accent thus becomes the badge for a range of qualities attributable to the social context which gives rise to it. The accent becomes a social symbol.

This chapter examines the rise of language attitudes of this kind by looking at a case study of a specific prestigious accent of English within a UK context, from the consciousness fostered during the eighteenth century to the resistance to assumptions about a hierarchy of accent and social/cultural worth that is evident today. While the case study is undoubtedly culture specific, it illustrates the mechanisms by which some accents come to be regarded as more or less prestigious than others, and associated with particular qualities which are seen as desirable or otherwise. In this respect, it will be of particular interest for readers outside the UK sphere of reference to investigate whether similar mechanisms apply to accents within their own context.

5.2 The consciousness of correctness

> No man can amend a fault of which he is not conscious, and consciousness cannot exert itself when barred up by habit.
>
> (Thomas Sheridan, 1762, *A Course of Lectures on Elocution*, p. 37)

Thomas Sheridan's *A Course of Lectures on Elocution* was intended to announce a fundamental shift within contemporary attitudes to accent. Sheridan was writing in an era often characterised by its interest in linguistic regulation, and it was the still unregulated state of English pronunciation which was to inspire Sheridan (and others) in their crusade for the establishment of a standard speech.

As we have seen in Chapter 3, eighteenth-century dictionaries and grammars had increasingly sought to establish a reference model for the 'proper' use of syntax and lexis for English. Nevertheless, pronunciation had largely remained outside these paradigms of correctness, conspicuously continuing to vary through time and space. Though notions of a 'best speech' had been located in London usage since at least the sixteenth century, widespread pressures for convergent behaviour had been noticeably absent. If prescriptivism is the view 'that one variety of language has an inherently higher value than others, and that this ought to be imposed on the whole of the speech community' (Crystal, 1987, p. 2), then it appears that at this stage it was not extended to pronunciation. Indeed, use of a local and regionally marked accent was common for all speakers in society, even for those higher in the social spectrum. 'Sounds are too volatile and subtle for legal restraints; to enchain syllables, and to lash the wind, are equally the undertakings of pride, unwilling to measure its desires by its strength,' as Samuel Johnson had declared in the Preface to his *A Dictionary of the English Language* of 1755.

However, Sheridan was now challenging Johnson's attitude, seeing it as the abdication of proper prescriptive responsibility. In this period, such tolerance of spoken diversity was therefore to be challenged by writers on spoken language and brought into line with their prescriptive rhetoric on other domains of language use. Regionalities of spelling or of grammar were not regarded as acceptable; why, Sheridan demanded, should matters be any different when it came to the management of the voice, and the non-localised uniformities which articulation too should involve?

As in the extract below, Sheridan's work is interesting in its deliberate assimilation of pronunciation within contemporary ideologies of standardisation. His stress on the need to raise the linguistic consciousness in this context is, in this sense, both ideological as well as practical – he desired to change the prevailing mind-set, to sensitise speakers to notions of correct pronunciation (and the need to accommodate individual speech behaviour to this) and, just as in other areas of language comment at this time, to constrain change and variability in the interests of a clear and regulated norm. Tellingly, the title page of his own dictionary of 1780 would affirm a very different agenda from that of Johnson's earlier work. It read: *A Complete Dictionary of the English Language, both with regard to Sound and Meaning. One main Object of which is, to Establish a Plain and Permanent Standard of Pronunciation.*

ACTIVITY 5.1

Allow about
30 minutes

Look carefully at the following extract from Sheridan's *Course of Lectures in Elocution* (1762). Select some of the key terms through which he constructs a persuasive argument.

> But it is not so with regard to pronunciation; in which tho' there be as great a difference between men, as in any other article, yet this difference, is not so much between individuals, as whole bodies of men; inhabitants of different countries [i.e. counties, regions], and speaking one common language, without agreeing in the manner of pronouncing it. Thus not only the Scotch, Irish, and Welsh, have each their own idioms, which uniformly prevail in those countries, but almost every county in England, has its peculiar dialect. Nay in the very metropolis two different modes of pronunciation prevail, by which the inhabitants of one part of the town, are distinguished from those of the other. One is current in the city, and is called the cockney; the other at the court-end, and is called the polite pronunciation. As amongst these various dialects, one must have the preference, and become fashionable, it will of course fall to the lot of that which prevails at court, the source of fashions of all kinds. All other dialects, are sure marks, either of a provincial, rustic, pedantic, or mechanic education; and therefore have some degree of disgrace annexed to them. And as the court pronunciation is no where methodically taught, and can be acquired only by conversing with people in polite life, it is a sort of proof that a person has kept good company, and on that account is sought after by all, who wish to be considered as fashionable people, or members of the beau monde. This is the true reason that the article of pronunciation has been the chief, or rather the only object of attention, in the whole affair of delivery. Yet tho' this is a point, the attainment of which is ardently desired by an infinite number of individuals, there are few who succeed in the attempt, thro' want of method, rules, and assistance of masters: without which old habits can not easily be removed.
>
> The difficulties to those who endeavour to cure themselves of a provincial or vicious pronunciation are chiefly three. 1st, The want of knowing exactly where the fault lies. 2dly, Want of method in removing it, and of due application. 3dly, Want of consciousness of their defects in this point.

(Sheridan, 1762, pp. 30–31)

Comment

I have previously mentioned standardisation as a 'rhetoric' and as an 'ideology'.
Both are in evidence here. As a rhetoric, the work of Sheridan (Figure 5.1)
seeks to persuade of the superiority of one form of speech, and the inferiority
of others. The pronunciation of the social elite in London is described in terms
which stress its politeness and desirability, affirming its intended status as
a model and, as in his *Dictionary* of 1780, as a 'standard' for all speakers,
wherever they might be located (in both social and geographical terms).
Regional pronunciation is, by contrast, described in terms which trade on
a markedly negative set of connotations, setting the 'provincial' against the
metropolitan, and the 'vicious' against the fashionable. The disparaging
associations of 'provincial' were, in this respect, a new development of the
eighteenth century; Johnson's *Dictionary* had glossed 'provincial' as 'rude,
unpolished' and, as the *Oxford English Dictionary* (OED) explains of this
particularly loaded development, the associations were those of deficit,
'wanting [in the sense of lacking] the culture or manners of the capital'.
'Vicious' was another popular prescriptive term, its application here again
intentionally serving to remove regional enunciation from the linguistic virtues
of the polite. Metaphors of sickness (and necessary remedy) are prominent – a
provincial accent is in need of 'cure' and is, as Sheridan elsewhere notes, the
product of 'infection': 'there are few gentlemen of England who have received
their education at country schools, that are not infected with a false
pronunciation of certain words peculiar to each county' (Sheridan, 1762,
p. 33). 'Disgrace' is moreover given as seemingly inseparable from the use of
regionally marked pronunciation of any kind.

Sheridan's prose also importantly engages with the idea of the 'best'
pronunciation as a sociolect, a social variety of discourse, or as Sheridan (1762,
p. 30) writes, a 'proof that a person has kept good company' (with the
additionally persuasive implication, of course, that someone without such an
accent must have kept company with those who might, in a variety of ways, be
judged to be less 'good'). Such deft manipulations of social nuance work well
in terms of Sheridan's avowed aims to raise the linguistic consciousness in
terms of accent, sensitising his readers not only to the stated – if entirely
subjective – values of one form of speech above others, but to the varied
demerits of failing to assimilate in this way. The 'right' accent is depicted as a
prized possession, one 'ardently desired by an infinite number of individuals'
(assumed here to include those who are well-born but who reside outside the
capital, as well as speakers less socially fortunate wherever they might be
located).

M.ͬ SHERIDAN.

PROLOGUE to CATO.

"A brave Man struggling in the Storms of Fate,
And greatly falling with a falling State".

Figure 5.1   Thomas Sheridan (1719–1788) was an actor throughout his life. For a time he became a prominent Dublin theatre manager. After that career ended in financial ruin through riots promulgated by supporters of a well-known 'gentleman' whom Sheridan had expelled for a drunken assault on an actress, he turned to a new career in English language education. He was the godson of Jonathan Swift, whose influence he readily acknowledged, and the father of several prominent children including the playwright and politician, Richard Brinsley Sheridan.

5.3 'Want of method'

As Sheridan recognised, assimilating speech within the standardisation process was potentially problematic, not least with reference to the means by which this designated 'proper' accent might be disseminated. While his own lectures might be spectacularly well-attended (some 300 gentlemen attended the course he delivered in Edinburgh in four weeks in 1761; those delivered in London had an audience of over 1500), even Sheridan could not reach the populace as a whole. As he acknowledged, the acquisition of a still largely localised (if undoubtedly socially prestigious) London norm was circumscribed by the limited number of people who might gain contact with its forms. The level – and the means – of linguistic exposure was the crux. For Sheridan and the other writers of this period who shared his concerns, this prompted two major developments: first, the rise of elocution as a new, and newly profitable, white-collar profession; and second, the rise of the pronouncing dictionary.

Both developments attested a widespread public appetite for information on accent and pronunciation, as well as affirming the increasing sensitisation to matters of speech that Sheridan had craved. Five times as many manuals of elocution appeared in the forty years after 1760 than had been published before this date. Perhaps still more significant was the incorporation of such concerns within the easily affordable manuals of linguistic etiquette aimed at 'the million' ('the multitude or the bulk of the population' in contemporary terms). *P's and Q's. Grammatical Hints for the Million*, in its second edition by 1855, displayed, for example, a stringent concern for correct pronunciation, giving popular language attitudes the appearance of hard facts. Readers were informed, for instance, that 'a defective pronunciation' was 'displeasing to the ear' and indicated that the speaker 'belongs to a class which is careless of the rights of letters'. Popular journals and magazines, tracts on pronunciation, works on elocution, and even textbooks intended for use in schools (discussed in Section 5.5) all regularly came to engage with ideas of this kind.

'Consciousness can be awoken only by information', Sheridan had stressed (1762, p. 38). As the wealth (and variety) of such publications indicate, information was henceforth to be provided in abundance, detailing in unprecedented detail the social as well as linguistic properties of the stated norm. Readers were moreover often encouraged to work systematically through the guidance provided; rather than a passive reference book upon a shelf, the dictates of pronouncing dictionaries were to be actively assimilated into an everyday form of self-improvement.

5.4 An educated accent

> Ay, ay; I know, I know; but I let other folks talk. I've laid by now, and gev up to the young uns. Ask them as have been to school at Tarley: they've learnt pernouncing; that's come up since my day.
>
> (George Eliot, *Silas Marner: The Weaver of Raveloe*, 1861, p. 90)

Learning 'pernouncing' was, as George Eliot indicates (not least by the strategic indications of regional pronunciation which Eliot allocates to Mr Macey, the tailor and parish clark of Raveloe), something of a new development in eighteenth- and nineteenth-century education. While a national education system did not come into operation in the UK until 1870 (when the Education Act 1870 established compulsory primary education for children up to the age of thirteen), educational provision in a variety of forms had been increasing over the previous decades. Private schools, dame schools, public schools, church schools and evening schools among others testify to the range of educational experiences that were on offer. John Walker, known as 'Elocution Walker' for much of the nineteenth century, established his own school in Kensington in London in 1769; Sheridan himself wrote a primer for elementary instruction (*Elements of English*, 1786) which, as might be expected, set out the necessary paradigms for the early acquisition of a standard accent. Sheridan's first work was, in fact, on the subject of education or, to give its full title: *British Education or The Source of the Disorders of Great Britain.* Language – and specifically the teaching of the spoken language – was depicted as central to the remedy of such 'disorder'. While it is, of course, difficult to pinpoint any one individual as instrumental in the shift of attitudes in this respect, Sheridan's influence was undoubted. Individual schools, such as Enmore School in Somerset, actively implemented Sheridan's ideas, as is illustrated in the following extract on teaching methodology.

> If a child omits, or mistakes, a word, or even a letter, he is liable to degradation; as it is the duty of the teacher instantly to [pass on] to the next child, and, if necessary, to all the children in succession; and on no account to rectify the mistake himself, until the whole class has been tried. Even a coarse or provincial way of pronouncing a word, though sanctioned by the general practice of the district, is immediately noticed by the teacher; and exposes the child, who uses it, as much to the correction of those below him, and consequently the loss of his place, as any other impropriety in reading would do.
>
> (Poole, 1813, p. 29)

Texts such as these clearly give a new reality to the modern idiom of the 'educated accent'.

'Standard English', as the sociolinguist Peter Trudgill affirms, 'is the dialect of education' (Trudgill, 1983c, p. 57). While, as he stresses, Standard English can in reality be spoken with any accent, nineteenth-century pupils were, in contrast, often given explicit instruction in the means by which one accent, and one alone, was to be acquired. Nineteenth-century conceptions of standard speech – often based on prescriptive models of language could, as this indicates, differ considerably from contemporary British. We can see this particularly clearly if we examine manuals of teaching practice, aimed at instructing teachers in the precepts of proper instruction. These not only enshrine the 'educated accent' as something which education should impart but also encode a number of shibboleths.

Shibboleth

The word shibboleth derives from a story in the Bible (Judges, 12) about a conflict between two tribes, the Gileadites and the Ephraimites. Trying to establish the identity of some escaped Ephraimites, the Gileadites set them a test, which was to say the word 'shibboleth'. The Ephraimites would give themselves away by saying 'siboleth' and be killed as a result. In this way the term 'shibboleth' has come to mean a feature of (usually) speech which somehow establishes identity, or distinguishes one identity from another.

Activity 5.2 includes a section from one of the most popular teaching manuals of the mid nineteenth century, tellingly headed 'Defective intelligence', which focuses on some of the emergent shibboleths of nineteenth-century speech.

ACTIVITY 5.2

Allow about
15 minutes

John Gill's *Introductory Text-Book to School Education, Method and School Management* went through a number of editions between 1857 and 1882; over 18,000 copies had been printed by 1870. It was a popular text in the training colleges for teachers, established in the wake of the Education Act 1870, as well as being used in thousands of individual teaching establishments both before and after that date. Read through the following extract carefully. How does Gill see the role of the teacher regarding the speech of pupils? What comparisons does he draw between an individual's accent and other qualities?

> *Defective intelligence.*   1)   Pronunciation. ... The most troublesome class of incorrect pronunciations are provincialisms; the substitution of one sound for another, as û for ŭ [i.e. the 'u' sound in 'push' for the 'u' sound in 'cut'], and vice versâ; the addition of a sound, such as idea-r, and the omission of sounds, as of the aspirate [/h/ sound]. These faults partake of a mechanical character, belonging to the ear and habit as much as to defective intelligence. The best mode of dealing with them is to take up a systematic course of orthoepy ... The cure is with the teacher, who alone is to blame if there exists much incorrectness in his first class. The teacher should take means to secure the accuracy of his own pronunciation and that of his subordinates. An aid to this would be to mark the quantities and accents in the 'Teacher's Lesson Book,' – the doing so being a part of the reading lesson.
>
> (Gill, 1863, pp. 155–6)

Comment

Gill's textbook places a categorical emphasis on correct pronunciation ('orthoepy') as one of the prime objectives of instruction within the school. Differences of pronunciation are, however, framed by notions of subjective inequality, by which certain pronunciations are depicted as intrinsically 'inferior'. In Gill's own words, these are 'faults', indicating 'defective intelligence' and 'incorrectness'. Features of pronunciation are given not just as markers of difference per se, but as emblematic of non-linguistic – and intensely negative – qualities. In this instance, this is given as connoting not just the absence of education, but also a deficit in intelligence. This image of cognitive inadequacy is profoundly discriminatory in its implications, actively stigmatising particular modes of speech (and particular speakers) in a form of clear-cut accent prejudice.

The problem of subjective inequality

The fact that nineteenth-century school inspectors often reinforced such ideas in their own assessments reveals just how pervasive such assumptions were; comments on regional 'peculiarities' and the corresponding need for 'good pronunciation' often litter their reports (Mugglestone, 2003, pp. 212–57). The role of the public schools, attended by the wealthy and socially well-to-do (as well as the offspring of the aspirational new rich), was not insignificant in this context. While in origin the public schools had catered for the poor and needy with a dominantly local intake, by the end of the nineteenth century a number of decisive shifts had taken place. As boarding schools (Figure 5.2), they came to provide a non-localised education for the emergent and existing upper classes of the day, separating pupils from the local community in which they had been born (and from the local forms of language which they might otherwise have acquired). Meanwhile the patterns of peer pressure they enforced were extremely effective in maintaining and consolidating norms of behaviour – including those of language. Formal tuition could also play its part, and a number of minor public schools produced their own handbooks for instilling the due proprieties of language. The 'public-school accent' duly came to act as yet another euphemism for 'talking proper'.

Such notions of subjective inequality are based purely on language attitudes – on how people think about language. As Richard Hudson notes:

> In some societies (but by no means all) people are credited with different amounts of intelligence, friendliness and other virtues according to the way they speak, although such a judgement based on speech may be quite wrong. Consequently, whatever virtues are highly valued, some speakers are thought to have more of them than they really have, simply

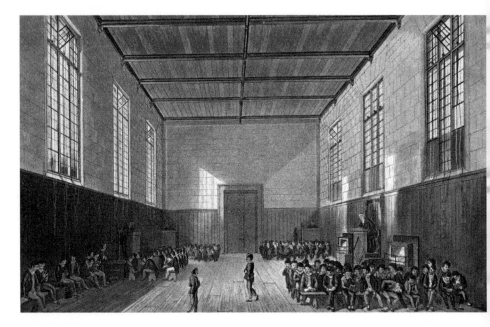

Figure 5.2   The Great School Room of Rugby in the nineteenth century. Founded in 1567, Rugby School had become a leading public school by the nineteenth century. Especially through the actions of its famous early nineteenth-century headmaster, Thomas Arnold, it became well known for an emphasis on religious and moral education combined with scholarship.

> because they have the 'right' way of speaking, and others are thought to have less because their speech conveys the wrong impression.
>
> (Hudson, 1986, pp. 193–4)

As Hudson explains, there are in fact no intrinsic links between prevalent images of intelligence, aesthetic value or culture with the underlying sounds, even though different modes of pronunciation are often seen as suggesting qualities of this kind. Such essentially arbitrary – and unfounded – affiliations need to be remembered when we seek to look behind language attitudes in this and other contexts. (You might like to consider whether similar language attitudes pertain within your own context if it differs from the one being described.) Whereas modern educational practice has moved on – 'it is no longer permitted in British society to be seen to discriminate against someone on the basis of their accent' (Trudgill, 2002, p. 176) – the legacies of such attitudes do still disturbingly persist.

5.5 Received Pronunciation

> In the present day we may ... recognise a received pronunciation all over the country, not widely differing in any particular locality, and admitting a certain degree of variety.
>
> (Ellis, 1869a, p. 23)

The words of pioneering phonetician Alexander Ellis have often been taken as providing the first formal analysis of the non-regional accent which is still referred to as **Received Pronunciation (RP)** – a mode of speech which, just as Sheridan had wished, is employed irrespective of the geographical origins of the speaker. As Ellis noted, RP seemed, for many, to be the logical culmination of the widespread belief 'that it is possible to erect a standard of pronunciation which should be acknowledged and followed throughout the countries where English is spoken as a native tongue'. Moreover, as Ellis added, by the late nineteenth century there was a clear conviction that such a 'standard already exists, and is the norm unconsciously followed by persons who, by rank or education, have most right to establish the custom of speech' (Ellis, 1869b, p. 624).

Such ideas were certainly widespread by this point. The elocutionist Arthur Burrell, for example, pointed out to his own readers in 1891 that 'it is the business of educated people to speak so that no one may be able to tell in what county their childhood was passed' (Burrell, 1891, p. 24). Education was assumed to preclude regional usage (and particularly, as we have seen, when this involved attendance at a public school which carried its own values of status). Henry Sweet – another pioneering phonetician upon whom Shaw reputedly based the character of Professor Henry Higgins (Eliza's tutor) in *Pygmalion* – also provided confirmation of this role of the 'received' in 1881, commenting (in his work *The Elementary Sounds of English)* on a form of speech which was 'approximated to, all over Great Britain, by those who do not keep to their own local dialects' (Sweet, 1881, p. 7).

However, as we have noted at other points throughout this chapter, in terms of language there can be a considerable distance between rhetoric and reality, and between belief and behaviour. Certainly, accent was heavily imbued with social meanings by this point. Fostered in literature as much as in popular works on language, features such as /h/-loss, the pronunciation of *-ing*, or the 'improper' sounding of /r/ in words such as *car, cart*, could all operate as a ready form of social shorthand, effectively discriminating between speakers on the basis of widely prevalent language attitudes. It is in such terms that Charles Dickens, for instance, chose to stigmatise the wife of John Bradbury, the publisher of his novels. Dickens had himself acquired the accent appropriate to the 'educated' (rather than one that signalled his own childhood experiences, which included working in a blacking factory in London for six shillings a week). In depicting Mrs Bradbury's voice in his private letters, Dickens conspicuously drew on familiar notions of ridicule. The following comes from a letter which Dickens sent to his wife in December 1855:

> Mrs Bradburys account of Bradbury's setting fire to the Bed ... was wonderful ... It seems that, she being hat Brihteen [i.e. Brighton] hat the time, he kept the secret of what had happened, until she came home. Then, on composing that luxuriant and gorgeous figure of hers between the sheets, she started and said, 'William, where his me bed? – *This* is not

me bed – wot has append William – wot ave you dun with me bed – I
know the feelin of me bed, and *this* is not me bed.'

(Dickens, 1855, quoted in Storey et al., 1993, p. 770)

Mrs Bradbury's voice is here made to unite a highly class-conscious set of
stigmatised features of speech. Her insecurities over /h/-usage, as in *append*
(for *happened*) and *hat* (for *at*), illustrate one of the foremost shibboleths of
Victorian speech patterns, and one which enabled a form of social segregation
to take place, allocating speakers to 'higher' or 'baser' spheres. To drop an /h/,
and to pronounce *house* as *ouse*, was, as the phonetician Alexander Ellis
stressed in 1869, to commit social suicide in polite circles. Mrs Bradbury also,
according to Dickens, uses *-in* rather than *-ing* in *feel**in***, and the stereotypical
wot (rather than *what*), which trades on the perceived and 'superior' delicacy
of pronouncing the initial sound as [hw] rather than [w].

As in one of the entries which Ellis was to write for the first fascicle of the
OED, even the word 'accent' had come to be synonymous with (negative)
marking of some kind: 'This utterance consists mainly in a prevailing quality of
tone, or in a peculiar alteration of pitch, but may include mispronunciation of
vowels or consonants, misplacing of stress, and misinflection of a sentence.
The locality of a speaker is generally clearly marked by this kind of accent'
(quoted in Murray, 1884, section 7.2).

Significantly, other speakers were assumed to speak 'without an accent', a
feature often given as one of the essential attributes of the emergent RP of the
day. It is, of course, a linguistic impossibility to speak without any accent at all,
but labellings of this kind reveal the wider meanings at stake. For instance, the
term '/h/-dropping' conceals an ideological slant by which such usage is
measured (and found wanting) against an implied and /h/-full norm. Similarly,
'speaking with an accent' signals an opposing (and preferable) norm in the
'accentless' – an implied ideal of regionally neutral speech. It was conveniently
ignored that the salient properties of this 'regionally neutral speech' were
more characteristic of the affluent south-east of England than, say, the north or
the west of the country.

The realities of RP

While writers within the prescriptive tradition continued to stress the
normative value of RP, Ellis was keener to analyse its actual properties,
emphasising the absence of fixity and uniformity which close examination of
its characteristics revealed. If such a norm existed, he made plain, then it had
to be seen as one which was open to change and variation. His own
transcriptions taken from a range of speakers in London confirmed the
amount of variability which existed, even within those who might be judged
to assimilate to this stated speech-form. 'A large number of words are
pronounced with differences very perceptible to those who care to observe,
even among educated London speakers', he noted (Ellis, 1869b, p. 629).

An 'educated' accent clearly in this sense wasn't monolithic; indeed, the very term 'educated pronunciation' was, to Ellis's mind, deeply troubling. 'There is no such thing as educated English pronunciation. There are pronunciations of English people more or less educated in a variety of things, but not in pronunciation', he insisted (Ellis, 1875, p. 23), stripping away common value judgements to focus on the characteristics of speech alone.

Ellis's status as phonetician lends him a welcome – and dispassionate – commitment to engage with the facts of usage. A single and rigidly codified accent for all speakers clearly remained the stuff of prescriptive myth. On the other hand, a non-localised and prestigious accent, albeit one used by a minority, had undoubtedly come into being. The 'Received Pronunciation' described by Ellis and Sweet was, however, fundamentally a social accent – one which confirmed not the egalitarian utopia which had originally been envisaged by Sheridan, but instead the hierarchical images of division.

5.6 The broadcast voice

> One hears the most appalling travesties of vowel pronunciation. This is a matter in which broadcasting can be of immense assistance.
>
> (John Reith, 1924, p. 161)

The British Broadcasting Corporation (BBC) was founded in 1922, initially as the British Broadcasting Company; John Reith was its first Director General. From the outset, the precise nature of the voices to be heard on the airwaves was a matter of urgent discussion, as is evident from Reith's words quoted above. Such notions of beneficial assistance were, however, to operate primarily in terms of the wider dissemination of RP. Those who were chosen to present programmes or to read the news bulletins were required to eradicate all traces of regionality from their speech. As Reith explained, 'We have made a special effort to secure in our various stations men who ... can be relied upon to employ the correct pronunciation of the English tongue' (Reith, 1924, p. 161). Convinced of the 'great advantage of a standard pronunciation', Reith saw the potential of broadcasting for increasing linguistic exposure to his chosen norm. Just like Sheridan, he saw the national transmission of one accent as a potential means of standardisation, fostering awareness of 'good' English' over the whole of Great Britain. As he commented approvingly in *Broadcast over Britain* (Reith, 1924, p. 162), 'children particularly have acquired the habit of copying the announcer's articulation; this has been observed by their teachers, and so long as the announcer is talking good English, and without affectation, I find it is much to be desired that [the announcer] should be copied'.

Parameters of acceptability were further clarified by the BBC Advisory Committee on Spoken English established in 1926. While the regional voice was not to be excluded altogether, its varied manifestations tended to be restricted to the domains of comedy and light entertainment, a distribution which tended to reinforce prevalent social and cultural stereotypes. RP was the voice of authority, used for all 'serious' broadcasting and the national news. In an appropriate image of status (and status consciousness), news announcers were required, from 1925, to wear dinner jackets while broadcasting. In terms of language, it was RP which was felt to provide a corresponding decorum for the spoken voice.

Consciousness of its perceived merits was such that, when the broadcaster Wilfred Pickles (Figure 5.3) – born in Halifax in Yorkshire in the north of England and with the regional accent of his birthplace – was chosen to read the news during the Second World War, there were complaints from listeners that they felt that they couldn't believe the information that they were being given. The BBC's motives in using Pickles as a London announcer in 1941 were perhaps even more discriminatory in the underlying assumption that the Germans would find it more difficult to imitate his Yorkshire tones, complete with a short northern [a] in words such as *bath* and *path*, and with prominent use of /h/-less realisations. National newspapers satirised Pickles's accent and caricatured him wearing the stereotypical (from the southern British point of view) dress of the less affluent northern male: flat cap, boots and woolly muffler or scarf. As Pickles (1949, p. 132) noted in his autobiography: 'The B.B.C.'s standard English had become a firmly rooted national institution like cricket and the pub and, Hitler or no Hitler, it meant something when there was a threat of departure from the habit'.

Figure 5.3 Wilfred Pickles (1904–1978) was a newsreader during the Second World War and later became one of the most popular broadcasters in the history of radio. His audience participation quiz show *Have a Go* ran from 1946 to 1967 and attracted audiences of up to twenty-six million.

Pickles's regionally marked accent in the context of national broadcasting indicates the state of language attitudes in the middle of the twentieth century, with still very strong feelings about the appropriacy and the 'proper' cultural dominance of RP on the airwaves, at least in authoritative spheres of usage such as the news. By this time, RP had gained another synonym – BBC English – originally used, as Tom McArthur notes (1992, p. 109), by regional BBC staff who resented the better prospects of those speakers who possessed public-school accents. The term came to assume a far more general currency: as the OED confirms, it came to signify 'standard English as maintained by BBC announcers'.

5.7 Contesting voices

You might like to compare the culture which ridiculed Pickles's accent as a newsreader with those expressed in the poem *The 6 O'Clock News* which appeared in 1984 in a series called *Unrelated Incidents* by the Scottish poet Tom Leonard. The programme *The Six O'Clock News* was Pickles's first national broadcast, on 27 November 1941. To emphasise his point, Leonard uses 'eye-dialect', where the spelling is intended to suggest a Scottish pronunciation. Alongside his poem below is a version using standard spelling.

this is thi	This is the
six a clock	six o'clock
news thi	news, the
man said n	man said and
thi reason	the reason
a talk wia	I talk with a
BBC accent	BBC accent
iz coz yi	is because you
widny wahnt	wouldn't want
mi ti talk	me to talk
aboot thi	about the
trooth wia	truth with a
voice lik	voice like
wanno yoo	one of you
scruff. if	scruffs. If
a toktaboot	I talked about
thi trooth	the truth
lik wanna yoo	like one of you
scruff yi	scruffs you
widny thingk	wouldn't think
it wuz troo.	it was true.
jist wonna yoo	Just one of you
scruff tokn.	scruffs talking.
thirza right	There's a right

way ti spell	way to spell
ana right way	and a right way
ti tok it. this	to talk it. This
is me tokn yir	is me talking your
right way a	right way of
spelling. this	spelling. This
is ma trooth.	Is my truth.
yooz doant no	You don't know
thi trooth	the truth
yirsellz cawz	yourselves because
yi canny talk	you can't talk
right. this is	right. This is
the six a clock	the six o'clock
nyooz. belt up	news. Belt up.

(Leonard, 1984, p. 88)

Leonard's poem provides an explicit challenge to the often-perceived superiority of RP. In such images of linguistic rebellion, Leonard has by no means been alone. Why should 'talking right' be vested in one mode of speech and not others, he demands. Many writers and speakers in the 1960s and 1970s came to express similar ideas, voicing resistance in their expressed attitudes as well as in their linguistic behaviour.

The social and linguistic context to such resistance was sought in a series of experiments which were conducted from the 1960s onwards to help build a broad picture of the way in which accents were evaluated across the UK (see for instance Giles and Powesland, 1975; Giles et al., 1990, pp. 191–211; and Honey, 1989). The experiments made use of 'matched-guise' technique, which 'involves the presentation of tape-recorded voices of one speaker reading the same factually-neutral passage of prose' (Giles, 1970, p. 211) in different accents to a range of audiences in a variety of UK locations. The audiences (themselves representing a wide range of accents and social class) were asked to assess the accents along a range of personal attributes.

Results showed that 'stereotyped impressions of an individual's personality may be formulated by listeners when presented with a speaker's voice whose vocal contours are representative of phonological patterns peculiar to specific group membership' (Giles et al., 1990). In other words, the responses were remarkably uniform wherever the experiment was conducted. RP came consistently top of the league on features such as communicative effectiveness and social status, being linked regularly to terms such as 'well-spoken', and leading the field in attributed qualities such as intelligence, ambition, leadership, self-confidence, wealth, and occupational status. However, RP often did less well than competing regional accents in qualities such as friendliness, generosity, honesty, integrity and sense of humour. Next to RP in the table came educated Scottish, followed by educated varieties of Welsh and Irish. These three accents refer to a hybrid of social and regional features, making them adoptive rather than native RP. These adoptive RP accents retain recognisable regional features, though '[s]ome phoneticians, on the basis that part of the definition of RP is that it should not tell you where someone comes from, would regard "Regional RP" as a contradiction in terms' (Cruttenden, 1994, p. 80). Equally consistently at the bottom of the table came four urban accents: those associated with the working-class natives of Liverpool, Birmingham, Glasgow and London.

Audiences in experiments of this nature will generally insist that they are responding to the aesthetic quality of each individual accent, encoding what is known as the **inherent value hypothesis**: the belief that one form of speech is intrinsically better than others. Doubt is cast on this belief, however, as the consistency observed above disappears when the audience is selected from outside the UK. This suggests that the judgement, far from being aesthetic, is instead associative, with audiences attaching to particular accents certain generalised assumptions about the values and qualities widely considered typical of certain social groups. In other words, accents are judged by the stereotypes which listeners already hold about their speakers. When the listener does not share the context which produces the stereotype, all signs of consistency disappear.

Such a view supports the way RP scores highly on qualities associated with a social elite (intelligence, ambition, leadership, self-confidence, wealth, and occupational status), while the distancing effect of such social superiority would account for the lower scoring on more personable qualities of friendliness, generosity, honesty, integrity and sense of humour (see Giles et al., 1990, for a summary). Interestingly, an alternative stereotype is revealed by the long history in US films of menacing villains with RP accents (from George Sanders in *Rebecca* and *The Jungle Book* to Jeremy Irons in *The Lion King* and *The Time Machine*), which a BBC website explains as follows:

> [T]he connotations of the accent come from centuries of anti-imperialistic fashionable thought. Even so, modern Americans don't necessarily associate modern Britons with the big, bad Empire of yesteryear. It's the accent that's seen as evil, not the nationality. It has become merely a stereotypical way of indicating the bad guy, a job once done by white and black cowboy hats or the glow of a cigarette in a dark alley.

(BBC, 2005)

5.8 The changing situation of modern Britain

Language attitudes, as we have seen, are by no means static; sounds once regarded with apparent indifference – such as /h/ – may develop into what the phonetician John Wells has described as 'the single most powerful pronunciation shibboleth in England' (Wells, 1982, p. 254). Other variants, such as the lengthened and lowered [ɑː] of *grass* and *bath*, were once regarded with abhorrence (this was widely stigmatised as a feature of cockney 'vulgarity' for much of the nineteenth century) before emerging as a feature of RP. Other features which have joined the RP repertoire are intrusive *r* (an /r/ is articulated where it doesn't appear in the orthography, usually between two vowel sounds, as in *lawr and order*), the shortening of the formerly characteristically long vowel sounds in words such as *off* and *lost,* and the replacement of the consonant [t] by a glottal stop [ʔ] (usually represented in print by *but* going to *bu'*).

This latter feature, also known as /t/-glottalisation, was examined by Anne Fabricius (2002) as part of her study into the changing face of RP. Using former public-school pupils who were students at Cambridge University – thus exploiting two predominant sources of RP speakers – she conducted a quantitative study examining the use of /t/-glottalisation in word-final position, that is, where [ʔ] replaced [t] at the end of a word. Subjects were recorded both in an interview and also reading prepared material, to see whether 'style shifting' (in this case more or less glottalisation) would take place between the more careful reading situation and the less formal speech of the interview. Results suggested that significant factors included: (1) the speech style; (2) the phonetic environment (whether the [t] was followed by a pause, a vowel or another consonant); and (3) where the speaker actually came from. For instance, word-final glottalisation before a following consonant was uniformly high in the interview, whereas before a pause (pre-pausal) there was much variation. Before a vowel (prevocalic), only subjects from London used [ʔ] rather than [t]. In reading style, on the other hand, all subjects widely avoided [ʔ] before the pause and the vowel.

These results suggest a number of possible trends in younger RP speakers. First, it seems that the once-stigmatised glottal stop is now becoming more generally acceptable, particularly in specific phonetic environments. Second, those environments seem greater for RP speakers from London than elsewhere in the UK, which means London is acting as the source of innovation for this accent (as indeed for others, see below). The probability is that pre-pausal glottalisation will be the next widely acceptable environment, moving outward from London, followed by the prevocalic. These latter two environments have not yet surfaced in more formal speech – not even the London-based RP speakers used them in the reading situation.

This last factor has led Fabricius to posit two different types of RP: native-RP, which is the type spoken in reasonably normal circumstances by RP speakers, as for instance in the interview reported above; and construct-RP, which is the codified, normative pronunciation which we find in dictionaries (particularly pronouncing dictionaries). We have to be careful, then, what we mean when we talk of changes in RP. As Fabricius explains:

> ... either it is change in [native]-RP or it is change in [construct]-RP. The two processes are related, but separate. The former is change in language form over time, the latter change in language evaluation ... over time ...

> Successive waves of change in the forms of [native]-RP gradually become part of [construct]-RP.

> (Fabricius, 2002, p. 119)

Popular attitudes to accent may also shift over time. While this chapter has traced the changing attitudes to regionality and status as manifested through pronunciation (and the concomitant pressures for a 'standard' accent), it is clear that issues of fashionability are as salient as ever, though for some speakers RP no longer reigns unchallenged. Indeed, it is not difficult to find evidence of negative reactions to RP, both among those who speak it and those who don't. The London-based newspaper *The Times* published an article by the journalist Victoria Moore which she entitled 'Why RP doesn't fit in'. In it, Moore discussed the disadvantages she faced in having displaced her native Yorkshire with adoptive RP. 'There is a great irony in my predicament,' she notes: 'I picked up RP in an attempt to fit in, and now I have it I don't' (Moore, 2000, p. 6). One year earlier John Morrish, writing in another UK newspaper *The Independent*, had confirmed this reversal in language attitudes. For Morrish, RP was 'the accent that dare not speak its name'; as he added, 'a posh voice is seen as naff and unfashionable' (Morrish, 1999).

RP in current Britain, then, may no longer be the passport to a certain type of employment that it once was. The BBC has long liberalised the range of voices on the airwaves, while telesales companies and call centres research the effectiveness (or affectiveness) of regional accents when hiring staff. Nevertheless, it would be unwise to conclude that prejudice against certain regional accents has disappeared altogether. In her book on changing attitudes to and practices of talk, Cameron notes that a term such as 'effective communication' is often no more than a euphemism for speaking with a prestigious accent:

> It cannot be assumed that 'communication skills' are wholly unrelated to more traditional notions of 'correctness' and 'well-spokenness' ... In the course of research I was told a number of stories about employers, managers and examiners for vocational qualifications labelling people poor communicators because they used non-standard grammar or had 'broad' accents.

> (Cameron, 2000, p. 197)

Trudgill (2002, p. 176) also observes that discrimination against accents from a lowly evaluative status persists, and since such discrimination is no longer outwardly permitted within British society, 'it has to masquerade as something else'. 'This hypocrisy is a sign of progress, of an increase in democratic and egalitarian ideals', comments Trudgill, tongue firmly in cheek.

Estuary English

Popular comment has increasingly shifted the limelight from RP on to 'Estuary English', a mode of speech first identified in 1984 by the linguist David Rosewarne as: 'a variety of modified regional speech. It is a mixture of non-regional and local south-eastern English pronunciation and intonation. If one imagines a continuum with RP and London speech at either end, 'Estuary English' speakers are to be grouped in the middle ground' (Rosewarne, 1984).

This has been widely discussed as a potentially new non-localised accent for the UK – one which is egalitarian where RP is elitist in its dominant connotations. Estuary English has been observed – mainly by journalists – spreading out from the regions of the Thames Estuary and is popularly hallmarked by the pronunciation of words such as *milk* with a vocalised /l/ which makes it sound like *miwk*, and of glottal stops rather than /t/ in utterances of, for instance, *partly* or *quite nice*. Newspapers have reported the move of Estuary English across the country into locations as diverse as Cornwall and Liverpool. Linguists, however, have questioned the empirical basis of such reports.

This popularly claimed displacement of RP by Estuary English implies, to begin with, the spread of Estuary English and the corresponding wane in the use of RP. It is perfectly possible that both these processes are perceived to be taking place. For instance, where it would have been the default accent in decades gone by in wide-reaching contexts such as broadcasting, RP is no longer so frequently heard. A Yorkshire accent in mainstream broadcasting no longer makes the headlines as it did in 1941 when Wilfred Pickles first read the national news. Further, with the decrease in overt prestige value, fewer people are displacing their native accent with RP, so there are fewer adoptive speakers. This admittedly leads to fewer speakers overall, though not necessarily fewer native speakers. Thirdly, the changing nature of RP itself, with previously stigmatised features like intrusive *r*, may lead to its more modern incarnations being dismissed as Estuary (just as, in the nineteenth century, features which were regarded as on the borders of acceptability were stigmatised as 'cockney'). As Trudgill (2002, p. 177) notes, such forms of RP have 'some new features, but the features are all, including /t/-glottaling, non-regional features and therefore must still be considered as being RP'.

Trudgill (2002) puts forward a number of reasons for the apparent advance of Estuary English. First, as was said above, the waning prestige of RP has ensured that those who would in earlier times have become adoptive RP speakers no longer do so. They continue to rid their speech of many of its regional features but not all. The consequence is that more people with what could be called lower middle-class accents are heard in public situations, and the most prominent of these within the UK would be from the south-east of England because this is the largest population area; and because there is considerable metropolitan bias in the British media due in no small part to the fact that this is where most of the media is based. Second, the increase in upward mobility over the last couple of decades has projected many more people from lower middle-class backgrounds into prominent positions, thereby increasing the exposure outlined above. Third, the phonological features of the south-east or Estuary English are spreading outwards in all directions, in the same way that London-based phonological features have done for centuries. It is hardly surprising, then, that the features associated with Estuary English cover a wider geographical area than formerly, and will probably continue to spread.

Terms such as 'geographical spread' and 'lower middle-class accent' lend credence to Rosewarne's definition of Estuary English as 'a mixture of non-regional and local south-eastern English pronunciation and intonation'. Trudgill, for instance, sees the accent as belonging to the lower middle classes from what are known as the Home Counties of England – those counties which surround London, such as Essex, Kent, Surrey, Berkshire, Buckinghamshire and Hertfordshire. That few of these are anywhere near the estuary in question (that of the Thames) is an interesting point, and it is eminently possible that they may quite soon be joined by the wider band of Sussex, Hampshire, Bedfordshire, Cambridge, Suffolk and Northamptonshire. This, of course, makes for a huge region, but it is still a region.

The geographical spread of Estuary English signals a wider trend in the UK (and arguably beyond) known as accent levelling. Indicators of this trend include the demise of traditional accents which belonged to smaller areas and to a time referred to by Wilfred Pickles when 'folks talk differently in places only five miles apart, a phenomenon that has its roots in the times when it took many days to ride from London to York by coach' (Pickles, 1949, p. 147). The process of levelling is dealt with in more detail from the viewpoint of grammar in the next chapter on dialect variation in English, but Reading A provides an excellent illustration of accent levelling as it has taken place in Milton Keynes in south-east England.

ACTIVITY 5.3

Work through Reading A, 'Milton Keynes and dialect levelling in south-eastern British English' by Paul Kerswill. Note that the term 'dialect' refers to elements of a language variety which include its grammar, vocabulary and accent. So while dialect can be taken to include accent, the converse does not hold. Kerswill's reading is taken from a larger piece of work which includes work on grammar and vocabulary, though here the focus is on accent. It is worth paying attention to the research methodology, the results of this and how Kerswill arrives at his conclusions, since these provide an insight into how sociolinguists work.

Comment

Kerswill finds that it is his twelve-year-old informants who are in the vanguard of linguistic change. He suggests that younger children are still following their parents' pronunciation, whereas the older children – a group for whom approval and acceptance of their peers is most important – are converging on a new pronunciation. Similar conclusions with regard to new dialect formation among colonial Englishes (e.g Australian, New Zealand, South African English) are discussed in some detail in the next chapter.

The methodology adopted in this study consists of identifying a set of sociolinguistic variables, or features of language that are used variably in a community, and investigating how the different forms, or variants, of these variables are used by different groups of speakers in different contexts. As such, this methodology has much in common with other research designed to investigate social variation in dialect and is dealt with in more detail in Chapter 6.

5.9 Accent evaluation revisited

The linguistic, empirical view of Estuary English is that it is fundamentally a regional accent with social overtones. However, the gap between this and lay opinion is as stark as it ever was. The popular view of language remains overtly prescriptive, as evidenced by the following question, which was put in July 2005 to the Culture Secretary at the British Parliament by David Taylor, Labour Member of Parliament for North-West Leicestershire in the east Midlands of England.

> The rich variety of British accents and dialects is one of our great cultural assets, which should be preserved and enhanced. Does the [Minister] agree [with me] that not enough is done to combat the slow sociolinguistic convergence towards effete estuarial English, leading to its dominance in the broadcast media and around the Cabinet table? Is not that the sort of class barrier that inclusive New Labour was set up to break down?

(Hansard, 2005)

The question reveals interesting similarities to and differences from the versions of linguistic prescriptivism expressed across the centuries as documented in this chapter. There remains in the above question, for instance, an underlying belief that language is something which can be regulated in some way by a given authority, in this case the government. Similarly, in 1712 Sheridan's godfather, the novelist Jonathan Swift, urged the foundation of a language academy for English on the model of the Académie Française.

Accents continue to arouse strong feelings of a negative nature – here Estuary English is described as 'effete', while /h/-dropping in the nineteenth century was both 'vulgar' and a sign of 'defective intelligence'. Just as striking is the continuing power of an accent to open doors of opportunity and admit its speakers to rewards proscribed to others, though, at least in the questioner's view, Estuary seems to have supplanted RP in this regard.

The association of accent with stereotype also continues: those in power are perceived to share a common badge (Estuary English) which admits them to the inner circle and acts as a 'class barrier'. On the other hand, the badge is also worthy of contempt ('effete') – it has retreated from the unambiguously high social status signalled by RP to one designed to identify the powerful more closely with those they represent. It may be significant that, while Prime Minister Margaret Thatcher adjusted her accent to adoptive RP from one which bore traits of her lower middle-class upbringing as a grammar-school pupil in Lincolnshire, Prime Minister Tony Blair adjusted his in the opposite direction: the former public-school pupil's RP which he spoke as a Labour candidate in the 1980s shows noticeable differences from his current accent, which the questioner may be including in his characterisation of Cabinet speech as 'effete Estuarial'.

ACTIVITY 5.4

Allow about
20 minutes

The parliamentary question quoted above was included in a weekend radio programme which rounded up the more interesting issues arising from that week's political debates. Below are some extracts from the discussion.

What similarities do you notice between the popular attitudes to accent from the twenty-first century as illustrated in the discussion below and those expressed over the past three centuries as described in this chapter? Are there any major differences?

> You will note that this extract contains many cultural references which are assumed to be shared by the audience. This sort of discussion about accent evaluation can only really take place in a situation where all participants share or are aware of a specific cultural context. Similar discussions no doubt take place along similar lines elsewhere in the world, but with a different set of cultural references.
>
> For those unfamiliar with the context, here are some brief explanatory notes. The participants are: David Taylor (DT), Labour Member of Parliament for North-West Leicestershire in the east Midlands of England; Michael Gove (MG), Conservative MP for Surrey Heath, an affluent area of south-east England; and the programme presenter (PP).
>
> Clare Short who is mentioned in the transcript was, at the time of recording, Labour MP for Birmingham and is, indeed, a 'Brummy' (native of Birmingham) herself. She is known for her forthright opposition to several aspects of her party's policies.

DT   Estuary English is used as a dialect disguise for the independently educated elite at the heart of our party or its imitative intonation from those who are on the make or on the way up ... By and large, the dominance of Estuary English, not just in politics but ... in the broadcast media as well – regional broadcasting quite rarely has people who are broadcasting to their listeners in the accent with which their listeners will communicate, and that's a shame. Regional accents are not museum pieces to be pinned to a board and examined with amusement. They're a means of communication which should be preserved and enhanced – one of our great cultural assets as a nation, I think.

MG   ... the United Kingdom overall is a much more mobile place, and it's a good thing too, than it was twenty or thirty years ago. ... But I think we've also got to accept the fact that some of the people who make Leicestershire lively and entertaining are not people who speak like the sons of the Leicestershire soil would have done fifty years ago. And that's no bad thing.

DT   I agree with Michael to a certain extent that we are a more mobile society both geographically and socially and therefore accents will change as times move on and as people move on, but I would not like to be in a position where we're all speaking some sort of monochrome mush that owes more to Essex than it does to the English regions.

MG   Clare Short – she's got a great Brummy accent and it adds to the authenticity in the sense that she's always speaking from the heart and it enhances her popularity.

PP   Would you agree that it is a disadvantage these days for politicians to have a posh accent?

MG   I don't think it's necessarily a huge disadvantage to speak in a way that is RP, cultured, the Queen's English, for want of a better word. I mean they're all slightly pejorative phrases, I know, but I think a clear and authoritative diction can help. I think, though, the one thing that can kill anyone is affectation, affectation that is too obviously an upwardly mobile strain, or ... affectation that is too clearly slumming it. I think one of the things about Tony Blair that has made him such a difficult politician is the fact that there's a chameleon tendency to him. But at the beginning I think that part of Blair's appeal was the fact that he was someone from a public school who was a middle class professional who could lead a party of the left, and I suspect that Blair's slumming it is actually a double weakness for him: it blunts the edge of the appeal that he has to middle class voters, and also makes him seem far more a phoney-Tony figure.

(The Week in Westminster, 2005)

Comment

The most obvious difference is that the discussion centres on, not the accent which denotes membership of the highest social class (RP), but one lower down the scale (Estuary English). The context has also changed, mainly in terms of more widespread social and geographical mobility. This has brought in its wake the fact that convergence towards Estuary can be in two directions: upwards, for those aspiring to positions of power (or in Taylor's terms 'on the make'); or downwards for the powerful who wish to reassure the electorate that they understand the problems of ordinary people. The accent becomes a strategy for aspiration, on the one hand, and a claimed solidarity, on the other. The aspirational motive at least resonates with Sheridan's vision of a codified speech which would no longer divide the country by inequities of access or hazards of birth.

Taylor's plea for the preservation of accent differences in the face of Estuary assault – which he emotively characterises as 'monochrome mush' – strongly echoes similar sentiments expressed by Wilfred Pickles, who perceived the danger coming from RP: 'May it be forbidden that we should ever speak like B.B.C. announcers, for our rich contrast of voices is a local tapestry of great beauty and incalculable value, handed down to us by our forefathers' (Pickles, 1949, pp. 146–7). But increase in mobility undermines any such linguistic stability, insists Gove, who associates the more traditional Leicestershire accent with the 'sons of the Leicestershire soil', thereby highlighting the continuing association between regional accents and low provincial status.

Conversely, Clare Short's provincial accent is seen as a sign of honesty and sincerity (such warm support from an Opposition MP may not be unrelated to the fact that Short was one of Prime Minister Tony Blair's sternest critics). On one hand, this is consistent with the accent evaluation testing of the 1970s where provincial accents scored better than RP on such personal qualities; on the other, the Birmingham accent came out consistently badly in those tests. This implies either that the Birmingham accent has become less unpopular or that any provincial accent would have served to make Gove's point.

Acknowledging that while RP and the Queen's English are currently endowed with pejorative connotations, Gove reveals his faith in RP as 'clear and authoritative diction', both setting it apart from a regional accent's 'mispronunciation of vowels or consonants' (as defined by Ellis, see Section 5.5), as well as endorsing the BBC's choice of RP as the voice of authority, used for all serious broadcasting and the news (see Section 5.6). His stigmatisation of affectation not only recalls Reith's depiction of his announcers as 'talking good English, and without affectation', but also quite interestingly raises the whole issue of an adoptive accent, which is arguably by definition a form of affectation, whichever social direction the speaker is taking. The depiction of Tony Blair's adoptive accent as 'slumming it' is possibly an involuntary revelation of RP's continuing reign as the UK's most prestigious accent among many in the most powerful social classes.

5.10 Conclusion

This chapter has surveyed the shifting language attitudes to accent and pronunciation over the past two centuries, tracing the flux of assumptions about acceptability as well as the varying pressures to standardise one accent for all speakers. Nevertheless, as sociolinguistic research continues to reveal, a single pronunciation model for all speakers is as remote as – or perhaps even more remote than – when Sheridan began his campaign to raise the linguistic consciousness on the matter of 'proper' pronunciation in the late eighteenth century. RP, on the other hand, is far from dead, though its use continues to characterise a minority of speakers. As might be expected in a living language, its constituent features are demonstrably in the process of change. Such changes are, moreover, taking place within a social context which may be more fluid than in the past. Some, such as Coulmas (2005, p. 31), argue: 'Postmodern societies are more mobile, have fewer class markers and are more tolerant of heterogeneity. Achievement is more important than class ... Variation is acceptable and identities are multidimensional'. However, even if society itself may be more 'mobile', attitudes towards social symbols and markers of identity arguably remain as sharply felt as ever. Adonis and Pollard assert: 'Cultural distinctions and nuances remain legion. Accents, houses, cars, schools, sports, food, fashion, drink, smoking, supermarkets, soap operas, holiday destinations, even training shoes: virtually everything in life is graded with subtle or unsubtle class tags attached ... And underpinning these distinctions are fundamental differences in upbringing, education and occupations' (Adonis and Pollard, 1997, p. 10).

READING A: Milton Keynes and dialect levelling in south-eastern British English

Paul Kerswill
(Paul Kerswill is a lecturer in the Department of Linguistic Science at the University of Reading.)

Specially commissioned for Wright (1996, pp. 292–300).

The role of dialect contact in language change

English, like all living languages, has undergone change throughout its history. Language change does not always occur at the same rate, however, and it is reasonable to suppose that the speed of language change depends in no small measure on the social changes affecting the speakers of the language. Here, I look at one kind of social change – the increase in geographical and social mobility of recent years – and consider its possible effects on the pronunciation of British English.

From the point of view of language change, it is probably the geographical aspect of mobility that has the more far-reaching effect. As people move to new areas, they may form social and ethnic groups with distinct ways of speaking, as in the case of immigrants from overseas. Migration within a single language area, such as Britain, leads to prolonged contact between speakers of different dialects of the same language (termed 'dialect contact' – see Trudgill, 1986).

In the south-east of England, as elsewhere, there has long been geographical and social mobility, leading (we must presume) to dialect contact. Mobility has increased markedly since the Second World War, and has probably led to the fact that young people in the south and south-east are beginning to sound more and more like each other. (This reduction of differences between dialects has been termed 'dialect levelling'.) Such mobility is perhaps typified by the rise of 'new towns', including Hemel Hempstead, Stevenage, Peterlee, Telford and Milton Keynes – all of which were established as a matter of government policy.

Below I describe a study I carried out with a colleague, Ann Williams, in Milton Keynes, the most recent and fastest expanding of these new towns. Our intention in the study was to see if there is evidence for the rise of a 'new dialect' in Milton Keynes, distinct from those of other places and from those of the people who moved into the town.

The Milton Keynes study

The role of children in the formation of new dialects

The Milton Keynes project follows a research tradition established by William Labov, who with his 1966 New York City research published the first systematic large-scale study of urban speech. However, the approach we took in the Milton Keynes project necessarily differed from Labov's. A tenet of his methodology is that by comparing the speech of older and younger people we can get a 'snapshot' of language change. In Milton Keynes this is clearly not possible, since there are few older 'native' inhabitants. In any case, our aim was a different one, as I suggested above.

Instead, we focused mainly on children, in whose speech we might expect to find evidence of a new dialect: children's speech is less fixed, more malleable than that of adults, most of whom will only change their speech in minor ways when they move to another area. It is the children of the in-migrants who, on encountering age-mates in nursery and at school, will have to 'settle on' a set of features that will be characteristic of speech in the new town.

A crucial further question is at what age children begin and complete their convergence on a new dialect. Most of us can tell anecdotes of young children losing their parents' accents on associating with other children, and of teenagers picking up strong local accents as they come under peer pressure to conform in all matters of behaviour. These changes in children's speech are part of what we can term 'sociolinguistic maturation': how do children acquire the sociolinguistic skills adults have that enable them to speak in different ways according to context? The project aimed to throw some light on this issue.

Choice of location

Milton Keynes is in the county of Buckinghamshire in England, close to the borders with two other counties, Bedfordshire and Northamptonshire. It lies near the towns of Bedford and Northampton, some 90 kilometres north-west of London. Milton Keynes was designated a new town in 1969, when there was already an existing population in this area of about 44,000 living mainly in the towns of Wolverton and Bletchley. By the 1991 census, the population had risen to 176,330. Table 1 shows where the new arrivals came from. Over three quarters were from the south-east, and nearly half of these were from London. Obviously, this fact will have repercussions for any 'new dialect' we might find in the town.

Table 1 Percentage of resident households moving to Milton Keynes since its designation as a new town, in 1969

Area of previous residence	% households
London	35.2
Immediate sub-region (approx. 15 minute drive)	3.4
Rest of Buckinghamshire	5.2
Rest of Bedfordshire/Northamptonshire	9.8
Rest of south-east	22.6
Total from south-east	76.2
Rest of England	16.2
Rest of UK	3.7
Overseas	3.9
Total	100.0

(Milton Keynes Development Corporation (MKDC), 1990, p. 31)

Methodology

Sociolinguistic variables

In the Milton Keynes project, we investigated ten sociolinguistic variables: in this case, speech sounds that had different pronunciations within the speech community. Five of these variables are discussed in this reading; they are summarised in Table 2. (I follow the usual practice of putting sociolinguistic variables in curved brackets.)

Table 2 The sociolinguistic variables used in the study

Consonants

(t)   word medial *t* which is often replaced by a glottal stop [ʔ], as in *letter*, *bottle*, ([leʔə], [bɒʔl]).

(th)   word initial, word medial, word final voiceless *th*, as in **th**ree, no**th**ing, too**th**, where the dental fricative [θ] can be replaced with the sound [f].

Vowels

(ou)   the diphthong vowel in *coat*, *moan*, etc. The second part of this diphthong can be 'fronted' (pronounced further forward in the mouth), to give the impression of received pronunciation *kite* or *mine*. Fronting may lead to *Coke* resembling *cake* in RP.

(uː)   the long vowel in *move*, *shoe*, etc., which can be fronted to a vowel close to that of French *tu* or German *grün*.

(au)   the diphthong in *house*, *now*, etc.; this can have a wide range of pronunciations in south-east England, ranging from the vowel [ɛɪ], which resembles the vowel in RP **rain**, through an RP [aʊ], to a broad London [ɛː], which resembles the vowel in RP *scarce*.

Speakers

In selecting our speakers, we decided to focus on children from three age groups: four-year-olds (when children are still largely under the influence of their caretakers' speech), eight-years-olds and twelve-year-olds (when they are verging on adolescence, with its associated peer group structures and orientation away from parental values). Additionally, we interviewed one caretaker for each child – in almost every case the mother. Once we had obtained the relevant permissions, we arranged recordings in one nursery and two schools in two of the earliest housing estates of the post-1969 new town. Our final sample consisted of forty-eight children who were either born in Milton Keynes or who had arrived there by the age of two. The children were equally divided between the sexes and the age groups, so that there were eight children in each group or 'cell' (i.e. eight girls aged four, eight aged eight, and so on). Sex and age were, then, the primary 'social variables' of the study. We felt that social class was less relevant to the central aims; it was held roughly constant by virtue of the fact that the schools and the nursery shared the same, fairly homogeneous catchment area.

The recordings

The recordings were divided into two main sections: elicitation tasks and spontaneous speech. The elicitation tasks were intended to elicit particular words that contained our target sociolinguistic variables; some were reading lists, others games such as quizzes, 'spot-the-difference' pictures and map-reading tasks. The spontaneous speech was obtained by interviewing the children about their school, friends and homes and by making recordings in the playground using radio microphones. The children's caretakers were also interviewed. In analysing these speech samples, we noted down all the occurrences of different variants (i.e. actual pronunciations) for each sociolinguistic variable. We could then quantify our data and carry out various forms of statistical analysis.

Interpreting the results

Is there a distinctive Milton Keynes dialect?

There are a number of expectations that one might have of the emerging Milton Keynes dialect. For instance, it might resemble the traditional dialect of the area; or it might reflect the range of accents of the new inhabitants of the city (so, given that about 75 per cent of the incomers are from the south-east, three quarters of the emerging dialect features might be from the south-east, with the remainder divided between the other areas represented). Table 3 shows neither of these to be the case. The children's accents differ, in many respects, from those of the original inhabitants of Milton Keynes and the nearby area. Furthermore, in the speech of the children with parents from outside the south-east, there is practically no trace of the parents' accents. In fact, every one of the Milton Keynes children's pronunciation features, both old and more recent, is also found in London and elsewhere in the south-east.

Table 3 A comparison between pronunciations in Stewkley near Milton Keynes (recorded in the 1950s); among elderly Milton Keynes residents (recorded in 1991); and among Milton Keynes children (recorded in 1991)

	Stewkley 1950s	Elderly MK 1991	MK children 1991
arm	arrm	arrm	ahm
three	three	three	free
feather	feather	feather	fevver
night	noit	noit	naa-it
round	raind	raind	round
fill	fill	fiw	fiw
woman	umman	woman	woman
letter	le'er	le'er	le'er

Note: 'Arrm' indicates that the *r* is pronounced. 'Le'er' indicates a glottal stop for *t*. The information for older speech is from the *Survey of English Dialects* (SED), which investigated Stewkley in the 1950s, and from six elderly people we recorded who were born within what is now Milton Keynes.

So far, the impression we get is that the new Milton Keynes 'dialect' is simply 'Cockney' (or London dialect) transported; indeed, some residents talk about 'Milton Keynes Cockney'. Perhaps what lies behind this phrase is the recognition that Milton Keynes speech is not *exactly* Cockney, but has a 'flavour' of it. So what pronunciation features are the children converging towards?

We can start with a vowel variable, (ou) – (the diphthong in words such as *home, go, boat, know, don't*, etc). I indicated in Table 2 that the second part of this could be 'fronted', so that the word *Coke* might be mistaken for *cake*. We quantified the fronting of (ou) on a four-point scale running from 0–3. Figure 1 shows the degree of fronting for the forty-eight children, with each child's score plotted against that of her or his caretaker. This shows that the children on average 'front' their vowels considerably more than the adults. The figure confirms my earlier suggestion that the children's speech is different from that of their parents. The children's pronunciations are also far less variable than the adults'. Fronted (ou) is, then, likely to be a characteristic of the new Milton Keynes dialect.

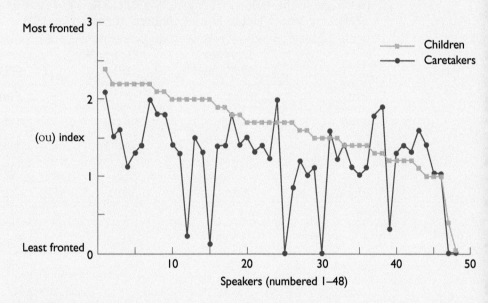

Figure 1　Association of children's (ou) scores with those of their caretakers

It's important to point out that this new feature, along with most of the other new features we have studied, is also found across broad swathes of southern England. For instance (ou)-fronting is observable in Reading, 90 kilometres to the south, as well as in Cambridge, 80 kilometres to the east. What we are observing is the convergence of accents, not just in the new town melting pot but throughout the south-east of England – as mentioned above. I return to this point below.

Who leads in the development of a new dialect?

We turn now to a consideration of which age group leads in linguistic developments, including the formation of a new dialect. We can again take the data for (ou) and compare it with that for (uː), the vowel in *move, spoon*, etc. As with (ou), (uː) is also being fronted. Figure 2 shows the percentage use among women and girls of 'fronted' pronunciations of both vowels in the words *home* and *move*. The patterns are not identical for each vowel, but it is clear that the oldest girls have by far the greatest degree of fronting, with the younger ones having scores similar to those of the caretakers. A likely explanation for this pattern is that the youngest girls still follow their mothers as far as these vowels are concerned, while the oldest, near-adolescent girls are converging on a different pronunciation.

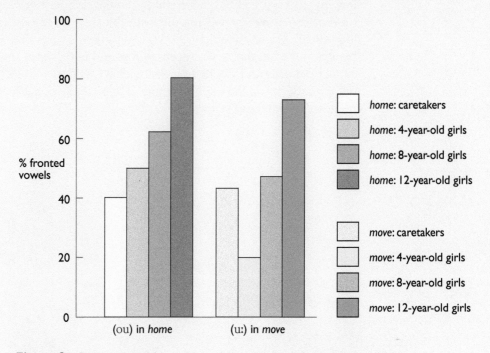

Figure 2   Percentage of fronted vowels in *home* and *move*, female subjects

New dialect formation and sociolinguistic maturation

It is apparent, then, that it is older children who do most of the sociolinguistic 'work' in new dialect formation. How does this relate to sociolinguistic maturation? We can now return to the variable (t), which we have defined as the alternation of [ʔ] and [t] within a word such as *letter*. Figure 3 shows the percentage use of the [t] pronunciation in three different elicitation tasks (reading and other tasks designed to elicit particular words), with the speakers divided according to sex and age group. Note first the fairly small differences between the tasks, with the most formal, the reading task, having the highest use of the 'standard' pronunciation [t] overall (the four-year-olds are, of course, omitted from this task). Secondly, it is striking how the girls consistently have a much higher score than the boys of the same age. This finding is consistent with much sociolinguistic research, which shows that female speakers often use more 'standard' features than male speakers. Thirdly, and most significantly for our discussion here, it is the oldest age group that has the highest frequency of [t]. We can assume that elicitation

tasks will encourage a rather formal speaking style, in which adults will feel
the need to use features characteristic of careful and standard speech. It is the
oldest children who seem to be adhering most closely to this expectation. The
connection between this finding and new dialect formation is this: older
children demonstrate patterns characteristic of adult communities in terms of
linguistic variation – here, style-shifting patterns. In a new community, it is
they, by contrast with younger children, who are the first 'natives' to establish
these patterns. We can couple this with the fact that the older children are
linguistically more alike than the younger children and thus may well
foreshadow what the 'new' accent will sound like. These results – the style-
shifting patterns and the degree of linguistic similarity – allow us to suggest
that the older children's speech quite closely represents the characteristics of
the new 'speech community'.

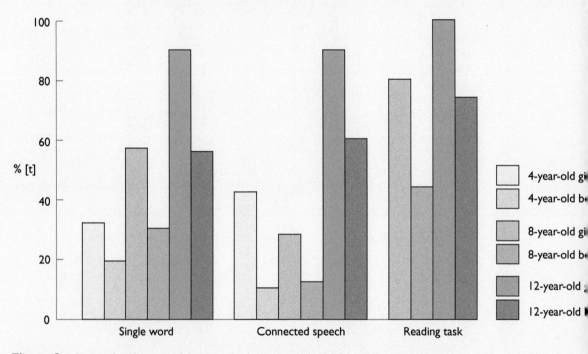

Figure 3   Scores for the use of the 'standard pronunciation' [t] by task, sex and age

Implications

Dialect levelling in the south-east of England

I suggested earlier that we may be witnessing the spread of a relatively
uniform pattern of speech across south-eastern England. If so, this means that
many features of the 'new' dialect we have been discussing in this chapter are
in fact common to a much wider area than just the one town. Let us consider
one further variable, the vowel (au), as in *house*, *round*, *now*, etc. In the

south-east of England, this vowel shows a large number of regional variants. Table 4 shows that the caretakers bring to Milton Keynes several different variants, all of which are found in the south-east. Interestingly, the children seem to favour the regionally neutral, RP-like variant, [aʊ], not the more regionally marked forms of their parents. Significantly, this vowel is gaining ground very strongly elsewhere too; for example, in Reading it has all but replaced the local vowel [eɪ], which is a striking feature of the old accent there.

Table 4 Percentage use of different pronunciations of the vowel in *house, round,* etc. (interviews)

	[hɛːs]	[haːəs]	[hæʊs]	[haʊs]
Children	11	8	13	66
Caretakers	12	17	39	31

Note: [hɛːs] represents a broad London monophthong; [haːəs] is a slightly diphthongised version of it. [hæʊs] is a diphthong starting with the vowel of 'hair' and finishing with the vowel of 'pull'. [haʊs] represents an RP-like form.

This and other variables, including (ou) and (uː) as well as the use of [f] for *th* in **th**ree, **th**in, etc., provide evidence of dialect levelling in the south-east: differences are becoming less and less marked, so that it is today more difficult to tell apart young speakers from Southampton, Reading, London and Cambridge than it was thirty years ago. Despite these strong tendencies, it is unlikely that regional differences will disappear altogether, since language differences have always been part of the armoury human beings use to maintain their own distinct social identities.

Milton Keynes, Estuary English and changes in spoken English

Several commentators have referred to a phenomenon known as 'Estuary English' (Rosewarne, 1984, 1994; Coggle, 1993). This is the notion that there is an increasingly widespread way of speaking 'Standard' English (without non-standard grammatical features) that contains a number of south-eastern pronunciations, such as the glottal stop and the vocalised *l*. The Estuary English phenomenon is an old one, since people have long been shifting to Standard English while retaining parts of their local pronunciation. What is news is the increasing acceptability of this form of speech in the media and the professions, where it is replacing RP, much to the annoyance of several newspaper columnists.

It is tempting to suppose that what we have observed in Milton Keynes is a form of Estuary English, since both are geographically levelled forms of speech. This is misleading, since young people native to Milton Keynes between them presumably cover a range of speech types, both non-standard and standard, that is similar to that found in other towns. If the Milton Keynes non-standard speakers do sound more Estuary English-like than their compeers elsewhere, this is because of the special sociolinguistic situation there, involving much more intensive dialect contact than in other parts of the south-east. What we see is possibly a sign of future changes in English: new towns are perhaps in the vanguard of the dialect levelling found in England as a whole.

Acknowledgement

Data for this reading is derived from the project 'A new dialect in a new city: children's and adults' speech in Milton Keynes', funded by the Economic and Social Research Council, 1990–4, ref. R000232376. Principal investigator: Dr P. Kerswill; Research Fellow: Dr A. Williams. Further information on the project can be found in Kerswill (1994), and Kerswill and Williams (1992, 1994).

References for this reading

Coggle, P. (1993) *Do You Speak Estuary?*, London, Bloomsbury.

Kerswill, P.E. (1994) 'Babel in Buckinghamshire? Pre-school children acquiring accent features in the new town of Milton Keynes' in Melchers, G. and Lennartsson, L. (eds) *Nonstandard Varieties of Language*, Acta Universitat is Stockholmiensis, Stockholm, Almqvist and Wiksell.

Kerswill, P.E. and Williams, A. (1992) 'Some principles of dialect contact: evidence from the new town of Milton Keynes' in Philippaki-Warburton, I. and Ingham, R. (eds) *Working Papers 1992*, Department of Linguistic Science, University of Reading.

Kerswill, P.E. and Williams, A. (1994) 'A new dialect in a new city: children's and adults' speech in Milton Keynes', final report and summary of research submitted to the Economic and Social Resource Council.

Labov, W. (1966) *The Social Stratification of English in New York City*, Washington DC, Center for Applied Linguistics.

Milton Keynes Development Corporation (MKDC) (1990) *Milton Keynes Population Bulletin*, 1990, MKDC.

Rosewarne, D. (1984) 'Estuary English', *The Times Educational Supplement*, 19 October 1984.

Rosewarne, D. (1994) 'Estuary English: tomorrow's RP?, *English Today* , vol. 10 no. 1, pp. 3–8.

Trudgill, P. (1986) *Dialects in Contact*, Oxford, Blackwell.

6 Dialect variation in English

Martin Rhys, based on the original chapter by Linda Thomas

6.1 Introduction

This book has traced the journey of English from its origins among the Germanic tribes of northern Europe to its current status as the world's most widely used language. Today's English appears in as many varieties as there are places where it is spoken. This chapter explores how these varieties – or dialects – differ from each other, as well as examining the factors which determine who speaks which dialect. First we need to be clear on what we mean by dialect.

Anyone who speaks, say, a Tyneside dialect of English will sometimes use different words from speakers of other dialects, such as *gang* instead of *go*. They may also use different grammatical structures, such as *might could* instead of *might be able to*. And if they use these features, the likelihood is that they will also pronounce words differently, for instance *lang* instead of *long*. In other words, dialect features can generally be described in terms of vocabulary, grammar and accent. It need not always be the case, though, that these three parameters invariably go together.

Whereas you could feel reasonably safe in predicting that someone who used the vocabulary and grammatical structures of Tyneside English would do so with a Tyneside accent, you would not feel the same confidence in predicting the accent of a speaker of Standard English, where vocabulary and grammar may be decoupled from pronunciation. Standard English, then, can be spoken in any accent.

The popular view of the term 'dialect' often sees it contrasted with the standard language. Standard English is popularly perceived as 'the language', while dialects are characterised by their deviations from it in terms of grammar or vocabulary. I could be said to have fallen into the same trap myself in illustrating Tyneside features in the opening paragraph by comparing them to forms which would be found in Standard English. As Swann et al. point out, however: 'This evaluative and hierarchical usage has been questioned by sociolinguists, who would see a language as a composite of all its dialects including its standard norm' (Swann *et al.*, 2004, p. 76).

The often quite contentious relationship between standard and non-standard varieties of English surfaces here regularly, but the chapter also indicates the common ground shared by these dialects and explores the social and regional factors which influence who speaks which. The chapter closes with a look at a selection of grammatical features (accent and vocabulary have already been

dealt with extensively in the book) in use across the vast range of English
dialects spoken throughout the world today.

6.2 Standard Englishes

A standard language has already been defined in Chapter 3 as the variety that
'provides agreed norms of usage, usually codified in dictionaries and
grammars, for a wide range of institutional purposes such as education,
government and science' (see 'The process of standardisation' in Section 3.2).
You will also recall from the same section in Chapter 3 that a key factor in the
development of a standard language is the selection of an existing variety as
the basis, and that the 'variety selected is usually that of the most powerful or
socially influential social or ethnic group'. Joseph confirms that: 'one thing is
constant: it is the people with power and prestige who determine the
prestigious dialect ... In social and geographical terms, prestige usually means
upper-class and urban (Joseph, 1987, p. 59, quoted in Bonfiglio, 2002, p. 17).

In England, for instance, the power derived from the south-eastern triangle
around London, where the Norman conquerors of the eleventh century
established both their court and the university towns of Oxford and
Cambridge. Had the final, successful invasion of England come from across
the North Sea instead of the English Channel, and the capital city established
as a consequence in Newcastle near the ancient universities of Sunderland
and Middlesbrough, Standard English might well have been closer to what we
now know as Geordie.

It seems, then, that while regional factors (where you're from) play a vitally
important role in determining the dialect you speak, even more significant
a role is played by social factors, such as your upbringing, education and
employment. In other words, Standard English is a social dialect. Whether you
use Standard English will depend on the degree of your access and exposure
to it, along with cultural attitudes to it at both the individual and community
levels. We will return to these points in more detail when we discuss the
different factors which govern the linguistic choices we make when we speak
'English'.

We might expect a language variety which has been selected, codified and
has agreed norms of usage to be constant, homogeneous – immutable even –
wherever it is spoken. As previous chapters have indicated, this is not the
case. Standard English varies according to where in the world it is spoken. In
fact, Standard English as an actual variety does not exist – it is an abstraction.
A standard variety of English can only actually exist – be realised in spoken or
written form – in the shape of one of its regional variations: hence we have
Standard British English, Standard American English, Standard Australian
English, and so on (see Figure 6.1). So when I compared Tyneside English to
Standard English, I should really have compared it to Standard British English.

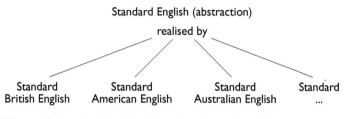

Figure 6.1   Standard English realised in regional form

Activity 6.1 will show how a socially determined standard dialect can have regional (worldwide) variations in its grammatical patterns.

ACTIVITY 6.1

Allow about
5 minutes

All six examples listed below are Standard English, but in which country are they used? See if you can match each example to one of the countries noted above the list. Whether or not you are able to complete this exercise will depend on your past experience. If you don't know, just guess.

Australia – Ireland – New Zealand – South Africa – Canada – USA

1	I'm playing tennis in the weekend.
2	The plastic is capable to withstand heat.
3	He usedn't go.
4	He just snuck in and burglarised the place.
5	This has always applied to men. As well, it now applies to women.
6	Is it stupid you are?

Comment

1   *I'm playing tennis in the weekend.*   (New Zealand)
   Use of the preposition *in* distinguishes Standard New Zealand usage. Most other standard varieties would use *at* or *over.*

2   *The plastic is capable to withstand heat.*   (South Africa)
   In Standard South African English, the infinitive form of the verb (*to* + verb root) can follow an adjective such as *capable*. In other standard varieties, we would probably see *of* + -ing (*capable **of** withstanding*).

3   *He usedn't go.*   (Australia)
   In Standard Australian English, the form *used to* is treated as an auxiliary, being negativised and contracted. Standard British English would be more likely to have *He didn't use to go.*

4   *He just snuck in and burglarised the place.*   (USA)
   Two features of verb formation in Standard American English strike us here. We have a 'strong' form of the verb *sneak* where the internal vowel

is changed. Standard British English would retain the weak form and just add *-ed* for the past tense – *sneaked*. Whereas Standard British English has the verb *burgle* (the root from which the agent *burglar*, *burgle* + *-ar*, comes), Standard American English takes the agent form and adds a verbal suffix (*burglar* + *-ise*). This is quite a productive means of generating verbs in Standard American English which has also become a trend for other varieties too (*citify*, *uglify*, *slenderise*).

5   *This has always applied to men. As well, it now applies to women.*   (Canada)
Standard Canadian English permits the phrase 'as well' to appear at the beginning of a sentence. Most other standard varieties would have it after the item it modifies (*It now applies to women as well*).

6   *Is it stupid you are?*   (Ireland)
The 'fronting' of the complement adjective *stupid* and the use of the dummy subject *it* is used as clefting. Whereas most standard varieties use clefting, only Standard Irish English uses it with the verb *to be* on its own.

6.3 Standard attitudes

There are, then, undeniable differences between these Standard Englishes, but they are relatively very few; relatively, that is, in comparison with the hundreds of regional varieties of non-Standard English spoken around the world. Before we sample some of these differences, however, it might be useful to raise the question of what 'standard' actually means in this context. Tom McArthur helpfully refers us to the first OED mention of the word:

> In the year 1138, the English and the Scots met in battle at Cowton Moor in Yorkshire ... [The English] rallying point was unusual: a cluster of flags on a ship's mast mounted on a carriage. When the contemporary observer Richard of Hexham later wrote about this strange device, he ... called it a 'standard', because 'it was there that valour took its stand'.

> (McArthur, 1998 p. 102)

From that first mention, the battle flag of England later became known as *the King's Standard*, and within three centuries the use of the term had broadened to include weights and measures which were guaranteed by the monarch. So, as well as a noun (*the King's **Standard***), it also became an adjective, describing invariant units which could be measured without dispute (*a **standard** yard, a **standard** pint*).

The word's etymology, then, seems to encourage a view of Standard English as both a bastion of correctness (Richard of Hexham's original use of taking a stand) and a model of intrinsic and fixed accuracy against which all other English usage is measured. Such a view of Standard English can even absorb those few variations we see in its international versions. The US yard and mile differ slightly from the British version – why can't each country have a (slightly) different version of Standard English too? The differences among Standard Englishes are, after all, relatively few, so that the accuracy and invariance of the standard version may still pertain for that particular section of the globe in which it is spoken.

But what about those varieties of English which differ from the standard? How do they fare with regard to notions of accuracy and correctness? Try the following activity.

ACTIVITY 6.2

Allow about
5 minutes

How would you classify instances such as *she won't do nothing about it* or *I might could do it* or *he did it hisself* or *six pound of potatoes*? Are they completely wrong? Or are they just different? It may be worth at this stage reflecting on your own views regarding the above points about the meaning of standard and the related notions of correctness and accuracy. There's no real need to write anything down – just be aware of your honest reaction to the questions, and whether those views are the same after reading this chapter:

Is *she won't do anything about it* correct, but *she won't do nothing about it* wrong?

Is *he did it himself* correct, but *he did it hisself* wrong?

ACTIVITY 6.3

In the light of your reaction, read 'Singlish and Standard Singaporean English' by Ann Hewings and Martin Hewings (Reading A). This reading outlines the attitude of the Singaporean government towards the variety of non-Standard English known locally as Singlish. As you read, consider how justifiable the measures of the Singaporean government are and what, if anything, would be lost if Singlish were to gradually disappear from use. Are you able to draw any comparisons with attitudes towards standard and non-standard varieties in your own part of the world?

Comment

As Hewings and Hewings state (in the last paragraph of the reading), the Singaporean government has been 'labelling one Singaporean English dialect as inferior to another'. Based on this judgement, it has used its authority to ban Singlish from two very influential contexts – broadcasting and advertising. The reasoning is that the variety acts as an obstacle to economic expansion, since people from outside Singapore find it difficult to understand. The Singaporean government has therefore adopted a prescriptive position: claiming that one variety of a language is superior to another.

A linguistic perspective on this issue would see Singlish as an insider variety of language for specific use by Singaporeans which functions to reinforce a linguistic and national identity as well as promote inter-ethnic links by drawing on local languages such as Mandarin and Malay. From many angles, this would appear easily as valuable a function as the international status claimed for Standard Singaporean English. Notions of correctness or superiority would simply not apply – Singlish would be accepted as a different variety of English which operated under a different set of rules which could be observed and systematically described. This would represent a descriptive approach to language analysis, taking the view that different varieties have different underlying rule systems without imposing any value judgements as to the relative merits of those systems.

This is clearly not the view adopted by the Singaporean government, which devotes considerable attention to language planning and language-related issues. Rather, there is a fear that such an ostensibly equitable approach to language varieties would disadvantage those who speak Singlish – especially as for many of these people, Singlish is the only variety in which they are proficient. Why this should be the case following a mandatory six years of primary school education and a further optional four to six years in secondary education through the medium of Standard Singaporean English is not easy to answer. But the situation is probably not dissimilar – except of course for the ban – to that of schoolchildren elsewhere in the English-speaking world where a non-standard variety is spoken at home. Success in education in most English-speaking countries entails mastery of the standard variety, further underlining the credentials of Standard English as a social dialect.

6.4 Variety and 'macro' social factors: class, gender and age

Much of the early work on the influence on language variation of 'macro' social factors such as class, gender and age centred on pronunciation or accent studies. Ground-breaking work by pioneers such as Labov in the USA and Trudgill in the UK provided the principles and methodology for later work on grammatical variation which concerns us in this chapter. For the sake of convenience, I will deal separately with each macro factor, but the interrelationships between them will soon become evident.

Social class

If Standard English is a social dialect and the vehicle of educational success, it follows that the social groups which will habitually use Standard English will be the educated middle and upper classes. It is among these groups, then, that we will find least dialect variety other than that noted in Standard Englishes (Section 6.2). Elsewhere along the social spectrum, where educational success has not so effectively imposed the habitual use of a Standard English, we would expect to find greater variety between regional non-standard varieties. Figure 6.2 clearly illustrates this point.

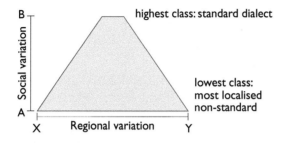

Figure 6.2   Social and regional dialect variation (Trudgill, 1983b, p. 41, Figure 1)

We need to bear in mind that Trudgill was working with a concept of social class (as in Figure 6.2) that conflated a number of parameters (background, education, work, etc.) which most sociolinguists today would prefer to separate out. The vertical axis extends from the lower end of the social scale (A) to the top (B). The horizontal axis (X–Y) represents the degree of variation in non-standard dialects of English. The trapezium-like figure suggests that the further up the social scale one travels, the less variation one finds among speakers as the educational and social demands of Standard English are applied. The summit is flattened somewhat to show the possibility of slight variation among different varieties of Standard Englishes, which we have already noted. The greatest point of variation among dialects is at the bottom of the social scale where the effects of education and the lure of social elevation via linguistic routes hold less sway.

Gender

In every social class, men use more non-standard forms than women, which Trudgill highlighted as 'the single most consistent finding to emerge from sociolinguistic work in the past two decades' (Trudgill, 1983b, p. 96). Why this should be so is less clear. Various explanations which have been offered are:

- Women are more status-conscious than men and therefore use more standard forms.
- From an early age, there is a greater expectation of women to conform to social norms and model acceptable or 'correct' behaviour.
- As a subordinate group, women's use of standard forms represents a desire to be polite and not to offend.

You'll notice immediately that all these points try to explain the speech behaviour of women, as though the use of more standard forms were deviant and needed explaining. What if we shift the focus a little and ask why men use more non-standard forms than women? It has been suggested that non-standard forms present a more masculine, tough and rebellious image, which declares its own superiority by disregarding demands to conform to social notions of correctness. It's not difficult to see that this is little more than the flip-side of the explanations summarised above for women's use of standard forms. What it does not explain is the overwhelming evidence that *all* speakers, irrespective of gender (and indeed social class), use more non-standard forms in a less formal context.

It is this response to the context which may offer a more convincing reason for gender disparity, at least in one set of research circumstances – the interview. Women tend generally to be more cooperative conversationalists than men (see, for instance, Maltz and Borker, 1998), accommodating or adjusting to the speech of their interlocutor. Given the probability that in most social dialect studies, the interviewers will be middle class and well educated, women will tend to respond to the formality of the situation by using more formal standard forms.

Age

Research suggests that there is a correlation between age and prestige language forms. Downes (1998) provides a diagrammatic account of this correlation, reproduced in Figure 6.3. The diagram suggests that the use of non-standard or non-prestige forms is high at adolescence moving towards greater use of standard or prestige forms as people grow older, this trend peaking at about middle age then reverting to non-standard forms for the older age groups.

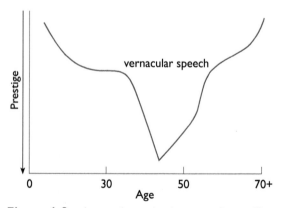

Figure 6.3   Age and prestige language forms (Downes, 1998, p. 224, Figure 6.9)

Downes argues that this is due to the 'pressures of different sorts of norms for different age groups'. It is at adolescence that we see the use of non-standard forms peak; Downes explains: 'Peer groups of young people exert great normative pressure on each other, and are correspondingly less susceptible to society-wide norms conveyed to them by the institutions of the adult and outside world' (Downes, 1998, p. 224). The middle age range – those most likely to be interested in improving their status both socially and professionally – is more susceptible to the outside pressures of work and societal values. As these pressures fade, so does the need to conform to prestige language forms.

This, of course, raises the question of perspective when we use a term such as 'prestige', and the perspective of adolescence in this respect is appreciably different from that of other age groups. This is confirmed in a case study by Eisikovits (1998) of adolescents in Sydney.

Eisikovits studied four groups from working-class inner-city areas: two groups of males and two of females, of which two groups were aged on average about fourteen years, and two about sixteen years. You will have noted already that, as well as age, we are taking account of two other macro parameters: social class and gender. The social class and age factors predict the wide use of non-standard forms among all of these groups, but it is the interaction of age and gender which provides the main interest.

Eisikovits found that, while both younger age groups had a high incidence of non-standard forms, such usage had declined in the older female group, but had increased in the older male group. It seemed that although these two groups were coming to the end of their schooling and were looking to the outside world, their perceptions of that world and their role within it were significantly different. The female acceptance of the more conservative responsibilities of adulthood and the jettisoning of rebellion was summed by one of the older group:

> I think I've settled down a lot. It's better not being in trouble anyway.

> (quoted in Eisikovits, 1998 p. 48)

The male perception of growing up on the other hand was more to do with aggressive self-assertion and an anti-establishment unwillingness to be dictated to, as shown by one interviewee's account of a confrontation with the police:

> You know, you can give 'em cheek, bit a cheek back 'n they can't say nothing.

> (quoted in Eisikovits, 1998 p. 51)

Linguistic evidence of the disparate views of what constituted prestige forms corresponding with these perspectives was clearest in the ways in which members of the two older groups corrected themselves. The females self-corrected towards the standard, while the males self-corrected away from it:

> [FEMALE]   An me and Kerry – or should I say, Kerry and I – are the only ones who've done the project.

> [MALE]   I didn't know what I did – what I done.

> (Eisikovits, 1998, p. 50)

The Eisikovits study shows how the macro social factors of social class, gender and age interweave to pattern the language choices of Australian adolescents, but the influence of such interweaving applies at other stages of life and not only between standard and non-standard choices. The following case study considers the effect of age, interwoven with gender and social class, on selections among standard forms.

Ito and Tagliamonte (2003) studied use of standard intensifiers in York. They focused on the use of the two most favoured intensifiers *very* and *really* by three different age groups, and found distinct patterns between the oldest and youngest.

> As the term suggests, intensifiers function to magnify or intensify the meaning of the following word, as in *the fall was **really** painful* or *your mother is **seriously** annoyed*. Intensifiers are generally the victims of their own success. The more they are used, the less they are able to fulfil their function of boosting or maximising the effect of the word they qualify. If someone reports the weather during a visit abroad as having been ***incredibly** hot*, do we take this to mean that the temperature was literally beyond belief? Or just that it was hotter than we would normally expect?

The oldest age-group (66+) were frequent users of *very*, but rarely used *really* as an intensifier. The younger age-group (17–34) provided the mirror image, using intensifying *really* as frequently as the oldest age group used *very*, but using *very* as rarely as their older counterparts had used *really*. In the middle age-range (35–65), use of *very* was maintained at the rate of the oldest group while *really* gained a little ground overall. See Figure 6.4.

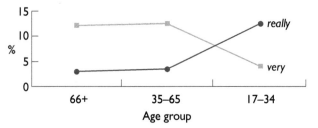

Figure 6.4 Distribution of *very/really* by age (adapted from Ito and Tagliamonte, 2003, p. 267)

It was when Ito and Tagliamonte looked at other factors such as gender and education that some interesting results emerged. In the middle age-range (35–65), there was gradual decline in usage of intensifying *really* along the cline from educated women (most use), to less educated women, to educated men, to less educated men (least use). In the younger age-range (17–34), both sets of women and educated men made substantially greater usage of *really* than less educated men. See Figure 6.5.

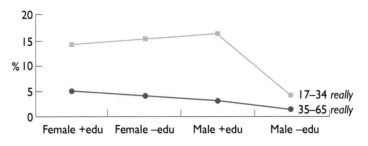

Figure 6.5 Distribution of *really* by age, gender and education (adapted from Ito and Tagliamonte, 2003, p. 276)

ACTIVITY 6.4

Allow about
10 minutes

These findings demonstrate how usage of a particular linguistic feature – in this case, a favoured intensifier – can change substantially from one generation to another. What else can you deduce from them?

Comment

They support the long-held view that women play a key role in implementing language change, a view which goes back to pioneering linguists like Otto Jespersen who ascribed women some double-edged credit in this particular respect: 'The fondness of women for hyperbole will very often lead the fashion with regard to adverbs of intensity' (Jespersen, 1922, p. 250).

They also seem to add further support to the patterns we've already observed among the interweaving influences of social class, gender and age. In particular, the less educated males in both age-groups are the closest in usage across the generations, suggesting greater linguistic continuity among this group, and within the younger age-group greater differentiation between this group and all the others. There is also the interesting question of whether the similarity in usage between the women and educated men in the younger age-group is an indication of greater equality between men and women in contemporary society.

Even allowing for their interrelatedness, what these macro factors of class, gender and age show us is a series of claims about systematic patterns of language variation within a population. They derive from quantitative studies of relatively large-scale collections of data and, put simply, suggest that speakers with a given combination of these factors (along with regional considerations) will use an appropriately corresponding group of linguistic forms, and that they will do this regularly. In other words, quantitative research of this nature is more concerned with general large-scale patterns, than with the reality of how individuals actually speak in a range of different circumstances. Data on the latter is more effectively gathered by localised qualitative research methods which seek to discover how speakers use varying linguistic forms in different contexts.

6.5 Variety and 'micro' factors: social networks

While the key or macro-level factors of social class, gender and age (and others such as ethnicity, which we haven't discussed here) may all have associated patterns of language use, they do not of themselves provide sufficient explanation for the wide variety of linguistic behaviour to be found in the day-to-day speech of most people. It may be possible to classify an individual in terms of social class, age and gender, but that individual may not display consistent speech patterns in all the interactions in which they are involved during the course of a week or even a day. In order to explain the ways in which speakers use different speech patterns in dynamic and creative ways in order to express various social identities, we need to look at the micro-level categories inherent in different social interactions.

Most people will have a variety of **social networks** in their daily lives: their families, colleagues at work, customers or clients, fellow students, teammates, drinking partners, members of the same club or organisation, and so on. For instance, Geraint and Iwan both play for the local cricket club which is at the heart of the community of my home town in south-west Wales. Let's consider how Geraint's and Iwan's social networks differ.

Geraint is a self-employed bricklayer; Iwan is a policeman. Geraint works on a regular basis with Peter, a member of the club's committee who is a plasterer, and employs Peter's son Gethin (who plays for the second XI) as a labourer. Geraint, Peter and Gethin have a drink after work unless there's a match or net practice. During the season there are usually two matches on a weekend, one midweek evening match and one net practice the same evening as the committee meeting. Geraint's local sporting profile ensures more than enough building work within the town. Iwan recently reached the rank of detective inspector. He is responsible for over thirty officers within a very large rural region which contains five medium-sized towns with police stations which he visits regularly. He gives media interviews on high profile crime enquiries. Pressure of work restricts him to one match per week and no practice. His wife, a civil servant, is a keen dancer and Iwan has discovered a gratifying talent in this direction. When work allows, they visit a dancing club in Swansea twice a week.

A sociolinguist would describe Iwan's social networks as **uniplex**: that is to say, they are largely unrelated to each other. He avoids mixing socially with his colleagues, only sees his cricketing teammates once a week, and his work involves contact with the media and the public. Geraint's networks on the other hand are interrelated or **multiplex**: his work and social life revolve around the same people.

It won't come as a great surprise to you that if you mix with the same people on a regular basis, the likelihood is that your speech is going to resemble theirs. By the same token, if your networks are mainly uniplex, you may alter your speech to accommodate the network in which you find yourself. This accommodation may be conscious or unconscious. I can most certainly recall my own experience returning home on vacation to South Wales after my first term as an undergraduate at an English university. I was left in no doubt by my friends at home that my newly acquired speech patterns were at odds with what they expected within that particular network (though they didn't word it quite like that). I made very sure that the aberration was not repeated on subsequent visits home.

ACTIVITY 6.5

Allow about
10 minutes

Based on your interaction during a typical week and/or weekend, work out what your own social networks are, and consider whether these are uniplex or multiplex. In other words, do you meet the same people in different contexts, or do the social and professional contexts in which you find yourself tend to be populated by different sets of people? More importantly, do you think your social networks give any clues to the way you speak? Can you identify the people whose speech your own most resembles? If not, what do you think is/are the main influence(s) on the way you speak?

Lesley Milroy (1980) conducted studies of various social networks in different districts of Belfast. In working-class Ballymacarrett, she found that the men worked in shipyards alongside their relatives and friends, whom they also met socially for a drink. Their networks therefore tended to be multiplex. The women, on the other hand, travelled to find better-paid work on the other side of the city where they mixed with different people in a uniplex professional network. Milroy found that the speech of the women contained fewer non-standard forms than that of the men.

In contrast, in another area of Belfast known as the Clonard, the men's work in the linen industry had come to an end with the result that they had to travel outside the area to find work. The women, however, had managed to stay in the area and find work together. The Clonard women's networks therefore resembled those of the Ballymacarrett men, and their speech likewise contained more non-standard features than that of the Clonard men. For both the Clonard women and the Ballymacarrett men, then, their multiplex networks meant that they were communicating with the same people regularly on a day-to-day basis, sharing the same speech patterns and thereby maintaining local non-standard varieties. The uniplex networks of the Clonard men and Ballymacarrett women exposed them to a greater variety of relationships and therefore different speech patterns which they incorporated into their own speech.

While the Ballymacarrett case study conforms to the macro expectations of social class and gender (the working-class men use a greater number of non-standard forms than the working-class women from the same community), the Clonard case study overturns those expectations entirely, with the Clonard women's linguistic behaviour being close to the macro male trend and vice versa. Such findings serve to underline the differences between the large-scale trends based on macro social factors thrown up by quantitative studies, and the varying language behaviour of individuals in different contexts as shown by localised qualitative research. They also show clearly that speakers are able to vary their language choices according to the situation in which they find themselves: they are not restricted to the patterns of a single dialect; and they are able to use language in order to construct particular social identities within day-to-day interactions. This 'style shifting' will be explored in more detail in the next chapter.

6.6 A core of English and dialect levelling

Up to now, I may have given the impression that Standard and non-Standard English are two separate entities with nothing in common, and that people will speak either one or the other. Neither of these is true. The distinction between standard and non-standard is not as hard and fast as it appears. Figure 6.2 provides a clue: the higher up the social scale one travels, the less variation one finds. The change from maximum variation to minimum variation is not sudden, it's gradual.

In the UK (for instance) the speaker of a non-standard variety is not using a totally different system from a standard speaker: these are interlinking systems which may have more similarities than differences. Figures 6.6, 6.7 and 6.8 may make this clearer.

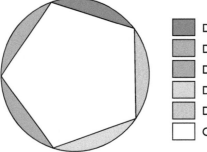

Distinctive features of Standard British English
Distinctive features of Tyneside English
Distinctive features of Dorset English
Distinctive features of Glasgow English
Distinctive features of East Anglia English
Common core of English

Figure 6.6　Common core of English plus varieties

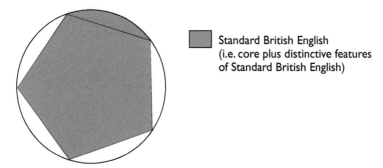

Figure 6.7 Standard British English including common core

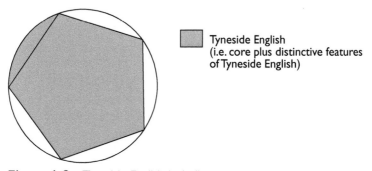

Figure 6.8 Tyneside English including common core

The three figures emphasise the large common ground of grammar and vocabulary which all dialects share. They also acknowledge that all dialects have distinctive features which distinguish them from other dialects. However, they fail to convey that some dialects contain more distinctive features than others, and also that some features, while distinctive, are common to more than one dialect. Several non-standard forms are now common in different geographical – particularly urban – areas. Coupland (1988) lists seven of these features; they are shown compared with standard usage to the right in Table 6.1 (below and overleaf).

Table 6.1 Common non-standard forms

	Non-standard	Standard
1	*I didn't do nothing to nobody* (multiple negation)	*I didn't do anything to anybody* (single negation)
2	*I never threw it* (*never* as a negative in the past tense)	*I didn't throw it* (*didn't* as a negative in the past tense)
3	*I'm not keen on them films* (*them* as demonstrative adjective)	*I'm not keen on those films* (*those* as demonstrative adjective)
4	*six pound of potatoes, please* (plural not indicated in word *pound*)	*six pounds of potatoes, please* (plural indicated by *s*)

5 *the boy played brilliant* (adjective form *brilliant* for adverb)	*the boy played brilliantly* (use of *-ly* adverb suffix)
6 *I'm going up London* (shortened form of preposition *up to*)	*I'm going up to London* (use of complex preposition *up to*)
7 *he did it hisself* (following pattern *my(self), your (self), his(self), our(selves)*)	*he did it himself* (breaking the pattern opposite, making it irregular)

(adapted from Coupland, 1988, p. 35)

Work by Cheshire and Milroy (1993) based on questionnaires sent to several urban schools throughout the UK confirmed 2, 3, 4 and 5 as the most widespread features, adding:

- *what* as a relative pronoun: *the book **what** was on sale* (Standard British English: *The book **that/which** was on sale*);
- *there's/there was* plus plural: *there **was loads** of them* (Standard British English: *there **were loads** of them*);
- *be + sat/stood*: *she **was sat/stood** on the other side of the room* (Standard British English: *she was **sitting/standing** on the other side of the room*).

The unexpected absence of multiple negation from Cheshire's list may be explained by the possibility that this feature remains so heavily stigmatised that pupils were unwilling to report it.

Such bunching of common non-standard features characterises a process known as **dialect levelling**. Dialect levelling occurs when speakers of different dialects come into regular contact with each other and lose some of the linguistic features of their dialect that are not widely shared with the others. The growth of cities, the urbanisation of former rural populations, transport links and broadcasting have driven the increase in dialect levelling and the accompanying reduction in the number of speakers of 'traditional' dialects.

6.7 Traditional dialects

Trudgill and Chambers (1991, p. 3) make the distinction between 'traditional' dialects – spoken by a shrinking minority 'in long settled and especially remote and peripheral rural areas' of the British Isles – and 'mainstream' dialects which include standard and modern non-standard varieties throughout the world. As examples of traditional dialect, Trudgill (1994, p. 16) offers *Hoo inno goin* or *She byun't a-goin* for standard *She isn't going* or (mainstream) non-standard *She ain't going*.

The substantial differences between the traditional versions reflect a time when language change developed along different lines within different communities, and the lack of easy transport links made communication between more distant communities difficult. At one time, a given community – let's label it community A – might have had reasonably close contact with communities B and Z, slightly less with communities C and Y, and very little with communities D, E, X and W. Consequently, the locals of A would have more language features in common with B and Z than with C and Y; and less again with D, E, X and W to the extent that they may even have had difficulty understanding each other. Such difficulties have for the most part evaporated considerably with the advent of the features listed above (the growth of cities, urbanisation, transport, broadcasting): those traditional features which remain will probably be in more isolated areas of the British Isles and even then used by older members of these communities.

One location where modernisation seems to have exerted less linguistic influence than elsewhere, however, is the small fishing town of Buckie on the north-east coast of Scotland between Aberdeen and Inverness. Geographically isolated, Buckie has nevertheless maintained a high degree of economic independence due to fishing and more recently oil. Inhabitants of Buckie have a very positive attitude to their home town and, significantly, a low percentage of young people leave the area, thereby going against the usual migratory trends. Marriage is largely endogamous with about ten surnames being shared by about 80 per cent of the population of approximately 8000. Factors such as these ensure that the Buckie dialect is less prone to dialect levelling than other similar areas. The sociolinguist Jennifer Smith, herself a Buckie exile and speaker of the Buckie dialect, says that it contains several features not shared by other non-standard Scottish varieties, such as the absence of the auxiliary verb *do* in negative statements, as in *I na see it*; compare this with the Standard British English, *I don't see it* (Steele and Smith, 2004). For instance, for Standard British English *I don't do that*, a Buckie speaker can say *I dinnae do that* or *I na do that* (where the *do* particle is absent). A Buckie speaker can also say *You dinnae dae it* or *You nae dae it*. However, the rules of Buckie English will not permit *She nae dae it*. In other words, whereas the *do* particle is optional for first- and second-person singular, it must appear in the third-person singular, another illustration of the patterning of non-standard dialects that at first sight seem simply irregular.

6.8 New-dialect formation

Traditional features such as those which persist in the Buckie dialect have no place in the Englishes of the southern hemisphere dominions such as Australia, New Zealand and South Africa (see Chapter 4, Section 4.2). Trudgill (2004) suggests that the process of new-dialect formation, far from being a haphazard affair, has a degree of determinism attached to it. As long as one knows the original dialect mix and demographic details of speakers, one can – within limits – predict the way a given dialect will develop. Trudgill uses a culinary analogy: 'If you bake cakes ... from roughly the same ingredients in roughly the same proportions in roughly similar conditions for roughly the same length of time, you will get roughly similar cakes' (Trudgill, 2004, p. 20).

A similar recipe pertains for new-dialect formation, which explains the similarities between the southern hemisphere Englishes, since they all developed from similar mixtures of British dialects. The normal time for this development to evolve is about fifty years, or two generations, and the key players in the formation of the new dialects are children under the age of eight, offspring of the first generation of English speakers born on the colony.

Trudgill's work arises from the Origins of New Zealand English (ONZE) project at Christchurch University. Building on the overview of new-dialect formation in Chapter 4 (Section 4.2), we will look at some of Trudgill's findings in order to illustrate in more linguistic detail the significant part played in the formation of a new dialect by processes such as accommodation (mentioned briefly in Section 6.5), levelling (see Section 6.6) and drift.

The ONZE project comprises a data archive of recordings of pioneer reminiscences from the children of the first European settlers in New Zealand, made between 1946 and 1948. Based on his analysis of several of these recordings, alongside documentary evidence of the British English dialects at the time of the initial emigrations and observation of current varieties of English, Trudgill proposes the following three stages in the process of new-dialect formation.

Stage 1   Emigrés born in about 1815 or after, leave the British Isles speaking their own varieties of English from about 1840 onwards. These varieties would have included traditional dialects, but the absence of such in the ONZE data showed that the more unusual (least widely used) features had been **levelled** out, either on the boat during the crossing or soon after arrival. Such levelling would be a result of **accommodating** speakers of dissimilar dialects in face-to-face interaction – part of the extremely powerful drive to 'talk like others talk' (Keller, 1994, p. 100), which lies at the heart of the process of accommodation within human communication. To put it another way:

- Speakers find themselves in the situation of needing to communicate with a wider circle of interactants, many of whom have very different speech patterns.
- They alter their own speech patterns in order to try to make communication as easy as possible for themselves and their interactants (accommodating).
- They do this by eliminating those features in their speech which are either irregular (don't follow consistent rules) or not shared by the majority of the wider circle (levelling).

Stage 2 English-speaking children born in New Zealand from about 1840 onwards – the offspring of the first settlers from the British Isles – had, despite the rudimentary levelling which had already taken place, a vast array of competing features to choose from the different dialects around them from all over the British Isles. The absence of a single dialect model meant that they acquired features derived from British varieties but in different combinations from those that pertained in the original dialects. Crucial in this process of acquisition was what Labov (2001, p. 191) calls 'frequencies of interaction' – shorthand for who interacts most often with whom (see Section 6.6). These frequencies of interaction would have determined that the proportions of variants collectively found in the speech of individuals were not random but reflected the proportions of variants in the dialects around them.

Stage 3 The first appearance of a distinctive New Zealand English came from those born between 1865 and 1890. Features typical of dialect levelling (such as the rejection of minority variants and the retention of regular forms), having continued throughout Stages 1 and 2, became stabilised to form a new dialect. Almost invariably, the features to survive in this new dialect were those features in the majority in the mixture spoken by the first generation of speakers born in New Zealand.

Though dealing specifically with New Zealand English, Trudgill also comments on the similarities in the developments of the other southern hemisphere colonial Englishes, and invokes the notion of **drift** as a significant factor in dialect evolution. Dialect drift was first mentioned by Edward Sapir: 'language moves down time in a current of its own making. It has a drift' (Sapir, 1921, p. 150).

In other words, dialects display a propensity to evolve along similar lines if they derive from the same source, due to the common structural properties that they inherit. An example from New Zealand English is the main verb *have*, which can appear as a stative or dynamic verb. Stative *have* implies a state of being or a state of affairs which pertains at a particular time, for example:

> *Do you have any money?*
> (where having money is a state of being at that juncture)

Dynamic *have* on the other hand implies a process taking place:

> *Do you have coffee with breakfast?*
> (where the taking of coffee would be a process rather than a state)

In the nineteenth century, the ONZE data showed that *have* didn't need the auxiliary *do*, whether the verb was used in a stative or dynamic sense. Both were used in the same way minus supporting *do*:

> *Have you any money?* (stative)

> *Have you coffee with breakfast?* (dynamic)

In the twentieth century, dynamic *have* took auxiliary *do* whereas its stative sense did not:

> *Do you have coffee with breakfast?* (dynamic)
>
> *Have you any money?* (stative)

Current evidence suggests that, in the twenty-first century, the situation is reverting back to both senses of the verb *have* being treated the same, but this time, as in most other varieties of English, both requiring auxiliary *do*:

> *Do you have coffee with breakfast?*
>
> *Do you have any money?*

Similar developments are observable in Australian and South African English. Trudgill concludes: 'We can regard these as changes in parallel in different parts of the anglophone world – changes in the language which have been set in motion and are continuing even after geographical separation' (Trudgill, 2004, p. 131).

6.9 Grammatical variety

The remainder of this chapter will examine a brief range of grammatical constructions to do with verb phrases found in varieties of English throughout the world, chosen for the interesting ways in which they illustrate how different varieties employ different grammatical rules which generate different forms and meanings. While the codification of Standard English has led to its being largely viewed as 'the' language, and English grammar in its most popular sense as the grammar of Standard English, deviations from that grammar are generally viewed as corruptions of the correct form.

As we have noted already in this chapter, such a position conforms to a prescriptive view of language rules and varieties. A very different view – a descriptive linguistic view – would hold that non-standard varieties are different from the standard (and each other) simply because they have different sets of rules which are able to convey different meanings, and that it is impossible on purely linguistic grounds to make any evaluative judgements on these systems (i.e. to say that some are 'better' or 'more correct' than others). You were asked for your own opinions on this issue in Activity 6.2. It would be interesting to reflect on those opinions after reading this section.

Strong verbs

ACTIVITY 6.6

Allow about
10 minutes

Table 6.2 compares some strong verb forms in Tyneside English, Irish English and Standard British English. Strong (or irregular) verbs indicate such things as tense by a change of vowel (e.g. *I sing, I sang, I have sung*) in contrast to weak (or regular) verbs which add an inflection like -ed (*I jump, I jumped, I have jumped*).

Three forms are shown for each variety: stem, past, and past participle. The stem is that used in the infinitive form of the verb; for example, to **break** things. 'Past' refers to the past tense; for example, I **broke** it yesterday in Standard British, Tyneside and Irish. The 'past participle' is used in constructions such as I'm afraid I've **broken** it in Standard British English, and I'm afraid I've **broke** it in Tyneside and Irish.

Where in the three varieties do you see the greatest regularity? Does the regularity make the meaning any less clear?

Table 6.2 Examples of strong verb forms

Tyneside			Irish			Standard		
Stem	Past	Past participle	Stem	Past	Past participle	Stem	Past	Past participle
break	broke	broke	break	broke	broke	break	broke	broken
bite	bit	bit	bite	bit	bit	bite	bit	bitten
go	went	went	go	went	went	go	went	gone
sing	sang	sang	sing	sung	sung	sing	sang	sung
do	done	done	do	done	done	do	did	done
come	come	came	come	come	come	come	came	come
beat	beat	beat	beat	beat	beat	beat	beat	beaten
give	give	give	give	give	give	give	gave	given

(based on Harris, 1993, and McDonald, 1981, quoted in Beal, 1993)

Comment

Old English had an extensive system of strong verb forms, many of which were subsequently lost or regularised as the language developed and changed. Of those that remain, many contemporary non-standard varieties of English have simpler strong verb systems than the standard. In Table 6.2, where Tyneside and/or Irish have two forms, Standard British English usually has three, and where Tyneside and/or Irish have one, Standard British English has two.

There is no loss of meaning in the more regular patterns, since the presence or absence of the auxiliary verb makes it clear whether the verb is a past tense form or past participle.

Harris (1993, p. 152) suggests that the simplification of the strong verb system was advanced in both literary and vernacular varieties of English by the eighteenth century. It was subsequently reversed, in part, in the standard system but not in non-standard dialects. Harris (1993, p. 152) compares the

Irish English example *He **would a went** on his own* (cf. this with Standard British English: *He **would've gone** on his own*) with Jane Austen's *the troubles we **had went** through (Sense and Sensibility)*, published at the beginning of the nineteenth century.

Age was found to be a significant factor in the simplification of strong verb forms in Smith's (2002) survey of past tense forms in Buckie, north-east Scotland. Smith found considerable variation across the town's entire population, such as:

> *And I **seen** his death in the paper*
> (Standard British English: *And I **saw** his death in the paper*)
>
> *And I mean, I had **drove** home fae Elgin heaps of times*
> (Standard British English: *And I mean, I had **driven** home from Elgin heaps of times*)
>
> *She's **gotten** a mixer but she winna use it*
> (Standard British English: *She's **obtained** a mixer but she won't use it*)
>
> *It was your granny that **telt** me on Sunday*
> (Standard British English: *It was your granny that **told** me on Sunday*)

However, it was the younger generation which exhibited the trend towards greater regularisation as they used the same form for past tense and past participle forms with most irregular verbs, as shown in Table 6.3.

Table 6.3 Strong verb paradigm for younger Buckie speakers

Stem	Past	Past participle
see	seen	seen
do	done	done
take	taen	taen
come	came	came
go	went	went
get	got	got
have	had	had
sell	selt	selt
tell	telt	telt
forget	forgot	forgot
fall	fell	fell

(adapted from Smith, 2002, p. 186)

From this we see that the younger speakers of the more traditional Buckie dialect are adopting a trait which we have already noted as prevalent in the more mainstream Tyneside and Irish dialects (Table 6.2), as well as New Zealand English (Trudgill, 2004). This supports both the theory of dialect drift (see Section 6.8) and the claim of Christian et al., (1988, p. 108, quoted in Smith, 2002, p. 186) that there is in English dialects worldwide a 'fairly strong tendency to reduce the number of form distinctions for a given irregular verb to two'. Pinker and Prince (1988, p. 122) suggest that irregular verbs exist in that area 'roughly where the grammar leaves off and memory begins'. Let me put that another way: while regular verbs are formed by the consistent application of a rule, irregular verbs on the other hand have to be remembered by rote. For instance, to form the past tense and past participle of a regular verb, you add -ed to the base form, so that *jump* + *-ed* = *jumped/ have jumped,* and *walk* + *-ed* = *walked/have walked.* The application of such a rule is systematic or grammatical and can be applied uniformly to regular verbs. No such systematic rule may be applied to strong or irregular verbs – how do you find a rule which derives both *went/have gone* from *go,* and *did/ have done* from *do?*

Smith suggests that having the same form for past tense and past participle decreases 'the cognitive burden on memory' (Smith, 2005, p. 185). Instead of having to learn the rather arbitrary and unsystematic differences in the paradigm employed by, say, Standard British English, analogical drift towards a single form for both past tense and past participle makes for a more efficient grammatical system by reducing the degree of irregularity.

Indeed, Viv Edwards (1993) suggests that this process of simplification continues to affect some verb forms in Standard British English, with many speakers now unsure of the distinction between 'past tense' and 'past participle' forms such as *drank/drunk or swam/swum.* So instead of the profile *swim – swam – swum,* and *drink – drank – drunk,* it is very possible that before long Standard British English will, due to widening usage, have simplified these to *swim – swam – swam and drink – drunk – drunk.* The principle underlying such change illustrates the continuing change even within Standard English, and how a feature which at one time might have been stigmatised as non-standard may eventually become an accepted standard form, thus supporting Trudgill's (2002) claim that features spread from low-status dialects to prestige varieties, and not the other way around. Such acceptance depends, of course, on sufficient usage by the appropriate section of the social spectrum, a social process neatly articulated by the dictum: 'When enough of the right people get it wrong, it becomes right'.

Present tense: with or without verbal -*s*

Table 6.4 shows different forms of the present tense in three dialects: Standard British English and two non-standard regional varieties of British English. From this table, we can see that there is only one present tense form in the non-standard varieties spoken by some people in south-west England and in East Anglia, whereas the standard variety distinguishes between the third person singular (*she, he* and *it* forms) and other verb forms in the present tense.

Table 6.4 Varying forms of the present tense

South-west England	East Anglia	Standard English
I loves	I love	I love
you loves	you love	you love
she, he, it loves	she, he, it love	she, he, it loves
we loves	we love	we love
they loves	they love	they love

(Cheshire and Milroy, 1993, p. 16)

Despite prescriptive claims about the superiority of the standard variety in terms of its logicality and systematicity, it seems here that the two non-standard varieties observe a regularity of verb-ending rules which is absent from the standard due to what seems to be an almost arbitrary -*s* ending for the third person singular. The reason for this is probably to be found – as so often when exploring such differences – in the history of the dialects' development. In Chapter 2 (Section 2.4), you saw how Old English had a whole series of inflections, or verb endings, that changed according to the subject of the verb (the verb ending would change according to whether the subject was *I, you, he, we*, etc). These inflections have been mostly lost in Modern English but there seem to have been different patterns of development. Cheshire and Milroy (1993, p. 17) comment: 'Because non-standard varieties of English have not been codified, they have sometimes been affected by processes of language change that have not influenced the development of Standard English. In some cases, this means that the rules for the non-standard feature are more regular than the rules for Standard English'.

Other varieties of English also show differences in present-tense verb forms. For instance, in Singapore (as in East Anglia) verbal -*s* as third person marker is usually absent from colloquial speech. It may be, as John Platt (1991) has suggested, that this is due to the influence of the local languages, Chinese and Malay, which do not mark verbs according to subject. But this process also occurs elsewhere when speakers of other languages learn English, irrespective of whether these other languages themselves mark verbs according to subject. It seems perfectly logical that learners should opt for the more consistent pattern.

Godfrey and Tagliamonte (1999) used a study of verbal -*s* in Devon, south-west England, to suggest a strong link between this feature in British non-standard varieties and African American Vernacular English (AAVE). Its usage in Devon is governed by several constraints to do with the sounds, meaning and grammar of the context in which it appears, as illustrated in the following examples.

Verbal -s is favoured in verb stems ending in consonants, such as *get*:

> *I don't know, it all depends how I gets on when I gets older innit.*

- Verbal *-s* is favoured if the subject of the verb is anything other than a pronoun, such as the noun *tractors* below

  > *Tractors **runs** away.*

- Verbal *-s* is favoured if the subject is somehow separated from the verb, even by a single word such as *that* below:

  > *That's me two grandsons that lives here.*

- Verbal *-s* is disfavoured in third person singular forms of *have* and *do*:

  > *He still do all this bacon and eggs and stuff.*

- Verbal *-s* is disfavoured after verb stems ending in sibilants:

  > *You lose every time you goes there.*

The conditioning factors which were found to still exist in Devon English corresponded in considerable detail to those found in AAVE, enough to eliminate chance as an explanation and establishing that 'verbal "-s" is a linguistic feature of AAVE that originated in British dialects' (Godfrey and Tagliamonte (1999, p. 115).

Tense and time

The relationship between **tense** and time in English is not altogether firm. The present tense can be used for events which have happened in the past:

> *So I walk up to the policeman, and I tap him on the shoulder.*

or in the future:

> *when you arrive at your destination.*

The first example above illustrates what is known as the historic present and is widely used for narrative purposes, usually in spoken English. Equally widely used is the present tense, shown in the second example, to indicate a future event, though some varieties, such as Indian English, prefer the more explicit use of the future tense with *will*:

> *when you will arrive at your destination.*

Past time is often signalled by adverbial expressions, such as *yesterday* or *two days ago*. In several varieties of British English, the past tense need not be used when there is an adverbial that indicates a reference to past time, as in:

> *She come home last week.*

The view could be taken that since the feature of pastness is already signalled by the presence of the adverbial *last week*, the additional use of the past tense of the verb to indicate pastness is redundant, and therefore in linguistic terms the non-standard version may be seen as more efficient than the standard.

Other varieties frequently rely on adverbial and other contextual information, rather than the past tense form, to indicate past time:

> He **walk** home **yesterday** [Jamaican English]

> It was **during that time** these people **make** some arrangement ... [West African English]

> **Before** I always go to that market [Malaysian English]

> **Last time** she **come** on Thursday [Singaporean English]

> (quoted in Platt et al., 1984, pp. 69–70)

Some of the other languages of the regions in the above examples do not mark verbs for tense, and it's possible that they have influenced the structure of the English variety. Platt et al. (1984, p. 70) suggest that it is thus 'quite common to "set the scene" by specifying that something took place in the past and then to use all the verbs unmarked for past tense'.

Aspect as well as tense has a time-related role for English verbs, in that it provides information such as whether an event or situation is continuing:

> *I'm **finishing** it off.*

> *She's **thinking** about it.*

or completed:

> *I've **finished** it off.*

> *She's **thought** about it, and she's **decided** ...*

Different standard varieties of English denote this sense of completion in different ways:

> *We've already eaten.* (Standard British English)

> *We already ate.* (Standard American English)

In some varieties of English, such as Malaysian and Singaporean English, adverbs alone may be used to mark aspect:

> *My father **already** pass away.*
> (Standard British English: *My father has passed away.*)

whereas Irish English is able to convey something which has very recently happened (the so-called 'hot-news' aspect) by a construction which has probably been borrowed straight from Irish Gaelic, using the preposition *after* following the verb *be*:

> *She's **after** selling the boat.*
> (Standard British English: *She's just sold the boat.*)

Interestingly, though not surprisingly, the same construction using the preposition *after* exists in Welsh, though it has never been transplanted into any variety of Welsh English.

Some varieties are able to exploit aspect to convey a sense of habitual or repeated action. In south-east Wales and the west of England, for instance, the auxiliary verb *do* is used to convey habitual events:

> *They do go down there all the time.*

Some varieties of Irish English require both *do* and *be* to convey the sense of habitual action:

> *They do be shooting in the woods.*

Singaporean and Malaysian English have a further alternative means of indicating a current habitual action with *use to*:

> *My mother, she use to go to Pulau Tikus market.*

> (quoted in Platt et al., 1984, p. 71)

Whereas the above example implies *she still does*, similar use of this construction in the past tense (*used to*) in most other varieties of English indicates past habitual action which no longer continues:

> *We **used to** go there every summer.*
> (i.e. 'we don't any more')

So the tense/aspect system in English is not the same for all speakers. Different elements of verb structures are present in different combinations to signify different meanings and are subject to different grammatical constraints. Some of these structures are exclusive to varieties other than Standard English and they create meanings or shades of meanings which are not available in a similar form in the standard.

Modal auxiliary verbs

Modal auxiliary verbs provide a means for expressing obligation (*must, should, ought to*), volition (*will, would, shall*) and possibility (*can, could, might*). There is considerable variation in the use of modal verbs in English.

Even among standard varieties there are different preferences for usage, and changes in the system can be observed. We can take the distinction between *will* and *shall* as one example of this. In 1926, H.W. Fowler noted: 'there is an inclination, among those who are not to the manner born, to question the existence, besides denying the need, of distinctions between [*shall*] and [*will*]' (Fowler, 2002 [1926], p. 526).

ACTIVITY 6.7

Is Fowler being prescriptive or descriptive in the above quote?

Comment

Fowler was attempting to maintain a distinction in usage between *shall* and *will*, where, for the simple future tense, *shall* would be used for the first person:

> I **shall** write it tomorrow.

> We **shall** never surrender.

and *will* for second and third:

> You **will** be arriving tomorrow evening.

> They **will** win their next match.

Those who questioned the need for such a distinction were observed by Fowler to be 'not to the manner born', in other words unworthy on account of their social status to make such judgements about language. Their lowly standing made them unable to distinguish between correct and incorrect usage. Fowler was without doubt being quite prescriptive, and, like all fervent prescriptivists, he was fighting a losing battle. He quotes examples 'from newspapers of the better sort' in which 'one or other principle of its use has been outraged'; for instance:

> But if the re-shuffling of the world goes on producing new 'issues', I **will**, I fear, catch the fever again.

(quoted in Fowler, 2002 [1926], p. 527, emphasis added)

From the perspective of the early twenty-first century, where *shall* is increasingly rarely used in any variety of English including Standard British English, we are tempted to ask why Fowler made such a fuss? You may get your answer from the correspondence pages of several newspapers where readers complain regularly about what they perceive as language misuse. Today's misuse might well become tomorrow's standard use, as long as enough of the right people misuse it.

The effects of language change are therefore gradually but clearly felt in the world of modals. Take the expression of obligation, studied by Tagliamonte et al. (2004). Old English had only 'must', but corpus evidence (i.e. from extremely large electronically stored data banks of naturally occurring language) informs us that *must* as an expression of obligation (*you must turn up tomorrow*) is becoming obsolete, though its use for other meanings such as drawing conclusions (*you must be shattered*) remains healthy. *Must* was challenged (and lessened in usage) as an expression of obligation as early as the fifteenth century by the arrival of *have to*, which itself lost ground to *have got to*, and more recently *got to*. Instead of fading quietly into oblivion, however, *have to* has maintained its ground by finding another niche for itself in the shape of a different shade of meaning: *have to* expresses a stronger sense of obligation than either *have got to* or *got to*. In Scotland, obligation is also expressed by the modal *need to*.

Indian English often expresses possibility by *could* and *would* in constructions such as *We hope that you **could** join us.* Trudgill and Hannah (1994) argue that *could* and *would* are seen as more tentative and therefore more polite. Similarly, *may* is also found as a polite expression of obligation: *These mistakes **may** please be corrected* (= *should* in Standard British English) (Trudgill and Hannah, 1994, p. 109).

ACTIVITY 6.8

Now study Reading B, 'Modals on Tyneside' by Joan Beal. This is an extract from Beal's work on the grammar of Tyneside English, which has been referred to at several points in this chapter. What aspects of the reading make it clear that we are dealing with an efficient linguistic system rather than a haphazard series of aberrations?

Comment

The systematic nature of Tyneside grammar and the way it conveys meanings by different grammatical rules is highlighted by the almost complete absence of *shall* and *may* on the grounds that the work done by these modals in standard varieties is carried out by other modals in Tyneside. Some dialects, including Standard British English, use both *will* and *shall* for futurity, but Tyneside (as well as Scots and Irish) maintains the consistency of *will* throughout.

Double modals observe economy by avoiding for the most part the 'battery of "quasi-modal" verbs' which Standard English and other dialects need since their grammars forbid one modal following another, even though the meaning requires it. Example (4) for instance uses two words (*wouldn't could've*) where Standard English and others would have required five (*wouldn't have been able to*). You might could see other examples where the double modal cuts down the number of words. Please note that I have strictly observed the rules of Tyneside grammar in the preceding sentence since the second modal was one of the two permitted to occur in that position!

Quotative verbs

These are the verbs which are used to introduce dialogue, verbs such as *say, think, shout* and *go*, all of which have been around for a long time. To their ranks has recently been admitted a new member, consisting of a form of the verb *be* followed by *like*, as in the fictional narrative:

So my dad's like, you've got to sublet if you're going to Europe, and I'm like, I promised Anna she could stay there weekends when there's home games so she can sleep with Jason, right?

(quoted in Franzen, 2002, p. 525)

Be + like as a quotative was unattested in the UK and Canada in the early 1990s (Romaine and Lange, 1991), while in the USA its usage was found to be restricted to those under the age of forty (Blyth et al., 1990). Since then, its usage has expanded considerably and in interesting ways. Research by Tagliamonte and Hudson (1999) on oral narratives by university students in the UK (based on a 1996 sample) and Canada (based on a 1995 sample) showed usage of *be + like* growing amongst this social/age group, though mainly to introduce first person dialogue:

and I'm like, pleased to meet you.

This same function had been noted by Romaine and Lange (1991) in their investigation of the early stages of American *be + like* usage, though later surveys (Ferrara and Bell, 1995) showed that within four years the grammatical function of quotative *be + like* had expanded such that half the usages were third person. Further, Ferrara and Bell found that, whereas in 1990 *be + like* was favoured twice as much by women as by men, within two years as usage had mushroomed, both genders were seen to favour it equally. The UK and Canada research showed women to favour usage more than men. It seems that usage of *be + like* in the UK and Canada was following the template of development – both internally, in terms of its grammatical functions, and externally, in terms of the age and gender of its users – already laid out in the USA.

We have seen the role of women in linguistic innovation, and the instrumentality of age in dialect variation and change. These notwithstanding, the large-scale diffusion of *be + like* in such a short time among young people in such geographically separated territories indicates a degree of dialect levelling inexplicable solely by factors such as those of urbanisation and transport mentioned earlier. Face-to-face interaction on its own could never achieve so geographically widespread a pattern of usage so quickly. Further research on the role of film, television and the internet may yield greater insight into future developments within the varieties of English across the world: 'Thus, the diffusion of *be like* may be a very good linguistic indicator of the types of developments and changes we might expect from the putative ongoing globalization of English' (Tagliamonte and Hudson, 1999, p. 168).

Tag questions

Tag questions, so called since they are tagged on to the end of a main clause (*You are staying*, **aren't you?**), are prone to variation across a range of English dialects, as the following activity will show.

ACTIVITY 6.9

Allow about
20 minutes

Which of the following are from standard varieties of English? From these examples, are you able to write a rule which produces a standard tag? Do you recognise any of the non-standard examples? Which examples do you think you might hear from other speakers in the area where you live? Which do you think you might use?

1   Are you still working at Woolies, are you?
2   She has gone home, is it?
3   You did see it, didn't you?
4   She can come, can't she?
5   You're going tomorrow, isn't it?
6   You didn't see it, did you?
7   She can't come, can she not?
8   She can't come, can't she not?
9   He isn't going there, isn't it?
10 I am coming, aren't I?
11 I am coming, amn't I?

(examples from Milroy and Milroy, 1993; Trudgill and Hannah, 1994; Platt et al., 1984; and independent observation)

Comment

The standard examples are 3, 4, 6 and 10. You can see that the verb in the tag corresponds to the verb in the main clause (3 and 6, the auxiliary *did*; 4 the modal *can*; 10 has different forms – *am* and *are* – of the verb *be*):

3   You **did** see it, **did**n't you?
4   She **can** come, **can't** she?
6   You **did**n't see it, **did** you?
10 I **am** coming, **are**n't I?

When the verb is repeated in the tag, it undergoes a polarity shift, which is to say that if it is positive in the main clause (She **can** come), it becomes negative in the tag (*can't*); if it is negative in the main clause (you **didn't** see it), it becomes positive in the tag (*did*). The subject pronoun then follows the verb in the tag (*can't* **she**, *did* **you**). Interestingly, however, if we try to apply this rule to 10, the standard version, we end up with 11, a non-standard version.

Example 1, in which a positive main clause (a question) occurs with a positive tag, is a Scottish English construction not found in Standard British English. It also expects the answer yes. This construction is also found in Tyneside and Liverpool English.

Examples 7 and 8 come from Tyneside English and the relationship between them is slightly more complex. Beal (1993) suggests that in the case of 7, the speaker is requesting information, while in 8, the speaker is asking for confirmation (presumably of something already known or suspected).

Examples 2, 5 and 9 exemplify 'invariant tags': the form of the tag remains the same (*is it* or *isn't it*) regardless of the verb used in the main clause. This construction occurs in several varieties, including Welsh, Indian, West African, Malaysian and Singaporean English. Both positive and negative tags are free to appear in combination with either a positive or a negative main clause, to seek information or confirmation. The invariant tag is the same as that found in several other languages, including Hindi and Urdu *na*?, German *nicht wahr* and French *n'est-ce pas*?

6.10 Conclusion

In this chapter we have looked at just a few aspects of English grammar, focusing on grammatical features that have been both shared and found to vary among different varieties of English. As earlier chapters have shown, there are no really discrete varieties of English, but a great deal of overlap between them. Standardised varieties of language tend to show only limited variation, and most studies of variation have been based on non-standard varieties. The codification of standardised varieties has often led to a deceleration of change allowing non-standard varieties to drift more quickly towards regularising certain grammatical features.

Social considerations are to the fore in determining who speaks the standard language, while the range of grammatical features in different varieties is regionally determined. The age of speakers is a key factor in dialect development, though gender can also figure since women seem to take a leading role in language innovation.

Many traditional features of older rural dialects have disappeared due to the effects of dialect levelling, a process which also plays a leading role in the creation of new dialects such as southern hemisphere colonial Englishes. Dialect drift can also motivate similar developments in geographically separated dialects. Mainstream modern non-standard dialects across the world share a number of grammatical features as a consequence of these drivers. The role of mass communication and broadcasting in this regard is still being investigated.

Possibly the key issue of this chapter, though, has been to acknowledge how the different varieties of English throughout the world vary from each other on a rule-governed, systematic basis. It is not only Standard English which has grammar rules; non-standard varieties also have them – these varieties simply follow different rules, and any variety can be developed for use in any situation. As Holmes puts it:

> A language used by a tribe buried in the mountains of Papua New Guinea or the depths of the Amazonian rain forests has the potential for use at the nuclear physics conferences of the Western world, or in the most sensitive diplomatic negotiations between warring nations. There are no differences of linguistic form between varieties which would prevent them developing the language required for such purposes. The barriers are social and cultural.

> (Holmes, 2001, p. 190)

They are, however, very real barriers, since varieties inevitably acquire the status of their users, a fact which often succeeds in obscuring the more objective, linguistic assessment.

READING A: Singlish and Standard Singaporean English

Ann Hewings and Martin Hewings
(Ann Hewings is Senior Lecturer, Centre for Language and Communications
The Open University; Martin Hewings is Senior Lecturer, English for
International Students' Unit, University of Birmingham.)

Source: Hewings, A. and Hewings, M. (2005) *Grammar and Context: An Advanced Resource Book*, London, Routledge, pp. 79–80.

[N]ew varieties of English are ... recognised, particularly in former British colonies like India and Singapore, although the status of these varieties is often a matter of contention in the countries in which they are spoken. In Singapore, for example, the local variety that has developed as a means of informal communication between the various ethnic and language groups in the country is known as 'Singlish'. It derives features from a number of local languages, particularly Chinese and Malay. However, it is often compared unfavourably with Standard Singaporean English, which is much closer grammatically and lexically to other standard varieties of English, notably Standard British English. For example, the National University of Singapore ha a 'Promotion of Standard English' (PROSE) website which highlights, in a clearly critical way, features of Singlish. Singlish is described as

> a layman's ... term that could mean any of the following:

- **Colloquial Singapore English** that is used in informal contexts by someone who is highly competent in educated Singaporean English or standard Singaporean English.
- **Lower (mesolectal and basilectal) varieties** of Singaporean English used by the less competent speakers, producing utterances such as 'He m teacher', 'Why you say me until like that?' and 'I got not enough money'. (Note: *Basilect* and *mesolect* are terms used by sociolinguists, usually in the study of creoles. A basilect is a variety most remote from the prestige variety – here Standard Singaporean English – and a mesolect is closer to the prestige variety.)
- **Interlanguage or developmental varieties** of English produced by some language learners at the beginning stages.

Standard English is defined as:

> English that is internationally acceptable in formal contexts. In other words, someone speaking Standard English should be understood easily by educated English speakers all over the world.

(It is worth noting here that the website does not make clear whether 'Standard English' refers to Standard Singaporean English or some other, unspecified, variety of English.)

Examples of Singlish with the Standard English equivalents are also given, including:

Singlish:	Why you never bring come?
Standard English alternative:	Why didn't you bring it?
Singlish:	He take go already
Standard English alternative:	He has taken it with him.
Singlish:	How come nobody tell us this exam is open book one?
Standard English alternative:	Why didn't anybody tell us this is an open book exam?

Regular criticisms of Singlish by Singapore government officials and in newspaper editorials are other strands of the authorities' promotion of the use of Standard Singaporean English over Singlish. Their argument is that while Singlish has assisted in promoting inter-ethnic exchange and the forging of a Singaporean identity, it fails as a language for international communication because it is difficult for non-Singaporeans to understand, and is therefore seen as a handicap in economic expansion. This policy has extended to banning Singlish from television and advertisements, while strongly promoting the use of Standard Singaporean English in schools and higher education. What we can observe happening here then is the government labelling one Singaporean English dialect as inferior to another and reducing the situations in which the less valued variety can be used.

READING B: Modals on Tyneside

Joan Beal
*(Joan Beal is Director of the National Centre for English Cultural Tradition,
University of Sheffield.)*

Source: Beal, J. (1993) 'The grammar of Tyneside and Northumbrian English' in
Milroy, J. and Milroy, L. (eds) *Real English: The Grammar of English Dialects
in the British Isles*, London, Longman, pp. 194–7.

The use and nature of modal verbs in Tyneside is markedly different from that
of Standard English in several important ways.

First, *may* and *shall* are hardly ever used in Tyneside English (as also in Scots
English), and have no important part to play in the grammar. As in many other
non-standard dialects, *can* is used rather than *may* to express permission, but
in Tyneside, even the sense of possibility normally expressed by *may* is
carried by *might* instead, as in

(1) Mind, it looks as though it might rain, doesn't it?

(McDonald, 1981, p. 284)

There is, therefore, no strictly grammatical need for *may* in Tyneside, as it
has no function that cannot equally well be performed by *can* or *might*. If it
is used at all, it is as an ultra-polite and formal stylistic variant of *can*. *Shall*,
likewise, rarely occurs in Tyneside: for the expression of futurity, *will* or *'ll*
are used. This is also true of most dialects of English, where *will* varies with
shall even in standardized varieties. However, in most dialects, *shall* is used
in first person questions, such as '*Shall I* put the kettle on?' In Tyneside, as in
Scots and Irish English, *will* is used even here, thus '*Will I* put the kettle on?'

Secondly, there is a rule of Standard English that only one modal verb can
appear in a single verb phrase. Thus 'He must do it' is grammatical whilst* 'He
must can do it' is not. Indeed, Standard English has developed a whole battery
of 'quasi-modal' verbs to 'stand in' for modals where the meaning requires
them but the above rule forbids them. The meaning of the sentence would
therefore be expressed in Standard English as 'He must be able to do it'.

In Tyneside English, the rule inhibiting double modals does not apply so long
as the second modal is *can* or *could*. Thus the asterisked sentence would
conform to the rules of Tyneside English. These double modals are also found
in Scots and some American dialects, but more combinations of modals are
allowed in these dialects than in Tyneside. Furthermore, more combinations
are allowed in the dialects of rural Northumberland than in those of urban
Tyneside. For instance, the combination of *would* and *could* appears in the

urban area – but only in a negative form – whilst in rural Northumberland the positive form may be found. Examples from McDonald (1981, pp. 186–7) are:

(2)   I can't play on Friday. I work late. I might could get it changed, though.

(3)   The girls usually make me some (toasted sandwiches) but they mustn't could have made any today.

(4)   He wouldn't could've worked, even if you had asked him. (Tyneside)

(5)   A good machine clipper would could do it in half a day. (Northumberland)

Thirdly, in Standard English, certain adverbs are placed *before* main verbs but *after* modals, thus 'I only asked' and 'I can only ask'. In Tyneside English, adverbs may be placed before *can* and *could*. Examples from McDonald (1981, p. 214) are:

(6)   That's what I say to people. If they only could walk a little bit, they should thank God.

(7)   She just can reach the gate.

Fourthly, in Tyneside, as in other nonstandard dialects of English, *can* and *could* are used in perfective constructions where Standard English has *be able to*:

(8)   He cannot get a job since he's left school.

(9)   I says it's a bit of a disappointment, nurse. I thought I could've brought it back again.

(McDonald, 1981, pp. 215–6)

These sentences could be 'translated' into Standard English respectively as:

(10) He has not been able to get a job since he left school

(11) I thought I would have been able to bring it back again

Fifthly, there are several cases in which a modal or quasi-modal verb has a meaning in Tyneside different from its Standard English meaning or where a different modal is used to express the same meaning. It is important for the outsider to be aware of these differences; after all a double modal immediately strikes a non-Tynesider as odd, and alerts him to the need for careful interpretation, but where a familiar syntactic structure has a different meaning, it may turn out to be a 'false friend'. For example, in a sentence with the meaning 'the evidence forces me to conclude that ... not', Standard English would use *can't*, whilst Tyneside would use *mustn't*. Thus:

(12) The lift can't be working (Standard)

(13) The lift mustn't be working (Tyneside)

...

On the other hand, where Standard English uses *mustn't* to mean 'it is necessary not to ...', Tyneside uses *haven't got to* . Here, misunderstandings could easily arise: a Tynesider saying:

(14) You haven't got to do that!

means, not that you are not obliged to do it, but that you are obliged *not* to do it!

Reference for this reading

McDonald, C. (1981) Variation in the Use of Modal Verbs with Special Reference to Tyneside English, ... PhD thesis, University of Newcastle.

Style shifting, codeswitching
Joan Swann and Indra Sinka

7.1 Introduction

ELIZABETH Do not really wish to marry? I? I will marry. I have said so.
I hope to have children, otherwise I shall never marry.

[Mary and Elizabeth come together.]

MARY Indeed I wish that Elizabeth was a man and I would willingly
marry her! And wouldn't that make an end of all debates!

LA CORBIE But she isny. Naw, she isny. There are two queens in one
island, both o' the wan language – mair or less. Baith young
... mair or less. Baith mair or less beautiful. Each the ither's
nearest kinswoman on earth. And baith queens. Caw.
Caw. Caw....

LA CORBIE *[Rhyming]* Ony queen has an army o' ladies and maids
That she juist snaps her fingers tae summon.
And yet ... I ask you, when's a queen a queen
And when's a queen juist a wummin?

*[She cracks her whip, and the hectic and garish but proud Elizabeth bobs
a curtsy, immediately becoming Bessie.]*

MARY Bessie, do you think she'll meet me?

BESSIE Aye, your majesty, she'll meet wi' ye face to face at York, an'
you're richt, gin ye talk thegither it'll a' be soarted oot. If ye
hunt a' they courtiers and politicians an' men awa!

(Lochhead, 1989, pp. 15–16)

In Liz Lochhead's play about Mary Queen of Scots the same actor plays
Elizabeth I of England and Bessie, a maid to Mary. A change of language
marks a change of persona. The change is deliberate, practised and explicit –
heralded by La Corbie and the crack of a whip. It is also, you might say,
pretence. The actor is actually neither Elizabeth nor Bessie, she is simply
playing a couple of parts.

In this chapter we explore how speakers routinely draw on different varieties
of English, or on English and other languages, to communicative effect – albeit
rather less dramatically and without the aid of a script. We look at variation
within English, which has often been represented as a range of speaking styles
associated with different contexts. And we also look at how speakers switch

between languages, or language varieties, during the course of a single interaction.

We suggest that, in both cases, questions of social identity are at issue. Previous chapters have discussed the social meanings associated with different languages, or language varieties: how the language variety you use conveys certain information about you, such as where you come from and what kind of person you are. But language diversity and variability do not serve simply as social indicators: they also constitute a resource that can be drawn on by speakers, to represent different aspects of their identity or to balance competing identities.

While a great deal of work on speakers' variable language use has been concerned with social issues, the way speakers manage switches between languages also has implications for grammar. How does the grammar of English and other languages allow you to switch from one to another? What happens when you switch between English and another language with a very different grammar? We explore such issues briefly in the course of this chapter.

Finally, we try to draw together some different theories of speakers' variable language use.

7.2 Stylistic variation in English

The Bishop of Sheffield had referred, in a meeting, to social and regional divisions in Britain and suggested that the Queen should have a greater presence in the north.

'By gum, tha's got a reet rum session ahead o' thee, an' as I were only saying t' Bishop o' Sheffield t'other day ... '
(*Guardian*, 6 November 1984, p. 1)

My sister, she's a right little snobby ... if she came here now she'd speak plain English, but she can speak Patois better than me. She speaks it to me, to some of her coloured friends who she knows speak Patois, but to her snobby coloured friends she speaks English. She talks Queen English, brebber. She's the snotty one of the family.

(quoted in Edwards, 1986, p. 121)

ACTIVITY 7.1

Allow about
5 minutes

Spend a few minutes thinking about the various contexts in which you use spoken English during the course of a day. Forgetting for the moment about any other languages you may speak, are there any differences in the type(s) of English you use in different contexts?

Comment

The answer you give to this activity will clearly depend upon your own circumstances. You may find that, in general, you use a more standard variety of English at, for example, work than at home. But 'work' and 'home' may not be two discrete contexts. At work, you may need to take part in meetings, to talk about work topics on the phone, or to chat to colleagues over lunch. Talk at home could involve colleagues who are also friends and it may involve a variety of different topics – including what has been happening at work.

The way people talk will differ according to several contextual factors (where speakers are, who they are speaking to, what they are speaking about). It will differ along several linguistic dimensions (pronunciation, grammatical structures, choice of words). Furthermore, although speech variation has often been related to the formality of a context (so that a meeting is more formal than a chat over lunch), degree of formality alone isn't enough to explain variation. One of the authors comes from Newcastle-on-Tyne, in the north-east of England, and her daughter comments that she uses many more 'Geordie' (Newcastle) pronunciations when talking on the phone to her parents than when chatting at home in Milton Keynes.

We want to go on now to look at how linguists have attempted to document and explain this kind of variability in speech. We draw on the notion of style to refer, initially, to aspects of dialect and accent: to the way in which the pronunciations, choice of words and grammatical features associated with different varieties of English are used variably by speakers in different contexts.

Linguists investigating **stylistic** (or **contextual**) **variation** in this sense usually identify a set of **sociolinguistic variables** and see how these are realised (i.e. what form they take) in different contexts. Some of the studies of English dialect discussed in Chapter 6 identified a stylistic continuum that was associated with degree of formality: speakers used more 'prestige' or high-status features in more formal contexts, and more vernacular features in more informal contexts. Here, we extend this earlier discussion by looking at further examples of research on speaking style. These confirm that speakers draw on different forms of English in different contexts, but they also suggest that there is no single stylistic continuum: speaking style is better regarded as multidimensional.

Style and audience

Researchers have traditionally isolated certain features of context in order to examine how these relate to speaking style. In a key study of style, Allan Bell developed a theory of **audience design** which suggests that the person or people you are speaking to will have the greatest effect on the type of language you use. Bell studied the varieties of English used by newsreaders on New Zealand radio stations and found that their pronunciation differed on different stations. (Bell, 1991).

Bell investigated several sociolinguistic variables, including how speakers pronounced the /t/ in words such as *writer* and *better* (in New Zealand English this may have a standard [t] proununciation, technically a voiceless alveolar plosive; or it may be voiced, so that the words begin to sound like *rider* and *bedder*).

Bell discovered that what he termed the more 'formal' [t] pronunciation was used most often on a station with a mainly 'educated' or 'professional' audience, less on 'general audience' stations, and least on rock music stations. Furthermore, some newsreaders worked for more than one station, and in this case their pronunciations differed on different stations: they seemed to converge on a 'station style'. Bell claims that it is the different audiences for each station that affect newsreaders' speech, while other factors, such as the topic mix of the news and the studio setting, remain constant.

Radio stations might seem to be a special context, because speakers are speaking on behalf of a station rather than in their own voices. But there is a great deal of evidence that in face-to-face interactions speakers use different varieties of English depending on the person they are speaking to. The British linguist Peter Trudgill (1986) discusses a particularly striking example of this in his own speech. As part of a sociolinguistic survey of English in Norwich in the east of England, Trudgill interviewed a range of informants from different social backgrounds. Later, he returned to this data to analyse his own speech, comparing his pronunciation with that of his informants. As Bell had done, one of the variables Trudgill looked at was the /t/ phoneme: in Norwich, as in several other parts of the UK, the pronunciation of /t/ in words such as *better* or *bet* may move towards a glottal stop [ʔ] (often represented in writing as *be'er*).

Figure 7.1 shows Trudgill's results for this variable. In most cases he tended to use slightly more glottal stops than the informant he was speaking to. He attributes this to his age: he was twenty-four at the time, younger than these informants, and glottal stops are used more frequently by younger speakers. Although numbers are small, Trudgill also seems to have used a higher number of glottal stops when talking to his male informants – a finding consistent with some other research that has shown speakers of both sexes use more non-standard features when talking to men than to women. The overall pattern of his speech, however, is remarkable for the way in which it mirrors that of his informants.

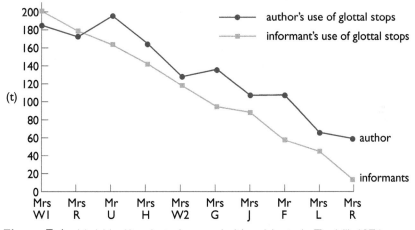

Figure 7.1   Variable (t): selected scores in Norwich study, Trudgill, 1974 (Trudgill, 1986, p. 8)

Nikolas Coupland (1984) found something very similar when he analysed the speech of a female assistant in a travel agency in Cardiff, in Wales. Here again, Coupland found her pronunciation of certain sounds mirrored that of her clients. In fact, he comments that the assistant's pronunciations were almost as good an indicator of the social class and educational background of her clients as the pronunciations of the clients themselves.

Both Trudgill and Coupland argue that these speakers were 'converging' towards the speech of their interlocutors: they were trying to sound similar to them. This notion of speech convergence derives from a theory concerned with motivations for stylistic variation known as **accommodation theory**, which was introduced in Chapter 6, Sections 6.5 and 6.8. The theory suggests that speakers will **converge** towards their interlocutor when they wish to reduce social distance, or get on with one another. They will **diverge** (i.e. become linguistically less similar) when they wish to emphasise their distinctiveness or increase social distance. It seems plausible to argue in each of these cases that the speakers wish to get on with their interlocutors because they need something from them: custom, in the case of the travel agency assistant; cooperation in carrying out the interview, in the case of the researcher. (Accommodation theory is consistent with Bell's theory of audience design. We return to both these theories in Section 7.4.)

Style and other factors

In the research we have discussed so far, the assumption was that speakers were in the same place, talking about similar topics – only the audience differed. Other research has set out to construct contexts so that the influence of different factors (including audience) may be examined. This was something attempted by Viv Edwards and her co-researchers in their study of the speech of young black people in Dudley, in the west Midlands area of England. Edwards's research (Edwards, 1986) was conducted as a set of interviews, with informants recorded in small single-sex groups in a researcher's flat. Within these constraints, five different 'situations' were created as follows.

1	Formal interview with white researcher	Group interviewed about education by older white researcher, smartly dressed and referred to as 'Mr Sutcliffe' by other researchers.
2	Formal interview with black fieldworker	Group interviewed by a black fieldworker of the same sex as group members; researcher uses a questionnaire and asks about interests and leisure pursuits.
3	Informal conversation with white student	Group left alone with Jeremy, a young white student from the same area. Jeremy is casually dressed and explains he is not part of the research team, but interested in some of the things they have been discussing.
4	Discussion by black peer group	Group left alone to talk about questionnaire they will be asked to complete later. Questions cover attitudes to mainstream white society; treatment of young black people by police, etc.
5	Informal conversation with black fieldworker	Group with black fieldworker in conversation over biscuits and drinks towards the end of the session.

Different terms are used for the varieties of English spoken by black people in Britain, as well as in the USA, and these have often aroused controversy. Older research has used terms such as 'Black Vernacular English' or, in Britain, 'British Black English'. The term 'Ebonics' has been used more recently for varieties spoken in the USA; linguists often prefer the term 'African American Vernacular English' or 'African American English'. British researchers often prefer 'creole', in recognition of the variety's origins in Jamaican Creole and other creoles. In this case, Edwards made the decision to retain the term used by informants.

Edwards was interested in the extent to which speakers used a variety they termed 'Patois', in these different contexts. She identified a number of features that varied (i.e. that occurred as either 'English' or 'Patois' variants). The entire list of variables is shown in Table 7.1. Some of these are pronunciation features; for example, whether the first sound in *then* is pronounced *th* or *d* (phonetically [ð] or [d]). But most are features of grammar; for example, whether a speaker says *John **swims** fast* or *John **swim** fast*.

Table 7.1 Linguistic variables in the Patois index

1 *Dentals*
   English variants: /θ/, /ð/ as in /θɪk/ (thick), /ðɛn / (then)
   Patois variants: /t/, /d/ as in /tɪk/ (thick), /dɛn/ (then)

2 *Vowels*
   English variants: /ʌ/ (Received Pronunciation), /ʊ/ (Midlands and north of England) as in /rʌn/, /rʊn/ (run)
   Patois variant: /o/ as in /ron/ (run)

3 *Third person singular present tense verbs*
   English variant: John *swims* fast; Kevin *eats* a lot
   Patois variant: John *swim* fast; Kevin *eat* a lot

4 *Plurals*
   English variant: six *cars;* all the *books*
   Patois variant: six *car;* all di *book*

5 *Simple past tense*
   English variants: Winston *saw* the boy; Beverley *walked* away
   Patois variant: Winston *see* di boy; Beverley *walk* away

6 *Copulas* (before adjectives and verbs)
   English variants: The man *is* happy; John *is* coming
   Patois variants: Di man happy; John *a* come

7 *First person singular pronoun*
   English variant: *I* feel happy
   Patois variant: *me* feel happy

8 *Third person singular pronouns*
   English variant: *he* put it away
   Patois variant: *im* put it away

9 *Third person plural pronouns and possessives*
   English variants: *they* like the baby; look at *their* hats
   Patois variant: *dem* like di baby; look at *dem* hat

10 *Infinitives*
   English variant: John asked *to* see it
   Patois variant: John aks *fi* see it

11 *Negatives*
   English variant: The boy *doesn't* want it
   Patois variant: Di boy *no* want it

(based on Edwards, 1986, p. 80)

Edwards noted how often English or Patois forms were used by different speakers and in different situations. The average scores for use of English/Patois variants in each situation are shown in Table 7.2.

Table 7.2 Average scores for English/Patois variants

Situation	1	2	3	4	5
Average score	94.43	87.05	92.37	56.71	69.89

Note: figures are expressed as a percentage, where a score of 100 would mean use of only English variants and a score of 0 would mean use of only Patois variants.

(Edwards, 1986, p. 81)

ACTIVITY 7.2

Allow 5–10 minutes

How does the young people's speech seem to vary in the five contexts just discussed? What might explain this variation?

Comment

The first thing that is striking is that audience seems to have an effect; in particular, the presence or absence of a white interlocutor affects the speakers' use of Patois features. Situation 3, the conversation with Jeremy, the white student, is designated informal but elicits very few Patois features – almost as few as the formal interview with the white researcher.

But the format of the interaction also seems to affect people's speech. In situation 2, a formal interview, there is far less use of Patois than in situation 5, an informal conversation, although the same person (a black fieldworker) is involved in each case.

Patois features occur least of all in situation 1, the formal interview with the white researcher; they occur most in Situation 4, the informal conversation with no outsider present.

We would also want to point out that we have no guarantee that the young speakers interpreted the situations in the same way as the researchers.

Finally, the results quoted are average figures: there were considerable differences among speakers (e.g. some used more Patois features throughout than others) and among the incidence of different features.

Edwards's research, like that of Bell, Trudgill and Coupland, is mainly quantitative; she identifies linguistic features that can be counted up to allow a numerical comparison between their use by different speakers and in different contexts. But she also presents us with case studies, which give a fuller account of individual speakers' use of language.

Below are extracts from the speech of two informants: Don, who is particularly hostile towards mainstream white society and whose life 'centres very firmly on the black community'; and Darleen, who has more connections within the white community and more limited knowledge of several aspects of black language and culture (Edwards, 1986). The author's commentary is included with the extracts of speech.

> After completing the questionnaire ... Don offers his candid opinions to the black fieldworker and the other participants:

> > Dem [the questions] alright in away, right. Dem reasonable. Dem coulda be lickle better, but dem reasonable. Me na bex (angry) wid dem, dem alright ... When white people ready fi write some rubbish bout black people, dem can do it, dem can do it, right. So dat's why me say dem reasonable. Notn wrong wid dem.

> This short extract illustrates a wide range of [Patois] features ... The phonology is consistently Patois; he uses Patois pronouns *mi* and *dem;* adjectival verbs *bex, reasonable* and *alright; fi* before an infinitive. ...

> [Don's] most 'English' performance ... is in the formal white interview. When talking about the origins of black culture, for instance, he says:

> > I say it come from Africa really. It started from dere tru slavery. Dat's di way I see it. It started from there, yeah. But those kids what born over here right, they don't want to admit it. Like Paddy, they don't want to admit it right that our culture started from Africa.

> Don's language in this situation is highly variable. Whereas in black peer-group conversation he shows an overwhelming preference for Patois variants, in the white interview he chooses a much higher proportion of English variants including inflected past tenses, negatives with *don't* and copulas. While he still uses Patois features like dental stops (*tru, dere, di*) and adjectival verbs (*born*), the number and range of these features is very limited.

> ...

> [Darleen's English is marked] by a high incidence of specifically Black Country dialect forms such as *her, wor, cor, ay* and copulas in (*a*) *m* [e.g. *you'm out* in the extract below]. In describing facilities for young people in Dudley, for instance, she says:

> > Just walk up the streets and you'm out of Dudley, know what I mean? In Birmingham, I don't know, I just get round a nice shop – I'm lost in it. But if you just walk up the High Street you'm out ... The other best thing in Dudley is the Trident Centre, that's what I think, there by Sainsbury's. You can sit down there. I said to Michael today, 'That's the best thing in Dudley, ay it?'

The only time when Darleen uses Patois is when left alone with her friends. ... She shows only a narrow range of Patois features, making variable use of Patois dentals and vowels and uninflected nouns and verbs. Otherwise Patois is limited to *mi, im, dem* and the continuative particle *a* [the particle marking continuous duration of action, as in the extract below]:

> Wa happen? Me a go say you a go get what you a look for? (*What happened? I'm going to say that you're going to get what you're looking for.*)

She is very aware of the limitations in her Patois:

> Tell the truth, we'm very up on our English. We talk slang sometime in Patois ... If I was in Jamaica now I'd be brought up to talk like that, but it's a white community.

(Edwards, 1986, pp. 88–92)

There is a danger, when presenting a generalised and quantitative account of speaker style, of seeing speakers as responding somewhat mechanically to context. Edwards's case studies suggest that things are more complex: that one needs to take account of speakers' feelings about language and about the contexts in which they are speaking. This is borne out by one or two other studies, such as some research carried out by Jenny Cheshire on the speech of young, white working-class speakers in Reading, in the south-east of England. Like Edwards, Cheshire was interested in the incidence of non-standard grammatical features, but these were features associated with Reading vernacular English, such as the non-standard present-tense verb forms in the following examples:

> I starts Monday, so shut your face
> You knows my sister, the one who's small
> They calls me all the names under the sun

(quoted in Cheshire, 1982)

Cheshire found that, on the whole, her young informants used fewer vernacular features when they were recorded at school than when they were recorded in a local adventure playground. But speakers differed in the extent to which they adapted their speech in the school context. She suggests that differences between speakers have to do with their familiarity with school and knowledge of school conventions (for instance, that Standard English is associated with talk in the classroom), and also with how they feel about school (so that pupils who identify with the school culture, or who get on with a teacher, are more likely to adapt their speech and produce fewer non-standard forms). Speakers, then, are making their own constructions of context: it is their perceptions of, and feelings about, people and situations that affect the way they speak. Nor are contexts fixed. Cheshire (1982, p. 125) comments that speakers continually reassess the context and adjust their speaking style accordingly.

Michael Huspek, similarly, had to take account of his informants' feelings about people and events in his study of the speech of lumber workers in a large industrial city in north-west USA. Huspek worked with a group of lumber workers for twenty-eight months over a four-year period, and recorded several interviews with them. From these, he was able to identify features that varied according to the linguistic context and to the topic the men were talking about (Huspek, 1986). One feature he identified was *-in/-ing* as a verb ending; for instance, whether a speaker said ***sittin*** or ***sitting***. This feature has often been selected as a sociolinguistic variable in English as it has been found to vary widely among different speakers and in different contexts. Huspek found that the men he studied most frequently used the *-in* variant, but did introduce *-ing* forms in certain circumstances. In the following passage the speaker switches from an informal to a more formal register to talk about a scientific topic (this switch is marked by the use of some *-ing* forms, shown in italics):

> I myself think it's where our source of energy is gonna come from. And nuclear power. I think we're gettin' into an area where we don't know that much about. And I myself feel we're gonna start sump'm that we're not gonna be able ta stop. Say a chain reaction, or somebody *splitting* some atom or other, that's gonna start *chain-reacting* an' it's not gonna be able to get stopped.

> (quoted in Huspek, 1986, p. 154, original emphasis)

Huspek argues that the *-ing* form may also be used in relation to someone who is respected by the speaker: *His engine was pur**ring** just like a kitten*. But also, presumably ironically, it may signal disrespect or resentment, as in the following example:

> We were jus' sittin' there on the beach tokin' away on this big doobie y'know when along comes this straight guy jogging along. He was all really decked out, y'know. He had lotsa bucks too. Y'know, I mean you could tell it by his clothes an' like that. So Jerry yells over at 'im: 'Heyman, you're *doing* real fine!'

> (quoted in Huspek, 1986, p. 155, original emphasis)

Huspek argues that the *-ing* variant is recognised as a prestige form, hence it is used when workers discuss the actions of 'high-prestige others'. But the workers' feelings about such people are somewhat ambivalent and so the 'prestige' form does not have entirely positive connotations.

More recent work by Willis (2002), which follows, in part, the research design set out by Edwards (1986), looks at codeswitching strategies among fifteen young (aged 15 to 30+) African-Caribbean people in Sheffield, in the north of England. Willis analysed recordings made between 1992 and 1994 to determine Sheffield Jamaican Creole usage and competence. The data were analysed both quantitatively (giving the number of types and tokens of creole used) and qualitatively (to look at interaction). The quantitative data show that the males used more creole than the females. Willis suggests that this may be as a result of a higher level of education among the females and a greater acceptance of standardised forms of English. The qualitative data provide further evidence for the need to take into account speakers' feelings: the older males interviewed were more critical about society than the females or younger males, sometimes showing anger or frustration regarding white superiors at work and using more creole to define their identity. Throughout the study it is evident that creole-English bilingualism 'plays a key role in defining the identity of its speakers, essentially that of being black African in a white society' (Willis, 2002, p. 127).

What else needs to be taken into account?

We have tried to select a range of studies that examine different features of English, that focus on different contexts, or aspects of context, and that, to some extent at least, employ different methods of investigating style. But this evidence still presents us with a rather limited picture of style in English. The evidence suggests that speakers vary the way they speak depending, at least, upon:

- the person or people they are speaking to (different clients in a travel agency)
- the setting (in school or an adventure playground)
- the format of the interaction (an interview or informal conversation)
- the topic being discussed (a switch to a scientific topic may produce a change in speaking style).

But evidence from any one study is extremely partial and what is found depends upon how the research is constructed – or what the researcher sets out to look for. However, the studies themselves do show that even more factors need to be taken into account, for instance the following ones.

- We have already suggested that these studies, perhaps necessarily, employ a simplified model of context: speakers are not merely responding to predetermined contextual features such as audience, setting and topic but to their own interpretations, or constructions of context. Different aspects of context will be more or less salient for different speakers. In addition, speaking style should not be seen simply as responsive: in using certain pronunciations when speaking about scientific research (for instance), speakers are also establishing this as a certain kind of topic (e.g. formal, high status).

- Each study has investigated variables that have 'prestige' and 'vernacular' forms. These have a cluster of associations. For instance, prestige varieties of English are associated with speakers and listeners with high socio-economic status and with settings and topics that have been characterised as formal, and perhaps also 'high status' (e.g. school setting, scientific topic). Vernacular varieties are set in opposition to these at the other end of the spectrum. We are presented with a unidimensional picture of style, in that speakers' variable use of language is seen to run along a single stylistic continuum.

- But it is also apparent from the studies that rather more is going on. Trudgill, in discussing his own variable pronunciation, mentions the potential influence of gender reflected in his use of more glottal stops to male than to female interlocutors. It is likely that he is responding to more than one aspect of his informants' social identities. In Edwards's study of speech in Dudley there are two vernaculars, Patois and local Black Country speech; Edwards contrasts only 'Patois' and 'English', but within the 'English' category speakers probably have access to more and less standard forms. The same can be said of Willis's study of creole and English use in Sheffield. Here again, style is likely to operate in more than one dimension, allowing speakers access to a more complex range of social meanings.

- Saying that styles have certain associations may suggest that their meanings are obvious or unambiguous. But one cannot simply 'read off' a certain meaning from a speaker's style. Huspek (1986), for instance, suggests that the same pronunciation feature (-*ing*) could convey either 'respect' or 'disrespect': you need a certain amount of contextual knowledge to interpret the use of different linguistic features.

- Studies of style, like studies of other aspects of variation discussed in Chapter 6, tend to isolate and quantify a small number of linguistic features. However, in varying the way they speak, people will draw on a whole set of features, including those that are less easy to measure (e.g. tone of voice). These will combine with, or be counterbalanced by, other non-verbal features (e.g. posture, facial expression); in practice, linguistic choices play a part in highly complex negotiations of social meanings.

Some research has adopted a more complex model of style, seeing this as multidimensional and as representing different, perhaps competing, aspects of social identity. We look at examples of this in the following section.

Multistyle

The individual creates for himself [*sic*] the patterns of his linguistic behaviour so as to resemble those of the group or groups with which from time to time he wishes to be identified, or so as to be unlike those from whom he wishes to be distinguished.

(Le Page and Tabouret-Keller, 1985, p. 181)

R.B. Le Page and Andrée Tabouret-Keller's work was carried out in multilingual communities, including several Caribbean countries, but their ideas have been influential among researchers with an interest in monolingual stylistic variation. They suggest that the desire to identify with, or distinguish oneself from, particular social groups is a major factor influencing speakers' choice of language variety. But they also allow for fluctuating patterns of usage (the phrase 'from time to time' is important here) and for the fact that speakers may have various (perhaps conflicting) motivations to speak in certain ways.

Trudgill (1983a) also draws on such ideas in order to analyse the way British rock and pop singers in the 1950s modified their pronunciations when singing in ways that were different from their usual speaking styles. The overall effect of this was to make the singers sound more 'American'. Trudgill compares this with other singing styles, such as folk singers attempting rural accents and reggae singers sounding more Jamaican.

Trudgill argues that US singers also modified their accents. The target in this case was the pronunciation used by southern or black singers, because 'it is in the American South and/or amongst Blacks that many types of popular music have their origin' (Trudgill, 1983a, p. 146). British singers were probably also aiming at this target, but they didn't always make it. For instance, British singers tended to pronounce an /r/ non-prevocalically in words such as *girl* in imitation of US pronunciation in speech; but US singers, who would use /r/ in this position in their speech, tended to omit it in singing in imitation of the target southern variety.

Slanging in Singapore

Americanised pronunciations occur in several contexts. For instance, in Singapore some individuals may adopt salient features of American English to transmit a Westernised identity. The features most commonly adopted are non-prevocalic /r/, and the replacement of intervocalic /t/ with /d/ in imitation of the US 'tap' pronunciation. This adoption of an Americanised accent, as opposed to a Singaporean accent, is called 'slanging' in Singapore. Those who do this have been satirised in comic books and in sketches.

(We are grateful to the sociolinguist Anthea Fraser Gupta for this observation.)

Trudgill found that, among British rock and pop groups, patterns fluctuated with different trends in pop music. An interesting pattern emerged in the 1970s with the advent of punk music, associated with urban working-class life and anti-mainstream values. When singing, punk-rock singers adopted certain low prestige southern English features that they did not necessarily use in speech. Such features were used alongside 'American' pronunciations, although they were in conflict with them:

> For [many punk-rock singers] there is a genuine split in motivation. The conflict is between a motivation towards a supposedly American model,

and towards a supposedly British working-class model – which can be glossed as a conflict between 'how to behave like a genuine pop singer' and 'how to behave like a British urban working-class youth'. The combination of linguistic forms that is typically found in punk-rock singing is an attempt to find a balance between the two.

(Trudgill, 1983a, p. 159)

ACTIVITY 7.3

Now read 'Hark, Hark the Lark: multiple voicing in DJ talk', by Nikolas Coupland (Reading A). This is a study of one speaker, Frank Hennessy (FH), a disc jockey in Cardiff, Wales, and how he uses accent during his radio programme.

Coupland's study is useful at this point because it both builds on and extends much of the work discussed above. Coupland is interested in stylistic variation; he begins by identifying a set of sociolinguistic variables (in this case, pronunciation features) and goes on to see how these are realised in different contexts. He assigns each pronunciation a numerical score, according to whether it is more or less vernacular.

But Coupland's analysis departs in significant ways from many previous studies, and takes account of most of the additional factors that we listed in the previous subsection. As you work through the reading we suggest you note particularly the results of Coupland's analysis and the interpretations he offers; for example:

- the notion of 'micro contexts': how FH's speaking style can be related to these
- Coupland's insistence on the creativity of this process; for example, FH as the 'orchestrator of contexts' (in the last sentence under 'Options for interpretation'), and his 'stylistic creativity' (opening sentence of the reading)
- the different sets of pronunciation features drawn on by FH (from Cardiff English and other varieties) and the interplay of meanings this gives rise to
- Coupland's concluding discussion of Cardiff English as a 'voice' – a way of speaking that has complex associations drawn from other speakers and other contexts, and that can be manipulated by speakers to express different identities and relate to listeners in different ways.

(Many of these points recur in Sections 7.3 and 7.4 of this chapter.)

Coupland refers to FH's status as a 'performer' and it is interesting that many ideas about speaking style have come from research on 'performers' of one sort or another, including newsreaders, pop singers and DJs. Such cases highlight the problematical nature of audience, as this has traditionally been investigated by sociolinguists. You may, for instance, question who the audience actually is that is being addressed in Coupland's study. Coupland himself has conceded that further work is needed on style in a wider range of contexts.

7.3 Switching in and out of English

Je suis une Canadienne-francaise I guess
(I'm a French-Canadian I guess)

(quoted in Heller, 1990, p. 67)

So far we have focused on style as a phenomenon that operates within English. But for a great many speakers, English is only one of a number of languages at their disposal. In bilingual and multilingual communities, style may be expressed by the selection of one language in preference to another. Chapter 1 discussed both patterns of language use, and the social meanings associated with English and other languages in several bilingual contexts. It was suggested there that, by opting for English or another language, speakers were tapping into a whole set of social meanings with which the language has become associated. But bilingual speakers need not keep their languages separate. One possibility open to them is to **codeswitch** – to switch back and forth between languages, thus capitalising on the associations of each language, or 'keeping a foot in each camp'.

It is worth noting here that definitions of codeswitching vary and that the term may also be used quite broadly in the literature to refer, for example, to switching between dialects. As Woolard (2004, p. 74) notes, codeswitching is generally seen in a positive light by today's researchers as use of language that is 'systematic, skilled and socially meaningful'. This has not always been the case, though, and in the past codeswitching was often viewed negatively, suggesting that 'the use of more than one linguistic variety in an exchange is neither grammatical nor meaningful but rather is indicative of a speaker's incomplete control of the language(s)' (Woolard, 2004, p. 74). Despite this academic change in direction, many communities still view codeswitching as a defective use of language and heated debate surrounding this issue continues (you may find it useful at this point to refer back to Chapter 1, Section 1.4, and the discussion surrounding the use of Sheng in Kenya).

A large amount of research on bilingual codeswitching has looked at the use of English alongside other languages. This no doubt reflects researchers' own backgrounds and the dominance of English within academic life, as well as the prevalence of English as a second (or third, etc.) language in so many parts of the world. Researchers have been interested both in the meanings and functions of codeswitching and in how switching works linguistically. We consider both aspects in the sections that follow.

Why switch?

ACTIVITY 7.4

Reading B, 'Codeswitching with English: types of switching, types of communities', is from Carol Myers-Scotton's paper on codeswitching in Zimbabwe and Kenya. (Remember that Chapter 1, Section 1.4, discussed patterns of language use in Kenya – focusing on the use of Kiswahili, English and Sheng; you may find it useful to refer back to this.)

Work through Reading B now, noting down what the researcher has to say about motivations for codeswitching. Our comments are included in the discussion that follows this activity.

The reading suggests that, like the use of different speaking styles by monolingual speakers, bilingual codeswitching is meaningful: it fulfils certain functions in an interaction. Myers-Scotton's **markedness model** suggests that particular codes (in this case, languages) are associated with, and therefore expected in, particular contexts (her Example 1 shows the use of Swahili with a security guard and English with a receptionist). Codeswitching itself may be the unmarked (expected) choice in certain contexts (as in Myers-Scotton's Examples 2 and 3).

A speaker's choice of language has to do with maintaining or negotiating a certain type of social identity. The use of a particular language also gives access to rights and obligations associated with that identity. Codeswitching between languages allows speakers (simultaneous) access to rights and obligations associated with different social identities. Myers-Scotton's examples of 'unmarked switching' from Kenya and Zimbabwe (Examples 2 and 3 respectively) show speakers balancing different aspects of their identity by switching between an African language and English.

Switching may sometimes operate to initiate a change to relationships, or to make salient different aspects of the context (for instance, Myers-Scotton's Example 4, of 'marked' – or unexpected – switching, in which a switch to English communicates authority).

Codeswitching is useful in cases of uncertainty about relationships: it allows speakers to feel their way and negotiate identities in relation to others (see, for instance, Myers-Scotton's illustration of 'exploratory switching' in Example 5, in which a young man attempts to negotiate higher status through English).

Researchers interested in the meanings or functions of codeswitching have sometimes tried to establish social meanings at a very general level. One of the best known examples of this is the distinction identified by John Gumperz (1982) between 'we' codes (associated with home and family) and 'they' codes (associated with more public contexts). In many bilingual and multilingual contexts it would be easy to suggest that English functions as the 'they' code because it is often associated with education, formality, and public rather than private arenas. This, however, suggests a view of meaning as something rather fixed and static. It is clear from the reading you have just studied that codeswitching needs to be interpreted in context. Myers-Scotton points out that in Kenya, English can encode both social distance and solidarity, depending on the context. Meanings are also subject to change and within any one context meanings are by no means unambiguous. In fact, one of the values of switching is that it permits a certain amount of ambiguity in contexts and in relations between people.

The research by Myers-Scotton looked at switching between English and other (distinct) languages, but switching also takes place between more closely related varieties. The following transcript, from research carried out by Mark Sebba, shows Brenda (B), a seventeen-year-old of Jamaican parentage, switching from London English to 'creole' (a London variety based on Jamaican Creole) to create an impression of a character in a narrative. (Transcripts of spoken language are not always easy to read! In this case the list of transcript conventions should help.)

1	B	now 'e ad everyfing if you was to sit down an
2		'ear that guy speak (.) ⌈ 'e (was going) to Jamaica
3		⌊ 'e was ni:ce (0.8) 'e was ni:ce
4	B	'e was going to *build 'is place* (0.6)
5		⌈ *'im a build 'is business (1.0)*
6	?	⌊ ye:h 'e was NI:CE man
7	B	an' it's the type of guy like that (0.6) I want

Transcription conventions
- each line of the transcript is numbered for ease of reference
- deep brackets [indicate overlapping speech
- (.) means a brief pause; (0.8) means a timed pause (0.8 seconds)
- switches to creole are in italics
- : indicates a lengthened vowel sound
- capitals indicate speaker emphasis

(Sebba, 1993, p. 113)

Brenda is talking about a man who is the type of man she would like to marry. She begins talking in London English about his plans to go to Jamaica, then switches to creole. She switches back to London English to describe her own feelings. Sebba quotes an earlier commentary he made on this extract, arguing that the switch to creole creates, or 'animates', the character Brenda is describing:

The switch to Creole occurs before the first instance of *'build 'is'* and this could be taken as a direct quotation of the man's words, rendered in Creole because he is apparently a Jamaican: cf. Brenda's 'if you was to sit down an' ear that guy speak'. More interestingly, however, this switch somehow indexes a culture for which this goal stands as an ideal: building your own place is a plausible goal in the Jamaican culture but very unusual in Britain, especially for a black person.

(Sebba, 1993, p. 121)

Sebba found that young British black speakers switched routinely between creole and London English in conversation with one another. He suggests, like Myers-Scotton, that codeswitching is related to different aspects of a speaker's identity – it gives them 'a foot in each camp'. It is also possible to attribute meaning to particular switches. During mainly creole conversation, a switch to English may be used for an aside. In contrast, a switch from English to creole marks out a sequence as salient: it stands out; it is the part of the utterance that other parties in the interaction respond to.

In the following transcript, Brenda has recounted to friends how she rebuffed the advances of a boy at a party who had been told by another boy that Brenda *had called him and wanted him*. Here, she adds that she did agree to dance with the boy but she had nothing else in mind.

B	1	then I just laughed (0.6) and then 'e – 'e just pulled me for a
	2	dance – I didn't mind dancin' ⌈ wiv 'im 'cause *me know say, me*
(J	3	⌊ yeah)
	4	*no 'ave nothin' inna my mind* ⌈ but to dance, and then we
(J	5	⌊ yeah)
	6	star?ed to talk and all the rest of ⌈ it and tha?s ⌈ it *full stop!*
(J	7	⌊ yeah ⌊ yeah)
(2.0)	8	
J	9	'e was a nice guy, but differently, right

Transcription conventions

- each line of the transcript is numbered for ease of reference
- ? represents a glottal stop
- deep brackets [indicate overlapping speech
- (.) means a brief pause; (0.6) means a timed pause (0.6 seconds)
- switches to Creole are in italics
- J's occasional contributions of 'yeah' have been placed in brackets because they give conversational support rather than being turns in their own right.

(adapted from Sebba, 1993, p. 111)

The salient parts of Brenda's story occur in the switches to creole in lines 2 and 4 and line 6, where she explains why she agreed to dance. Sebba suggests rather tentatively that, while speakers use both creole and English at home and among peers to discuss a range of topics, creole may feel closer to the 'heart and mind' and thus may impart greater salience to an utterance.

Codeswitching approaches have tended to be used to look at the variable language use of bilingual or bidialectal speakers where, even when two varieties are related, switches are relatively easy to identify. But in practice the distinction between (bilingual or bidialectal) codeswitching and (monolingual) style shifting becomes rather blurred. There is a problem, discussed in earlier chapters, of establishing clear linguistic boundaries between 'varieties' and attributing features unambiguously to one or another. Furthermore, as Coupland showed in Reading A, it's possible to apply an approach that looks very like an analysis of codeswitching to style shifting within English. Sebba's data is also quite similar to Edwards's examples of the use of Patois and English in Dudley. Edwards isolated certain features and counted how often they were realised as Patois or English variants, thus allowing her to make a numerical comparison between the language used by different speakers and in different contexts. Sebba, on the other hand, focused on how his speakers drew strategically on English and creole during conversations. Sebba comments on the analysis by Edwards: 'it tells us whether that person uses many or few Patois features overall in their talk, but nothing about how he or she uses Patois and English as part of a communicative strategy' (Sebba, 1993, p. 36).

Quantitative analyses of style and qualitative analyses of codeswitching can therefore be regarded as different methods, underpinned by different views of what is important about language, as much as responses to different sorts of data.

Switching and grammar

The examples of codeswitching quoted in this chapter and its associated readings show that, as well as fulfilling a number of social functions, switching can take a variety of different forms. Speakers may switch from one language to another at a clause boundary, or a long sequence in one language may be followed by a switch to another. But often switches occur within a clause and involve a more intimate mix of two or more languages. This poses an interesting question about grammar: when switches occur between two language varieties with distinct grammars, what is the grammar of the whole utterance? Are both grammars somehow involved, or does one win out – and if so, which one?

(As in Reading B, in the following transcriptions English is in normal type, a second language is in italics, a third language is in small capitals, and the English translation is on the right.)

J'ai la– la philosophie ancienne on va dire, que, tu sais, si tu as faim, get off your ass and go and work, *tu sais?*	I have the– the old philosophy, let's say, that, you know, if you're hungry, get off your ass and go and work, you know?

[Switching between French and English in Canada]

(Poplack et al., 1988, p. 53)

Yahāā kii kampaniyāā ejentō kō *baRaa paesaa detii hāē*	Companies here give a lot of money to the agents.

[Switching between Hindi and English in India]

(Kumar, 1986, p. 201)

NINDANGA NA KAKAMEGA, *watu huko wanatumia Kiswahili,* English, *na Luyia* . You know, this is a Luyia land and therefore most of the people who live in rural areas do visit this town often. *Kwa hiyvo huwa sana sana wanatumia Kiluyia na Kiswahili. Lakini wale ambao wanaishi katika town yenyewe, wanatumia Kiswahili sana.*	To start with Kakamega, people there use Swahili, English and Luyia. You know, this is a Luyia land and therefore most of the people who live in rural areas do visit this town often. Therefore they use Luyia and Swahili very much. But those who live in the town itself, they use Swahili very much.

[Switching between Luyia, Swahili and English in Kenya]

(Myers-Scotton, 1993a, p. 4)

ACTIVITY 7.5

Allow about
10 minutes

How do the switches into English differ in the examples above? What seems to happen to the grammar of the English switched items in each case?

Comment

In the switch from French to English, whole clauses are switched. English grammar is observed within the switched text.

In the Hindi/English example, single words from English are switched. The spellings *kampani* and *ejent* suggest that these words are drawing on the Hindi sound system. Neither word has the English plural marker s but they each have a Hindi morpheme attached to them. (In fact, ō and *yāā* are plural morphemes in Hindi.) An English speaker unfamiliar with Hindi might not even recognise these words as English.

The third example involves three languages, Luyia, Swahili and English. A whole English sentence is switched, which retains its own grammar. Later, the word *town* is switched. Since conventional spelling is used it is not clear whether this shows traces of the Swahili sound system.

These switches may look different, but while switching occurs at different points in an utterance, and involves different linguistic items, it is not random: switches follow certain patterns and so are subject to grammatical constraints. Over the years, a great deal of research effort has gone into determining these constraints and several proposals have been put forward in an attempt to understand the nature of bilingual codeswitching.

One model, which we shall focus on here, called the Matrix Language Frame (MLF) model, has been put forward by Myers-Scotton (1993a) and colleagues (Jake et al., 2002). Myers-Scotton argues that within any stretch of codeswitching one language can be seen as the main, 'matrix', language, in that it provides a frame into which items from the other language, or languages, may be embedded. It is the grammar of the matrix language that affects the form of codeswitching. When single words from another language are embedded, the matrix language word order applies, and the matrix language also supplies what Myers-Scotton terms 'syntactically relevant morphemes'. 'Content morphemes' (typically nouns, most verbs, and adjectives) are distinguished from 'system morphemes', which signal grammatical relationships rather than carrying semantic content (in English, items such as determiners, *the, a, all* and *any,* verb endings such as *-ed* and *-ing,* and the verb *be*). The MLF model predicts that any system morphemes that signal relations between items in a sentence will come from the matrix language (the 'system morpheme principle') and be in the surface order demanded by the matrix language (the 'morpheme order principle'). So, example A below is possible but B would not occur:

A	*Yule mtu ni*	*mtoto*	*w-a* boss	That person is the
		child	of	boss's child

B   **Yule mtu ni* the boss's *mtoto*

[Swahili and English]

(Myers-Scotton, 1993a, p. 109)

In the examples above, English words are used but they are not following the grammar of English: they have been temporarily assigned the grammar of another language. But on other occasions, English switched items do retain their own grammar. This usually occurs when sequences of words – 'embedded language islands' – are embedded in the matrix language. In Example C *this evening* is part of an island following English word order (the matrix language is Swahili):

C   *Wache mimi nielekee tauni,*   Let me go so that I may reach
      tukutane this evening ...   town, let's meet this evening....

(Myers-Scotton, 1993a, p. 140)

It is also possible to say *evening **hii***. This would not be an island. It follows
Swahili word order and consists of an English embedded item followed by
a Swahili system morpheme (*hii* = 'this'). Other Swahili-English combinations
are not possible: ***jioni** this* (*jioni* = 'evening') violates the system morpheme
principle and *this **jioni*** violates both the system morpheme principle and the
word order principle.

Myers-Scotton's explanation also covers some switches that are not included
as switches in other frameworks. For instance, single words that fit in with the
morphology of the matrix language have sometimes been relegated to a
separate category of 'nonce', or one-off, borrowings.

Codeswitching and borrowing

The inclusion of one-word switches within her framework allows Myers-
Scotton to posit a connection between codeswitching and borrowing.
Codeswitched items are regarded as belonging to another language, so
that someone who codeswitches has to have access to two linguistic
systems (though this doesn't imply they are equally competent in both
languages). Borrowed items, on the other hand, are felt to have become
part of the matrix language. All languages have borrowed terms (for
example, English has *amateur* from French; Swahili has *baisikeli*
('bicycle') from English). Terms such as *baisikeli* fill a gap in the matrix
language, but languages also borrow when they have equivalent terms
of their own (for instance, *town* in Swahili). Myers-Scotton argues that
words such as *baisikeli* (she terms these 'cultural borrowings') enter the
language abruptly as the need for them arises, whereas words such as
town ('core borrowings') enter gradually, via codeswitching: they are
subject to the same social motivations and grammatical constraints. As
they become used more frequently, they are on their way to becoming
borrowings, sometimes displacing original terms. There is, therefore, a
continuum operating between codeswitching and borrowing, rather than
a cut-and-dried distinction between the two.

Chapters 2 and 3 pointed to the large number of borrowed terms acquired by
English during its history (the term 'adoption' is used in these chapters).
Chapter 1 discusses attitudes in France towards borrowings from English.

In this section we have pointed out that embedded items may show greater
or less integration into the structure of the matrix language in terms of
phonology, syntax and morphology (and that researchers have used such

formal criteria to distinguish between different types of embedded items, for instance, to determine whether or not they count as codeswitching). We would like to conclude the discussion with a brief look at some research carried out by Rajeshwari Pandharipande in Maharashtra, a state in northern India. Pandharipande was interested in the extent to which English switched items were integrated into Marathi grammar, as in the following example:

D	*to*	office	*cyā*	work	*sāthii*	*ālā*	*hotā*	He had come for
	he	office	of	work	for	came	was	some office work

[English switch containing Marathi suffix]

E	*to* office work *sāthii ālā hotā*	He had come for
		some office work

[English switch without Marathi suffix]

(adapted from Pandharipande, 1990, p. 20)

In the above lines, Example D follows the Marathi construction *kāryālāyā cyā kāmā* (literally 'office of work'), whereas the switch in Example E retains English grammar, *office work*.

Pandharipande points out that in the community she studied, English is associated with a sense of modernity. Speakers frequently switch between Marathi and English when topics such as modern technology, higher education and media are discussed. But the degree of integration of English switched items is also important in this respect. In contexts in which modernity is particularly salient, English embedded items tend to retain more of their English form (word order and morphology). In contexts where modernity is less of an issue, or where other factors are important, English items take on more structural features from Marathi. Pandharipande's research therefore takes us back to the social meanings of codeswitching, showing how they may affect the linguistic form of an utterance.

7.4 Designer English?

We suggested earlier that qualitative studies of codeswitching highlighted speakers' strategic use of different language varieties – and that this was masked in quantitative studies totalling the occurrence of linguistic variants in different contexts. Quantitative comparisons seem to downplay any notion of individual agency: this is simply much less visible than in stretches of transcript showing how speakers utter certain words and phrases and how these are responded to by others. But despite these methodological biases, many interpretations of all studies of speaker style (applying this term in a generic sense to include monolingual style shifting and bilingual codeswitching) have seen this as a relatively creative enterprise: speakers, to a large extent, are able to design their speech to take on particular identities.

This suggests that speaker style has its origin in variation between groups of speakers (the patterns of social variation discussed in Chapter 6). There is some evidence for this view: research in English-speaking communities (and no doubt others) has found that most linguistic features that show variation do vary among social groups as well as stylistically. Some show only social variation, but none shows only stylistic variation. Furthermore, with rare exceptions, stylistic variation is always less extreme than social variation. Bell (1984, p. 153), in a review of this research, comments 'The explanation is that style variation ... derives from and mirrors the "social" variation. As is the habit of mirrors, the reflection is less distinct than the original: style differentiation is less sharp than the social'.

Features that show stylistic variation are subject to evaluation by speakers (i.e. when asked, speakers will make evaluative judgements about them so they are aware, at some level at least, of their connotations and associations). Therefore, the argument goes, they are able to draw on them to communicate social meanings.

Over the years, codeswitching has become more established as a central area of linguistic and sociolinguistic research and many different theoretical approaches to codeswitching have been developed. The discussion below addresses some of these models for the purposes of this chapter (MacSwann, 2004, provides a more comprehensive critique of current theoretical approaches).

Myers-Scotton's markedness model (which has been applied to variation in the speech of monolingual as well as bilingual speakers) seems to allow a more dynamic relationship between individual speaking style and established social meanings. She argues that speakers are aware of patterns of language use that are unmarked or expected in particular contexts from their experience of taking part in similar interactions. They usually choose a speaking style that fits in this context – that is consistent with the relationship they would expect to hold with other participants. But even here they are being creative in the limited sense of choosing one option, the unmarked pattern. In so doing, they are helping to re-establish this as 'normal' or expected. Sometimes they may make a marked choice in an attempt to redefine a relationship. For Myers-Scotton, this is equivalent to saying: 'Put aside any presumptions you have based on societal norms for these circumstances. I want your view of me, or of our relationship, to be otherwise' (Myers-Scotton, 1993b, p. 131). Of course, such marked choice may not succeed in redefining a relationship because it may be contested by others.

The work on bilingual codeswitching discussed here, as well as some studies of monolingual style shifting (such as Trudgill's study of British pop groups and Coupland's study of the Cardiff DJ) have focused on the role of style in managing or (re)negotiating speakers' social identities. Other interpretations have seen style as primarily a response to an audience. In Section 7.2, we mentioned two theories that took this approach: audience design and accommodation theory. These theories are consistent with one another, so here we discuss them together.

Accommodation theory developed from the work of the social psychologist Howard Giles and his associates in the 1970s. It has been enormously influential. We mentioned earlier some initial premises of accommodation theory: speakers will converge towards the speech of their interlocutor in order to emphasise solidarity, and diverge from their interlocutor's speech in order to increase social distance. This is based on the assumption that convergence will be positively evaluated and divergence negatively evaluated. Trudgill's study of his speech in a sociolinguistic interview and Coupland's study of a travel agency assistant's speech illustrate this theory. But some codeswitching can also be interpreted in this light: Myers-Scotton's example of a (marked) switch to English to communicate authority could be interpreted as divergence.

Bell's theory of audience design provides useful additional insights by distinguishing between different types of audience. It is not only the person addressed who will affect someone's speech but also (though to a lesser extent) others who are involved in the interaction. Like Myers-Scotton, Bell argues that style is not always responsive: it may have an initiative function – as when a speaker switches style to redefine a relationship. Bell suggests that on such occasions speakers are addressing their audience as if the audience were someone else. Often speakers are switching towards a 'referee', that is, someone not involved in the interaction but who is nevertheless salient. Speech divergence can be redefined as initiative shifting since the speaker is not simply diverging away from the addressee but towards another reference group. Finally, Bell argues that audience design provides a comprehensive and integrative model of speaker style: other contextual factors that influence people's speech may be re-interpreted in terms of audience. Here is what he says:

> ... speakers associate classes of topics or settings with classes of persons. They therefore shift style when talking on those topics or in those settings as if they were talking to addressees whom they associate with the topic or setting. Topics such as occupation or education, and settings such as office or school, cause shifts to a style suitable to address an employer or teacher. Similarly, intimate topics or a home setting elicit speech appropriate for intimate addressees – family or friends. The basis of all style shift according to nonpersonal factors lies then in audience-designed shift.
>
> (Bell, 1984, p. 181)

Accommodation theory itself has been considerably developed and refined since its early beginnings. Here we mention one or two developments that seem particularly relevant. An article by Giles et al. (1991) provides a more systematic review.

The theory now recognises that speakers do not always accommodate to how their addressee actually speaks. There are obvious limitations – speakers cannot put on any accent (or whatever) at will. But, in addition, speakers sometimes converge towards the variety they expect their addressee to speak, or that is associated with their addressee, rather than to the variety the addressee is actually speaking. (This could explain why Trudgill, in his sociolinguistic interviews, used more non-standard speech to his male informants than to his female informants.)

People will vary in the extent to which they converge. Difference in status between the speakers is likely to be a factor here (Giles et al. point to evidence that subordinates are more likely to converge towards a superior than vice versa). But there may be several reasons why it is more, or less, in a speaker's interests to converge. In some situations it may be important to maintain aspects of a distinctive identity, but without necessarily implying hostility; for example, a teacher in a classroom may use a standard variety of English because that's what is expected of a teacher, rather than simply to express social distance from pupils. Giles et al. term this 'complementarity'.

A related point is that the meanings of accommodation need to be interpreted in context; it is not always the case that convergent speakers intend to decrease social distance, nor that convergence will be positively evaluated. Giles et al. quote several examples of alternative interpretations.

Finally, Giles et al. concede that what is interpreted as accommodation may be an artefact. They give the example of an interviewee who converges towards the high-status language variety used by the interviewer: this may be because of a wish to appear in a certain way (e.g. as competent) rather than simply due to a desire to converge.

Identity-based theories such as the markedness model have different origins, and different emphases, from audience design and accommodation theory but they are not necessarily incompatible. Speakers do adopt certain language varieties in order to lay claim to a certain identity (or set of identities), but this is always in relation to other participants. At a general level, speakers are taking account both of their own identities and those of their interlocutors in 'designing' the way they speak. One common feature of the three theories is that design is seen most frequently as responsive, as when speakers fall into expected patterns of convergence or complementarity. But speakers may also make marked or divergent choices in a bid to redefine a relationship.

To conclude, Woolard (2004) raises important issues that question some of the basic assumptions made by the approaches discussed above. One of these, for example, addresses the nature of 'explanation': in all of the above discussions, the researchers concerned have sought to explain why switching occurs where it does; however, as Woolard states: 'Does a full explanation not also need to account for why [codeswitching] does not occur in seemingly similar circumstances?' (Woolard, 2004, p. 81). Research within this field should, therefore, also recognise that patterns of switching will differ across communities. In this way, research can encapsulate the bigger picture: looking beyond micro-social to macro-social structures and identities.

Divergent convergence?

Francophone shoppers in Montreal, Canada, were heard to address anglophone shop assistants in fluent English to ask for the services of a francophone assistant. While this is an example of linguistic convergence the act is clearly one of dissociation.

Jamaican schoolteachers, who usually use a standardised form of English in the classroom, sometimes 'converged' in mockery or disparagement of their pupils' creolised forms when the latter were being disruptive, inattentive or lacking in academic effort.

Attempts by an English-speaking tourist to use the language of the countries he was visiting did not always meet with success:

> In sojourns in Latin America and Southeast Asia, the author's use of inelegant but workable host-country language or expressions often was countered with requests to proceed in English, even when the host's competence in it was severely limited. Some people perceived the visitor's initiative as a pejorative reflection on their English ability; still others appeared pleased with the effort, but indicated that they preferred to practise their English.
>
> (Ellingsworth, 1988, p. 265)

(adapted from examples quoted in Giles et al., 1991, pp. 12, 36 and 75)

7.5 Conclusion

This chapter has discussed 'speaking style' in English: it has looked at how speakers draw on different varieties of English, and switch between English and other languages, to communicate aspects of their identity and to negotiate relationships with others. It has also looked at different traditions of research: research that has adopted a quantitative approach, identifying general patterns of variation; and qualitative research, emphasising the meanings of speakers' language use in different contexts. Such methodological considerations seem important, not least because different methods provide different kinds of evidence and allow different judgements to be made about the use of English and other languages (contrast, for instance, the rather different preoccupations of researchers such as Edwards and Sebba).

While most of this chapter has focused on issues to do with language and identity, we also discussed some of the grammatical constraints that operate when speakers switch between English and other languages (though even here social factors turned out to be an important influence on the extent to which English was integrated into another language's grammar).

Finally, we discussed some theories that have addressed the motivations for speakers' variable language use, suggesting that speakers can be seen as relatively creative 'designers' of language.

The research referred to throughout the chapter suggests that such design is not a simple process. Speakers are able to draw on a wide range of linguistic resources, the meanings of which are often subtle and ambiguous. They negotiate identities, relationships and contexts moment by moment. They may have to balance conflicting identities, and their attempts to initiate certain relationships may be contested. Furthermore, the project remains unfinished: relationships between individuals change, and social groups realign themselves; the English language also changes, in terms of both its structure and its relationship to other languages. Speaking style reflects these processes but also, necessarily, contributes to them.

READING A: *Hark, Hark the Lark*: multiple voicing in DJ talk

Nikolas Coupland
(Nikolas Coupland is Professor and Director of the Cardiff Centre for Language and Communication Research.)

Specially commissioned for Swann (1996, pp. 325–30). (Revised by the original author.)

In 1985 I published an exploratory paper focusing on the stylistic creativity of a radio disc jockey (DJ), Frank Hennessy (FH), who was at that time a local radio presenter in Cardiff (Coupland, 1985). FH is a broad-accented speaker of the Cardiff English dialect who is well known in the community not only as a radio presenter but also as an entertainer, folksinger/songwriter, social commentator and humorist. His popular image is built around his affiliation to, and promotion of, local Cardiff culture and folklore, in large measure through his dialect. For many, he typifies the vernacular Cardiff voice, perhaps even the stereotypical Cardiff worldview: a nostalgia for dockland streets and pubs, a systematic ambivalence to 'Welshness' (even though Cardiff is the capital city of Wales), a sharp, wry humour and a reverence for the local beers, in particular 'Brain's Dark Ale'. In general, his show is a celebration of in-group regional solidarity.

The transcript starting on the following page (transcription notes are given immediately below the transcription) is a continuous sequence from FH's radio show beginning with him reading out a letter from a listener. FH's speech is interspersed by the playing of a record (the Checkmates's '*Proud Mary*') at line 7. The extract ends when another record is cued and played.

Transcription conventions
- This is a verbatim transcript: it includes common expressions such as *um* and *er* and, like many research transcripts, it is not punctuated.
- The symbols in round brackets above certain words indicate sociolinguistic variables that were investigated. The numbers below show how they were scored. Both conventions are explained below.
- Wide spacing between words gives a rough indication of pauses.

1   dear Frank   would you please give a mention on your birthday spot for

       (au)   (h)
2   our brother whose birthday is on the second of June well that was
       0   0

                 (C)   (ou)(C) (h)
3   yesterday wasn't it so it's a happy birthday to (name) and lots of love
               0   1 0 0   0

                                                (ou)
4   from your sisters (names) and Mum of course   and also from all
                    0 1 0   1

             (h)   (h)   (ou)   (ou)
5   your family   his name is (name) and he lives at Seven Oaks Road
              0   1   1   1

       (aː)   (h)
6   Ely in Cardiff   happy birthday (name) (cues record)   here's the
            3   0   0   1

                  (au)   (r)
7   Checkmates   Proud Mary   yeah (record plays and fades) oh good
                      2   0

                      (au)   (r)
8   music there   the Checkmates and Proud Mary   and the wall of
                                    2   1

  (au)   (r)   (au)
9   sound there of Phil Spector   unmistakable of course   they sound
    2   1   2

             (ng)   (aː)   (C)   (au)   (aː)
10   as if they going bananas don't they   talk about bananas   we got
             1   4   1   9   4

    (aː)   (r)(aː)   (ng)   (t) (C)(ai)   (r)
11   Bananarama coming up next   but it's time to limber up this Sunday
    4   0 3   1   0 0 1   1

        (aː)   (r)   (C)   (C)
12   with the Margaret Morris Movement Special   that's a special day of
           1   0   0   0

  (ai)   (aː)
13   exercise and dance at the National Sports Centre for Wales   it
    2   3

  (aː)   (au)(t)   (au) (ou)   (ou)   (ai)
14   started about an hour ago at ten o'clock and it goes until five o'clock
    2   2 1   2   1   1   2

    (aː)   (au)   (aː)   (aː)   (r)
15   this afternoon   now the Margaret   Margaret Morris Movement is
     3   2   0   1   1

               (r)   (C)   (C)
16   a unique form of recreative   movement   and it's um   well it's a
                   0   0   0

      (ai)   (t) (C) (ou)
17   system of exercise   which achieves physical fitness   but it's also
             2   0 1   (R)

           (ng)   (t)   (t)   (t)   (t)
18   capable of developing creative and aesthetic qualities which make it
                   1   0   0   0   0

                                       (ng)   (aː)
19   exceptional   in physical education and training   are you with me
                                          0   (R)

        (ai)   (ou)(t)   (C)
20   ah   'cause I'm totally confused   anyway it's equally suitable for
         2   1 1   0

21   men and women of all ages as well as children even the kids can join

22   in with this   and er the muscular control and coordination make it
                                (ou)   (ou)   (t)
                                  1   1   0

23   an excellent preparation for all sporting and athletic activities   now
                    (r)   (r)   (ng)
                    0   1   0

24   all sessions today are absolutely free   so if the weather's a little bit
                    (aː)   (ou)
                    (R)   1

25   gone against you   and you fancy   well not running round in the
                                        (r)   (ng)(r)(au)
                                        0   1 0 2

26   rain   but er you fancy doing a bit of exercise it's all on at the
   (r)   (t)   (ng)   (t)   (ai) (C)
   0   0   1   1   2   1

27   National Sports Centre for Wales   that's at Pontcanna of course
                                      (C)
                                      0

28   started an hour ago you can go any time up until about five o'clock
   (aː)   (r) (ou)   (ou)   (ai)   (au) (ai)
   3   1   1   1   2   2   2

29   this evening   so there we are   as I said   Bananarama   here
        (ng)   (ou)   (aː)   (ai)   (aː) (r)(aː)
        1   1   4   2   0   0 4

30   they are   with a little touch of (cues record) Rough Justice I'll
   (aː)   (r)   (ai)
   4   (A)   (R)

31   have to get me r i g h t arm in training you know   the pints are
   (h)   (r)(ai)   (aː)   (ng)   (ou)   (ai) (aː)
   1   1 2   4   1   1   2   (R)

32   getting heavier ((have)) you noticed that   or is it me getting weaker
   (t)(ng)(h)   (ou)   (r)   (t)(ng)
   1 1 0   1   1   1 1

33   have to drink six h a l f s instead of me three usual darkies   ah (record)
   (h)   (h)(aː)   (aː)
   1   1 4   4

The extract conveys something of the in-group framing of the show. Many correspondents are regular contributors and have therefore become, to an extent, radio personalities in their own right. Some open their letters with ever more familiar forms of address than the *dear Frank* instance in the extract – *[h]ello, Franky Boy, [h]i, [h]i Frank, [h]ow's things, Our Kid*. The show often carries announcements of local events, such as the 'Margaret Morris Movement Special' introduced at line 12 of the extract. Other instances include a quiz feature asking listeners to supply the original name of Wimbourne Street in *lovely old Splott* (a long-established working-class Cardiff city district) and the names of six paddle steamers which operated in the Bristol Channel after the Second World War.

Cardiff English

The show can be said to be constituted dialectally. Cardiff dialect is not merely an incidental characteristic of FH's own speech; it permeates much of the performance and imbues it with a regional significance. For instance, vernacular Cardiff speech does not regularly distinguish between the quality of the long vowel sound in words such as *dark* and *park* and the short vowel sound in words such as *cat*. Cardiff pronunciation can be represented phonetically as [æ:] and [æ] and this vowel quality, particularly its long form, has become a stereotype of Cardiff speech (the [æ] represents a vowel quality somewhere between RP *man* and *men* while the diacritic [:] signifies the vowel is lengthened). FH's radio show draws on the associations of this pronunciation; it has the informal title *Hark, Hark, the Lark* and is introduced and punctuated by a distinctive jingle – a whimsical, sung fanfare of the words 'Hark, hark the lark in Cardiff Arms Park' with an [æ:] vowel quality predominating throughout. FH perpetuates this phonological theme in his own catchphrases, such as *it's remarkable, well there we are* and *that's half tidy*. Notice how the extract ends with a list of phono opportunities for [æ:] in highly prominent positions during the final three lines of transcript: *arm, halfs* meaning 'halves' or 'half-pints', and *Darkies* ('pints of Dark Ale').

Correspondents often make their own contribution to this dialectal theme, sometimes consciously ending their letters with an opportunity for FH to produce a broad Cardiff pronunciation; for example, *yours through a glass darkly, signed Prince of Darkness* (both of these are again oblique references to Dark Ale), *don't forget Derby day*, or simply the words *ta* ('thank you') or *tarra* ('goodbye'). This single sound, then, is a highly productive focus for the symbolic expression of shared Cardiff provenance and accompanying attitudes and allegiances.

The sound can be treated as a sociolinguistic variable (ɑ:) in analyses of variation in Cardiff speech: technically, ways of realising the variable can be represented as positions on a five-point scale running from 0 to 4, with 4 being maximally 'broad' or vernacular and 0 being the RP realisation. There is of course a full repertoire of other sociolinguistic variables available – in this case, sounds that have both more vernacular Cardiff and more RP-like pronunciations. These include (ai), the pronunciation of the first part of the diphthong in *like, time*, etc., and (au), the pronunciation of the first part of the diphthong in *now, house*, etc.; each of these variables is represented on a three-point scale running from 0 to 2, again with the higher numbers indicating more non-standard forms. Other variables can be represented as either RP-like (0) or vernacular (1):

(ng)   the pronunciation of *-ing* in words such as *running*, *something*, etc. as either *-ing* or *-in*;

(h)   the presence or absence of /h/ at the beginning of a word;

(C)   whether consonant clusters are simplified (or reduced) in certain positions (e.g. *next day*; *don't they*; *it's*);

(t)   the pronunciation of /t/ between vowels (e.g. *better*, *lot of*);

(r)   the pronunciation of /r/ before vowels;

(ou)   the pronunciation of the first part of the diphthong in *know*, *coal*, etc.

In the transcript, each possible realisation of a salient Cardiff English pronunciation feature is underlined. The relevant sociolingustic variable is set out above the line, and the number below the line shows how standard or non-standard each realisation is. ('R' means that the feature is too reduced phonetically to be scored; 'A' means that the realisation is an Americanised version.)

Options for interpretation

What are we to do with arrays of style-representing numbers such as those that appear in the transcript? In line with much conventional sociolinguistic research, we might want to aggregate the scores for particular pronunciation variables across many such extracts. If we do this, we reach the very unsurprising conclusion that, for all the variables we have listed above, FH's speech is generally quite 'non-standard'. But it is only uniformly 'non-standard' in the case of one variable (ou). For all others, we get high percentages but percentages that derive from varying stylistic performance from instance to instance.

A next step might therefore be to try to isolate the micro contexts of FH's speech. The context is, from one point of view, unvarying. After all, we have a single speaker who is speaking, ostensibly, to the same audience over the course of the show. But it seems possible and potentially productive to establish categories of context on the basis of topics of talk, or modes of discourse, or in relation to specific communicative activities within the show. We can see, even in this extract, how FH's performance involves him in reading listeners' letters (lines 1–6), making public announcements (presumably based on prepared written sources (the Margaret Morris episode) doing 'record-speak' (e.g. *here's the Checkmates Proud Mary*, lines 6–7) and being funny (e.g. *I'll have to get me right arm in training you know*, lines 30–31).

Some generalisations can be made on this basis. For instance, FH tends to use more consistent Cardiff pronunciations when talking about Cardiff people and events. He also does this when he makes joking references to his own incompetence. But he uses more RP-like pronunciations in connection with structuring and publicising the show, when 'competence' and 'expertise' become more salient aspects of his identity, as the italicised features in these other examples demonstrate:

> *we've got for the next two hours so stay with me until two o'clock*

> *Frank Hennessy here on CBC two two one metres medium wave and ninety-six VHF in stereo*

FH does not use RP-like forms for all the variables on such occasions: those that are 'corrected' are generally stigmatised features in social dialect terms (for example, /h/-dropping). Specifically Cardiff features such as (ɑː) are left in their local forms to continue marking in-group identity.

There are boundary problems inherent in this micro-contextual approach. Is the link between the two records in the extract (*they sound as if they going bananas don't they*, line 10) humour – and a phono-opportunity for (aː) – or record-speak? FH's announcement of the dance event is interspersed with humorous commentary on the announcement itself (*are you with me ah 'cause I'm totally confused*, lines 19–20). It also shows elements of spontaneous ad-libbing (*now all sessions today are absolutely free so if the weather's a little bit gone against you and you fancy well not running round in the rain*, lines 24–6). Any text-based typology, assigning utterances to contextual types, is therefore imprecise. Although it allows us to produce some interesting general correlations between stylistic 'levels' and contexts, the approach does not ultimately appear to do justice to the moment-to-moment creativity of FH's own performance.

This is so for at least three reasons. First, FH is not limited to the alternation between more and less RP-like realisations of Cardiff English. Sometimes he uses features from other dialects. He adopts American features to introduce some songs, including the 'yeah' in line 7 of the extract and, perhaps surprisingly (because they are a British band), the title of the Bananarama song in line 30. There are other features elsewhere in the recording; for instance, south-west of England dialect features in connection with a mention of Dorsetshire, and Cockney features to introduce a song by Joe Brown and His Bruvvers.

Second, a correlational account cannot capture the interplay between style, content and key. Some of the dialect mimicry is playful, as in the case of American features parodying slick DJ patter. Again, the 'social meaning' of broad Cardiff dialect seems different depending on whether the focus of the talk is Frank himself (in which case it conveys humour through self-deprecation) or cultural history (in which case it conjures up social solidarity and a sense of community).

But third and crucially, there is the theoretical consideration that the various configurations of 'context' do not exist independently of FH's speech forms. It is often the case that we can only identify a 'contextual type' by virtue of the stylistic attributes of FH's speech. He is the orchestrator of contexts, and this removes the empirical basis that justifies correlation.

A theoretical realignment for the study of style

I have referred above to FH's 'performance' in the DJ role. FH is clearly a media 'performer' in the specific sense of seeking to entertain and developing his media persona(s) with a degree of self-consciousness and overt planning and scripting. Variation in his speech and in particular his dialect can therefore be said to be, not only styled, but stylised. But 'performance' is also the appropriate term because of Frank's stylistic creativity. His styles are not situational reflexes. They are ways of drawing simultaneously on multiple sets of social meanings.

In this case, more than merely representing a speech community (Cardiff), dialect opens up a range of potential personal and social identities for FH, and diverse bases on which he can relate to his audience. Through stylistic choices in dialect, he can project but then momentarily undermine his 'ethnic Cardiff' persona with a pastiche of the slick American DJ ('yeah').

Conversely, he can undermine this 'DJ' projection with a strongly dialectised admission of personal incompetence (*I'll have to get me right arm in training*). He can manufacture the persona of the competent public announcer, then parody this role (and the announced event?) both referentially and through a dialect switch. Cardiff English is not merely 'Frank's voice' but one of many culturally loaded voices that FH, and presumably his audience too, can manipulate for relational and other interactional purposes.

These critical readings of stylistic shifts are far less consistent with the dominant tradition within sociolinguistics than with the work of the Russian theorist Mikhail Bakhtin. In his paper on 'The problem of speech genres' (written in 1952–3 and reproduced in Emerson and Holquist, 1992), Bakhtin writes of 'such fictions as "the listener"' (p. 68) and of how any speaker:

> ... presupposes not only the existence of the language system he [*sic*] is using, but also the existence of preceding utterances – his own and others' – with which his given utterance enters into one kind of relation or another (builds on them, polemicizes with them or simply presumes that they are already known to the listener)

> (Bakhtin, quoted in Emerson and Holquist, 1992 p. 69).

This idea of 'multiple voicing' arguably has a more direct relevance to the study of dialect style than to any other dimension of linguistic variation. Dialects are, indeed, Bakhtin said 'the drive belts from the history of society to the history of language' (Emerson and Holquist, 1992, p. 65), replete with social and cultural echoes, associations and 'dialogic reverberations' (1992, p. 94). Bakhtin writes that 'Our speech ... is filled with others' words, varying degrees of otherness and varying degrees of "our-own-ness", ... [which] carry with them their own evaluative tone, which we assimilate, rework and re-accentuate' (Emerson and Holquist, 1992, p. 89). The 'Hark, Hark' analysis is well summarised as FH borrowing, reworking and re-accentuating dialect styles, creatively and multidimensionally.

Acknowledgement

I am very grateful to Mr Frank Hennessy for his permission to use data from the radio show and for his interest and cooperation.

References for this reading

Coupland, N. (1985) ' "Hark, Hark the Lark": social motivations for phonological style-shifting', *Language and Communications*, vol. 5, no. 3, pp. 153–71.

Emerson, C. and Holquist, M. (eds) (1992) *M. M. Bakhtin: Speech Genres and Other Late Essays*, Austin, University of Texas Press.

READING B: Codeswitching with English: types of switching, types of communities

Carol Myers-Scotton
(Carol Myers-Scotton is Distinguished Professor Emeritus, Linguistics Program and Department of English, University of South Carolina.)

Source: Myers-Scotton, C. (1989) 'Codeswitching with English: types of switching, types of communities', *World Englishes*, vol. 8, no. 3, pp. 333–9.

[This extract draws on Carol Myers-Scotton's research on codeswitching in Kenya and Zimbabwe. Myers-Scotton's model of codeswitching suggests that languages (codes) are 'indexical' of social relationships: they establish a speaker as a certain kind of person in relation to others. More specifically, they index a particular set of rights and obligations that will hold between participants in an interaction. A speaker will, then, select a code that indexes the rights and obligations he/she wishes to be in force between him/herself and others. In this extract, Myers-Scotton identifies different patterns of codeswitching based on the notion of 'markedness'. An 'unmarked' choice means an expected choice, one that is associated with the type of interaction in which it occurs. A 'marked' choice means one that is not expected in that context. It is an attempt to redefine a relationship.

The conventions used for the different languages in the transcription examples in the reading are: English is in normal type, a second language is in italics, a third language is in small capitals, and you will find the English translation on the right.]

Sequential unmarked choices

This pattern consists of a switch from one unmarked choice to another one when external forces (e.g. a new participant, a new topic) alter the expected balance of rights and obligations and therefore the relative markedness of one code vs. another. ...

Example (1) illustrates sequences of unmarked choices in East Africa, with English as a component.

(1) A school principal who speaks English and Swahili in addition to his first language is in Nairobi on a visit. He wishes to call on a friend working for a large automobile sales and repair establishment. While speaking to the guard at the gate, he uses Swahili as an unmarked choice, but once inside the office, he switches to English as the unmarked choice there.

Guard (Swahili)	*Unapenda nikusaidie namna gain?*	In what way do you want me to help you?
Principal (Swahili)	*Ningependa kumwona Peter Mbaya*	I would like to see Peter Mbaya.
Guard (Swahili)	*Bwana Peter hayuko saa hii. Ingia na uende kwa* office ya inquiries *na umngoje. Atarudi.*	Mr Peter isn't here right now. Go inside to the inquiry office and wait for him. He'll return.
Receptionist (English)	Good morning. Can I help you?	
Principal (English)	Good morning. I came to see Mr Mbaya.	
Receptionist (English)	He is out but will soon be here. Have a seat and wait for him.	

Switching as an unmarked choice

When participants are bilingual peers, the unmarked choice may be switching but with no changes at all in setting, participants, topic, or any other situational feature. That is, for ingroup communication – especially in an informal setting – the pattern of alternating between two varieties may [itself] be unmarked ... When the unmarked state of affairs is simultaneous participation in two rights and obligations balances, each associated with a different social identity, speakers switch between two codes, each one being unmarked in the specific context for one of the identities. The overall pattern of switching is the major social message (i.e. dual identities) in this type of switching, each individual switch point need have no social significance at all ... [Examples 2 and 3 illustrate this type of switching.] Although the transcript does not show it, there are no hesitation phenomena and no change in the stress pattern.

(2) A school principal from Western Kenya is in Nairobi visiting a friend who is an administrator at the Government Printer. Their conversation has been in their shared mother tongue, Lwidakho, when a telephone call interrupts them.

Administrator (English, Lwidakho)	(on telephone) Good afternoon. This is Gabriel.	
	Oh, Elijah. *Mbulili unvele muwale uvira khulishi?*	How are you? I heard you were sick.
	Yes, with Henry. He's been here about an hour.	
Administrator (English)	(to Henry, the principal) When are you returning?	
Principal (English) The first week of next month – before schools reopen.	The first week of next month – before schools reopen.	
Administrator	(on telephone)	
(Lwidakho, English, Swahili)	*Alatsya lisitsa lyukhura mu mweli muluya.*	He'll go during the first week of the new month.
	Yes, I'll tell him that.	
	LAKINI, BWANA, SIKU HIZI HUONEKANI. UMEPOTEA WAPI?	But, mister, you aren't seen these days. Where are you lost?

(3) Two University of Zimbabwe students are chatting in their dormitory. Their shared mother tongue, the Karanja dialect of Shona, is the matrix language. [In a codeswitching context the matrix language is a kind of

bedrock language, heavily influencing the word order, word formation and other aspects of any switches from other languages that may be embedded in it.]

Student (Shona, English)	*Oramba a-chi-ngo-deliberat -a a-chi-ngo-deliberat -a kwava kuzoti tava kusvika pai muclass tava kutosvika pa-ma* classes.	She kept on deliberating up to a point when we were about to reach the classrooms.

(Note: At issue is the status of 'class' as a loan word or a switch.)

Codeswitching as a marked choice

Switching away from the expected, away from the unmarked choice ... is a negotiation to replace the current – and unmarked – rights and obligations set with another one. ...

Marked choices to ingroup varieties among group members typically encode solidarity. Quite another effect typically results from switching to varieties associated with education and/or authority. Such switches often encode more social distance between participants, sometimes out of anger or a desire to lower the addressee's or increase one's own status. Because it is associated with authority (either in former colonial regimes or in present governments or educational systems), English is often the language of such a marked switch, especially in the Third World. Note, however, that the indexical message of a code is context-specific: in some contexts English may encode solidarity, even though it is a second language, such as between highly educated peers. Example (4) illustrates two different marked choices, one to a mother tongue not shared by all (communicating solidarity with the speaker's ethnic group member, but distance from the others) and one to English (communicating authority).

(4) Four young office workers in the same government ministry in Nairobi are chatting. Two are Kikuyu, one is a Kisii, and one is a Kalenjin. Swahili-English switching has been the unmarked choice up to the switch to Kikuyu. The conversation about setting up a group 'emergency fund' has been proceeding when the Kikuyus switch to Kikuyu to make a negative comment about what has just been said, a marked choice communicating solidarity between the two Kikuyus but distancing them from the others. At this point, the Kisii complains in Swahili and English and the Kalenjin makes a switch from Swahili to a sentence entirely in English, a marked choice, to return the discussion to a more business-like plane.

Kikuyu II (Kikuyu)	*Andu amwe nimendaga, kwaria maundu maria matari na ma namo.*	Some people like talking about what they're not sure of.
Kikuyu I (Kikuyu)	*Wira wa muigi wa kigina ni kuiga mbeca. No tigucaria mbeca.*	The work of the treasurer is only to keep money, not to hunt for money.
Kisii (Swahili, English)	*Ubaya wenu ya Kikuyu ni ku- assume kila mtu anaelewa Kikuyu.*	The bad thing about Kikuyus is assuming that everyone understands Kikuyu.
Kalenjin (Swahili, English)	*Si mtumie lugha ambayo kila mtu hapa atasikia?* (said with some force): We are supposed to solve this issue.	Shouldn't you use a language which every person here understands?

Codeswitching as an exploratory choice presenting multiple identities

In non-conventionalized exchanges or simply when meeting someone for the first time and when all the relevant social identity factors of the other person or other situational factors are not known, multiple identities sometimes are presented via codeswitching as an exploratory choice. In these circumstances, since no unmarked choice is obvious, speakers may switch in order to settle upon a code which will be mutually acceptable as the unmarked choice of the exchange. Accepting a code as the basis for the conversation, of course, means accepting the balance of rights and obligations indexed by that code. Example (5) illustrates such switching in a community where English is a frequent component of exploratory switching. Note that this type of switching highlights the interactional nature of codeswitching as a negotiation of identities; while any speaker can switch to any code to negotiate a particular relationship, for the negotiation to succeed requires that the addressee reciprocate with this code.

(5) A young man has come into the manager's office in a Nairobi business establishment. The young man begins in English, but finally switches to Swahili, following the manager's lead. Either language would be a possible choice, but each communicating different relationships. The manager's insistence on Swahili denies the young man's negotiation of the higher status associated with English.

Young man (English)	Mr Muchuki has sent me to you about the job you put in the paper.	
Manager (Swahili)	*Ulituma barua ya* application?	Did you send a letter of application?

Young man (English)	Yes, I did. But he asked me to come to see you today.	
Manager (Swahili)	*Ikiwa ulituma barua, nenda ungojee majibu. Tutakuita ufike kwa interview siku itakapofika.*	If you've written a letter, then go and wait for a response. We will call you for an interview when the letter arrives.
	Leo sina la suma kuliko hayo.	Today I haven't anything else to say.
Young man (Swahili)	*Asante. Nitangoja majibu.*	Thank you. I'll wait for the response.

Codeswitching showing multiple identities in non-conventionalized exchanges is also used as a neutral strategy. Since each code communicates a particular identity in a given situation, when it is unclear which identity offers the speaker the most positive evaluation, the speaker may see codeswitching as a solution.

References

Abdulaziz, M.M.H. (1991) 'East Africa (Tanzania and Kenya)' in Cheshire, J. (ed.) *English Around the World,* Cambridge, Cambridge University Press.

Adonis, A. and Pollard, S. (1997) *A Class Act: The Myth of Britain's Classless Society*, London, Hamish Hamilton.

Aitken, A.J. (1984) 'Scots and English in Scotland' in Trudgill, P. (ed.) *Language in the British Isles*, Cambridge, Cambridge University Press.

Alexander, G. (1982) 'Politics of the pronoun in the literature of the English Revolution' in Carter, R. (ed.) *Language and Literature*, London, Allen & Unwin.

Allason-Jones, L. (1989) *Women in Roman Britain*, London, British Museum Publications.

Bailey, R.W. (1992) *Images of English*, Cambridge, Cambridge University Press.

Bartlett, R. (1993) *The Making of Europe*, Harmondsworth, Penguin.

Baugh, A.C. and Cable, T. (1978) *A History of the English Language* (3rd edn), London, Routledge & Kegan Paul.

BBC (2005) *Why Villains in Movies have English Accents* [online], http://www.bbc.co.uk/dna/h2g2 (Accessed 24 October 2005).

Beal, J. (1993) 'The grammar of Tyneside and Northumbrian English' in Milroy, J. and Milroy, L. (eds) *Real English: The Grammar of English Dialects in the British Isles*, London, Longman.

Bell, A. (1984) 'Language style as audience design', *Language in Society*, vol. 13, no. 2, pp. 145–204.

Bell, A. (1991) *The Language of News Media*, Oxford, Blackwell.

Bennett, J.A.W. and Smithers, G.V. (eds) (1968) *Early Middle English Verse and Prose*, Oxford, Oxford University Press.

Biber, D., Johansson, S., Leech, G., Conrad, S. and Finegan, E. (1999) *Longman Grammar of Spoken and Written English*, London, Longman.

Bliss, A. (1984) 'English in the south of Ireland' in Trudgill, P. (ed.) *Language in the British Isles*, Cambridge, Cambridge University Press.

Blyden, E. (1888) *Christianity, Islam and the Negro Race*, London, W.B. Whittingham.

Blyth, C. Jnr, Recktenwald, S. and Wang, J. (1990) 'I'm like, "say what?!": a new quotative in American oral narrative', *American Speech*, no. 65, pp. 215–27.

Bonfiglio, P.B. (2002) *Race and the Rise of Standard American*, Berlin, Mouton de Gruyter.

Boyle, R. (1927 [1675]) *Electricity and Magnetism*, Old Ashmolean Reprints, 7, Gunther, R.W.T. (series ed.), Oxford, Oxford University Press.

Brooks, C. (1985) *The Language of the American South*, Athens, GA, University of Georgia Press.

Bullokar, W. (1977 [1586]) *Bref Grammar for English*, Delman, NY, Scholars' Facsimiles & Reprints.

Burnley, D. (1992) *The History of the English Language: A Source Book*, London, Longman.

Burrell, A. (1891) *Recitation: A Handbook for Teachers in Public Elementary Schools*, London, Griffith, Farran, Okeden & Welsh.

Cameron, D. (2000) *Good to Talk? Living and Working in a Communication Culture*, London, Sage.

Carver, E.M. (1992) 'The Mayflower to the Model-T: the development of American English' in Machan, T.W. and Scott, C.T. (eds) *English in its Social Contexts: Essays in Historical Sociolinguistics*, Oxford, Oxford University Press.

Cheng, C.C. (1992) 'Chinese varieties of English' in Kachru, B.B. (ed.) *The Other Tongue: English across Cultures* (2nd edn), Urbana & Chicago, University of Illinois Press.

Cheshire, J. (1982) *Variation in an English Dialect*, Cambridge, Cambridge University Press.

Cheshire, J. and Milroy, J. (1993) 'Syntactic variation in non-standard dialects' in Milroy, J. and Milroy, L. (eds) *Real English: The Grammar of English Dialects in the British Isles*, London, Longman.

Christian, D., Wolfram, W. and Dube, N. (1988) *Variation and Change in Geographically Isolated Communities: Appalachian English and Ozark English*, Tuscaloosa, AL, American Dialect Society.

Clanchy, M.T. (1993) *From Memory to Written Record: England 1066–1307* (2nd edn), Oxford, Blackwell.

Coulmas, F. (2005) *Sociolinguistics: The Study of Speakers' Choices*, Cambridge, Cambridge University Press.

Coupland, N. (1984) 'Accommodation at work', *International Journal of the Sociology of Language*, no. 4–6, pp. 49–70.

Coupland, N. (1988) *Dialect in Use: Sociolinguistic Variation in Cardiff English*, Cardiff, University of Wales Press.

Crowley, T. (1989) *The Politics of Discourse: The Standard Language Question in British Cultural Debates*, Basingstoke, Macmillan Education.

Cruttenden, A. (1994) *Gimson's Pronunciation of English* (5th edn; revised by A. Cruttenden), London, Arnold.

Crystal, D. (1985) 'Commentary on the English language in a global context' in Quirk, R. and Widdowson, H.G. (eds) *English in the World: Teaching and Learning the Language and Literatures*, Cambridge, Cambridge University Press for the British Council.

Crystal, D. (1987) *The Cambridge Encyclopedia of Language*, Cambridge, Cambridge University Press.

Crystal, D. (1988) *The English Language*, Harmondsworth, Penguin.

Crystal, D. (2003) *English as a Global Language* (2nd edn), Cambridge, Cambridge University Press.

Crystal, D. (2004) *The Stories of English*, London, Penguin.

DeCamp, D. (1958) 'The genesis of the Old English dialects: a new hypothesis', *Language*, vol. 34, pp. 232–44.

Donaldson, W. (1986) *Popular Literature in Victorian Scotland*, Aberdeen, Aberdeen University Press.

Douglas, P. (2001) *Geordie English*, London, Abson Books.

Downes, W. (1998) *Language and Society* (2nd edn), Cambridge, Cambridge University Press.

Eagle, A. (2004) 'Stravaigin the Wab', *Lallans: The Journal o Scots Airts an Letters*, no. 64, pp. 103–7.

Edwards, V. (1986) *Language in a Black Community*, Clevedon, Multilingual Matters.

Edwards, V. (1993) 'The grammar of Southern British English' in Milroy J. and Milroy L. (eds) *Real English: The Grammar of English Dialects in the British Isles*, London, Longman.

Eisikovits, E. (1998) 'Girl-talk/boy-talk: sex differences in adolescent speech' in Coates, J. (ed.) *Language and Gender: A Reader*, Oxford, Blackwell.

Eliot, G. (1861) *Silas Marner: The Weaver of Raveloe*, London, William Blackwood.

Ellingsworth, H.W. (1988) 'A theory of adaptation in intercultural dyads' in Kim, Y.Y. and Gudykunst, W.G. (eds) *Theories in Intercultural Communication*, Newbury Park, CA, Sage.

Ellis, A.J. (1869a) *On Early English Pronunciation with Especial Reference to Shakspere and Chaucer*, Part I, London, Asher & Co.

Ellis, A.J. (1869b) *On Early English Pronunciation with Especial Reference to Shakspere and Chaucer*, Part II, London, Asher & Co.

Ellis, A.J. (1875) *On Early English Pronunciation with Especial Reference to Shakspere and Chaucer*, Part IV, London, Asher & Co.

Ellis, A. J. (1890) *English Dialects: Their Sounds and Homes*, London, Kegan Paul, French, Trübner & Co.

Fabricius, A. (2002) 'Ongoing change in modern RP: evidence for the disappearing stigma of t-glottalling', *English World-Wide*, vol. 23, no. 1, June, pp. 115–36.

Ferguson, G. (2003) 'Classroom code-switching in post-colonial contexts' in Makoni, S. and Meinhof, U. (eds) *Africa and Applied Linguistics*, AILA Review, no. 16, pp. 1–12.

Ferrara, K. and Bell B. (1995) 'Sociolinguistic variation and discourse function of constructed dialogue introducers: the case of be + like', *American Speech*, no. 70, pp. 265–89.

Filppula, M. (1991) 'Urban and rural varieties of Hiberno-English' in Cheshire, J. (ed.) *English around the World: Sociolinguistic Perspectives*, Cambridge, Cambridge University Press.

Fowler, H.W. (2002 [1926]) *A Dictionary of Modern English Usage*, Oxford, Oxford University Press.

Franzen, J. (2002) *The Corrections*, London, Fourth Estate.

Gelling, M. (1984) *Place-names in the Landscape*, London, Dent.

Gildas (1562 [?540]) 'The epistle of Gildas' in Abingdon, T. (ed.) *A Description of Great Britain Written Eleven Hundred Years Since*, London, John Hancock.

Giles, H. (1970) 'Evaluative reactions to accents', *Education Review,* vol. 22, no. 3, pp. 211–27.

Giles, H. and Powesland P.F. (1975) *Speech Style and Social Evaluation*, London, Academic Press.

Giles, H., Coupland, N. and Coupland, J. (1991) 'Accommodation theory: communication, context and consequence' in Giles, H. Coupland, J. and Coupland, N. (eds) *Contexts of Accommodation: Developments in Applied Sociolinguistics*, Cambridge, Cambridge University Press.

Giles, H., Coupland, N., Henwood, K., Hariman, J. and Coupland, J. (1990) 'The social meaning of RP: an intergenerational perspective' in Ramsaran, S. (ed.) *Studies in the Pronunciation of English: A Commemorative Volume in Honour of A.C. Gimson*, London, Routledge.

Gill, J. (1863) *Introductory Text-Book to School Education, Method and School Management* (9th edn), London, Longman, Green, Longman, Roberts & Green.

Godfrey, E. and Tagliamonte, S. (1999) 'Another piece for the verbal -s story: evidence from Devon in southwest England', *Language Variation and Change*, no. 11, pp. 87–121.

Görlach, M. (1991) *Introduction to Early Modern English*, Cambridge, Cambridge University Press.

Graddol, D., Goodman, S. and Lillis, T. (2007) (eds) *Redesigning English*, London, Routledge/Milton Keynes, The Open University.

Gumperz, J. (1982) *Discourse Strategies*, Cambridge, Cambridge University Press.

Gupta, R.S. (2001) 'English in post-colonial India: an appraisal' in Moore, B. (ed.) *Who's Centric Now? The Present State of Post-Colonial Englishes*, Oxford, Oxford University Press.

Halliday, M.A.K. (1993) 'On the language of physical science' in Halliday, M.A.K. and Martin, J.R. (eds) *Writing Science: Literacy and Discursive Power*, Basingstoke, Falmer.

Hansard, HC, vol. 436, cols 557 8 (11 July 2005) [online] http://www.publications.parliament.uk/pa/cm200506/cmhansrd/cm050711/debtext/50 (Accessed 31 October 2005).

Harris, J. (1991) 'Ireland' in Cheshire, J. (ed.) *English around the World: Sociolinguistic Perspectives*, Cambridge, Cambridge University Press.

Harris, J. (1993) 'The grammar of Irish English' in Milroy, J. and Milroy, L. (eds) *Real English: The Grammar of English Dialects in the British Isles*, London, Longman.

Haugen, E. (1972) 'Dialect, language, nation' in Pride, J.B. and Holmes, J. (eds) *Sociolinguistics*, Harmondsworth, Penguin.

Heller, M. (1990) 'The politics of codeswitching: processes and consequences of ethnic mobilization', workshop paper presented at 'Impact and Consequences: broader considerations', *Network on Codeswitching and Language Contact*, Brussels, 22–4 November.

Heller, M. (1992) 'The politics of codeswitching and language choice', *Journal of Multilingual and Multicultural Development*, vol. 13, no. 1/2, pp. 123–42.

Hogg, R. (1992) 'Introduction' in Hogg, R. (ed.) *Cambridge History of the English Language*, vol. 1, Cambridge, Cambridge University Press.

Holmes, J. (2001) *An Introduction to Sociolinguistics* (2nd edn), Harlow, Longman.

Honey, J. (1989) *Does Accent Matter? The Pygmalion Factor*, London, Faber & Faber.

Hooke, R. (1961 [1665]) 'Preface', *Micrographia or Some Physiological Descriptions of Minute Bodies made by Magnifying Glasses with Observations and Inquiries thereupon*, (ed. R.W.T. Gunther), Mineola, NY, Dover.

Houghton, B. (1975) *Scientific Periodicals: Their Historical Development, Characteristics and Control*, London, Clive Bingley.

Hudson, R.A. (1986) *Sociolinguistics*, Cambridge, Cambridge University Press.

Hunter, M.C.W. (1989) *Establishing the New Science: The Experience of the Early Royal Society*, Woodbridge, Boydell.

Huspek, M.R. (1986) 'Linguistic variation, context and meaning: a case of -ing/in' variation in North American workers' speech', *Language in Society*, no. 15, pp. 154–5.

Ito, R. and Tagliamonte, S. (2003) 'Well weird, right dodgy, very strange, really cool: layering and recycling in English intensifiers', *Language in Society*, no. 32, pp. 257–79, Cambridge, Cambridge University Press.

Jake, J., Myers-Scotton, C. and Gross, S. (2002) 'Making a minimalist approach to codeswitching work: adding the matrix language!' *Bilingualist: Language and Cognition*, vol. 5, no. 1, pp. 69–91.

Jespersen, O. (1922) *Language: Its Nature, Development and Origin*, London, George Allen & Unwin.

Johnson, S. (1755) *A Dictionary of the English Language*, Vol. I, London, W. Strachan.

Johnson, S. (2006 [1755]) 'Preface' in Johnson, S. *Dictionary*, http://www.bartleby.com/39/28.html (Accessed 8 May 2006).

Joseph, J.E. (1987) *Eloquence and Power*, London, Francis Pinter.

Joyce, P. (1991) *Visions of the People*, Cambridge, Cambridge University Press.

Kachru, B.B. (1992) *The Other Tongue: English across Cultures* (2nd edn), Urbana & Chicago, University of Illinois Press.

Kanyoro, M.R.A. (1991) 'The politics of the English language in Kenya and Tanzania' in Cheshire, J. (ed.) *English Around the World*, Cambridge, Cambridge University Press.

Kastovsky, D. (1992) 'Semantics and vocabulary' in Hogg, R. (ed.) *Cambridge History of the English Language*, vol. 1, Cambridge, Cambridge University Press.

Keller, R. (1994) *On Language Change: The Invisible Hand in Language*, London, Routledge.

Kemp, J.A. (trans.) (1972) *John Wallis's Grammar of the English Language*, London, Longman.

Kumar, A. (1986) 'Certain aspects of the form and function of Hindi-English code-switching', *Anthropological Linguistics*, summer.

Labov, W. (2001) 'Principles of Linguistic Change', *Social Factors*, Volume 2, Oxford, Blackwell.

Lass, R.G. (1992) 'Phonology and morphology' in Blake, N. (ed.) *Cambridge History of the English Language*, vol. 2, Cambridge, Cambridge University Press.

Le Page, R.B. and Tabouret-Keller, A, (1985) *Acts of Identity: Creole-based Approaches to Language and Ethnicity*, Cambridge, Cambridge University Press.

Leonard, T. (1984) *Intimate Voices*, Newcastle, Galloping Dog Press.

Ligon (1647) *A True and Exact History of the Island of Barbados*, London, Moseley.

Lily, W. (1945 [1542]) *A Shorte Introduction of Grammar*, Flynn, K.J. (ed.), Delman, NY, Scholars' Facsimiles & Reprints.

Lochhead, L. (1989) *Mary Queen of Scots Got Her Head Chopped Off and Dracula*, Harmondsworth, Penguin.

Lowth, R. (1968 [1762]) *A Shorter Introduction to English Grammar: With Critical Notes*, Menston, Scholar Press.

MacSwann, J. (2004) 'Code switching and grammatical theory' in Bhatia, T. and Ritchie, W.C. (eds) *The Handbook of Bilingualism*, Oxford, Blackwell.

Makoni, S. and Meinhof, U. (2003) 'Introducing applied linguistics in Africa', *Africa and Applied Linguistics*, AILA Review, no. 16, pp. 38–51.

Maltz, D.N. and Borker, R. (1998) 'A cultural approach to male–female mis-communication' in Holmes, J. (ed.) *Language and Gender: A Reader*, Oxford, Blackwell.

Mazrui, A. (1973) 'The English language and the origins of African nationalism' in Bailey, R. W. and Robinson, J. L. (eds) *Varieties of Present-Day English*, London, Macmillan.

McArthur, T. (1992) *The Oxford Companion to the English Language*, Oxford, Oxford University Press.

McArthur, T. (1998) *The English Languages*, Cambridge, Cambridge University Press.

McArthur, T. (2002) *The Oxford Guide to World English*, Oxford, Oxford University Press.

McClure, J.D. (1988) *Why Scots Matters: The Scots Language is a Priceless National Possession*, Edinburgh, Saltire Society.

McCrum, R., Cran, W. and MacNeil, R. (1992) *The Story of English* (2nd edn), London, Faber & Faber/BBC Books.

McCrum, R., Cran, W. and Macneil, R. (2002) *The Story of English* (3rd edn), London, Faber & Faber/BBC Books.

McDonald, C. (1981) 'Variation in the use of modal verbs with special reference to Tyneside English', PhD thesis, University of Newcastle.

Mehrotra, R.R. (1998) *Indian English: Texts and Interpretation*, Amsterdam, John Benjamins.

Milroy, J. (1992) 'The study of geographical variation in Middle English' in Blake, N. (ed.) *Cambridge History of the English Language*, vol. 2, Cambridge, Cambridge University Press.

Milroy, J. and Milroy, L. (1985) *Authority in Language: Investigating Language Prescription and Standardisation*, London, Routledge & Kegan Paul.

Milroy, J. and Milroy, L. (eds) (1993) *Real English: The Grammar of English Dialects in the British Isles*, London, Longman.

Milroy, L. (1980) *Language and Social Networks*, Oxford, Blackwell.

Moore, V. (2000) 'Why RP Doesn't Fit In', *The Times*, 27 July, p. 6.

Morrish, J. (1999) 'The accent that dare not speak its name', *The Independent on Sunday*, 21 March.

Mugglestone, L.C. (2003) *Talking Proper: The Rise of Accent as Social Symbol* (2nd edn), Oxford, Oxford University Press.

Mühlhäusler, P., Dutton, T. and Romaine, S. (eds) (2003) *Tok Pisin Texts: From the Beginning to the Present*, Amsterdam, John Benjamins.

Murray J.A.H. (1884) *A New English Dictionary on Historical Principles*, Part 1, A–ANT, Oxford, Clarendon.

Myers-Scotton, C. (1993a) *Duelling Languages: Grammatical Structure in Codeswitching*, Oxford, Clarendon.

Myers-Scotton, C. (1993b) *Social Motivations for Codeswitching: Evidence from Africa*, Oxford, Clarendon.

Njogu, K. (2005) 'National exams and the case of Kiswahili as a national language', *Africa News*, All Africa Inc., 9 January, Lexis-Nexis Executive database.

Pandharipande, P. (1990) 'Formal and functional constraints in code-mixing' in Jacobson, R. (ed.) *Codeswitching as a Worldwide Phenomenon*, New York, Peter Lang.

Pickles, W. (1949) *Between You and Me: The Autobiography of Wilfred Pickles*, London, Werner Laurie.

Pinker, S. and Prince, A. (1988) 'On language and connectionism: analysis of a parallel distributed processing model of language acquisition,' *Cognition*, no. 28, pp. 73–193.

Platt, J. (1991) 'Social and linguistic constraints on variation in the use of two grammatical variables in Singapore English' in Cheshire, J. (ed.) *English Around the World*, Cambridge, Cambridge University Press.

Platt, J., Weber, H. and Ho, M.L. (1984) *The New Englishes*, London, Routledge & Kegan Paul.

Poole, J. (1813) *The Village School Improved; or, The New System of Education Practically Explained, and Adapted to the Case of Country Parishes* (2nd edn), Oxford, Oxford University Press.

Poplack, S., Sankoff, D. and Miller, C. (1988) 'The social correlates and linguistic processes of lexical borrowing and assimilation', *Linguistics*, no. 26, pp. 47–104.

Pryor, F. (2004) *Britain A.D.: A Quest for Arthur, England and the Anglo-Saxons*, London, HarperCollins.

Puttenham, G. (1936 [1589]) *The Arte of English Poesie* in Willock, G.D. and Walker, A. (eds) Cambridge, Cambridge University Press.

Quirk, R. (1985) 'The English language in a global context' in Quirk, R. and Widdowson, H.G. (eds) *English in the World: Teaching and Learning the Language and Literatures*, Cambridge, Cambridge University Press for the British Council.

Quirk, R. (1990) 'Language varieties and standard language', *English Today*, vol. 6, no. 1, January, pp. 3–10.

Quirk, R., Greenbaum, S., Leech, G. and Svartvik, J. (1972) *A Grammar of Contemporary English*, London, Longman.

Reith, J.C.W. (1924) *Broadcast over Britain*, London, Hodder and Stoughton.

Robinson, R.N. (ed.) (1966) *The Works of Geoffrey Chaucer* (2nd edn), Oxford, Oxford University Press.

Romaine, S. and Lange, D. (1991) 'The use of like as a marker of reported speech and thought: a case of grammaticalisation in progress' *American Speech, no.* 66, pp. 227–79.

Rosewarne, D. (1984) 'Estuary English', *The Times Educational Supplement*, 19 October.

Samper, D.A. (2002a) 'Preview', 'Talking Sheng: the role of a hybrid language in the construction of identity and youth culture in Nairobi, Kenya', PhD thesis, University of Pennsylvania, http://wwwlib.umi.com/dissertations/preview-pickup/17/02/341702/1/00019.gif (Accessed 24 October 2005).

Samper, D.A. (2002b) 'Talking Sheng: the role of a hybrid language in the construction of identity and youth culture in Nairobi, Kenya', PhD thesis, University of Pennsylvania, http://wwwlib.umi.com/dissertations/fullcit/3043947 (Accessed 24 October 2005).

Sapir, E. (1921) *Language*, New York, Harcourt Brace.

Scott, W. (1986 [1815]) *Ivanhoe*, Harmondsworth, Penguin.

Sebba, M. (1993) *London Jamaican: Language Systems in Interaction*, London, Longman.

Shaw, G.B. (1941) *Pygmalion*, Harmondsworth, Penguin.

Shaw, G.B. (1972 [1910]) *Pygmalion* in *The Bodley Head Bernard Shaw: Collected Plays with their Prefaces*, vol. IV, London, Max Reinhardt/The Bodley Head.

Sheridan, T. (1762) *A Course of Lectures on Elocution*, London, W. Strachan.

Sherley-Price, L. (1968) *Bede, A History of the English Church and People*, Harmondsworth, Penguin.

Simpson, J.A. and Weiner, E.S.C. (eds) (1989) *Oxford English Dictionary* (2nd edn), Oxford, Oxford University Press.

Skeat, W. (1962 [1912]) *English Dialects from the Eighth Century to the Present Day*, www.gutenberg.net (Accessed 1 March 2006).

Smith, J. (2002) 'Accounting for vernacular features in a Scottish dialect: relic, innovation, analogy and drift' in Kay, C., Horobin, S. and Smith, J. (eds) *New Perspectives on English Historical Linguistics*, Selected papers from 12th ICEHL, Glasgow, August 2002, Amsterdam, John Benjamins.

Smith, J. (2005) 'The sociolinguistics of contemporary Scots: evidence from one community' in Kirk, J.M. and Ó Baoill, D.P. (eds). *The Fifth Symposium on the Politics and Languages of Scotland and Ireland*, Belfast, Queen's University.

Sprat, T. (1959 [1667]) *History of the Royal Society by Thomas Sprat* in Cope, J.I. and Jones, H.W. (eds), St. Louis, Washington University Press.

Stallybrass, P. (1988) 'An inclosure of the best people in the world: nationalism and imperialism in late sixteenth century England' in Samuel, R. (ed.) *Patriotism: The Making and Unmaking of British National Identities*, London, Routledge.

Steele, H. and Smith, J. (2004) *'I Ø ken fit you're saying': Acquisition of Variable Forms in a Scottish Dialect*, paper delivered at Sociolinguistics Symposium 15, Newcastle, April 2004.

Storey, G., Tillotson, K. and Easson, A. (eds) (1993) *The Letters of Charles Dickens, Volume Seven 1853–1855* in House, M., Storey, G. and Tillotson, K. (general eds), *The Letters of Charles Dickens*, Oxford, Oxford Clarendon.

Swann, J. (1996) 'English voices' in Graddol, D., Leith, D. and Swann, J. (eds) *English: History, Diversity and Change*, London, Routledge/Milton Keynes, The Open University.

Swann, J. (1996) 'Style shifting, codeswitching' in Graddol, D., Leith, D. and Swann, J. (eds) *English: History, Diversity and Change*, London, Routledge/Milton Keynes, The Open University.

Swann, J., Deumert, A., Lillis, T. and Mesthrie, R. (2004) *A Dictionary of Sociolinguistics*, Edinburgh, Edinburgh University Press.

Sweet, H. (1881) *The Elementary Sounds of English*, London, Adelphi.

Tagliamonte, S. and Hudson, R. (1999) 'Be like *et al.* beyond America: the quotative system in British and Canadian youth', *Journal of Sociolinguistics,* vol. 3, no. 2, Oxford, Blackwell.

Tagliamonte, S., Smith, J. and Lawrence, H. (2004): *'You've got to Speak Properly; You have to keep up with the Joneses': The Changing Modals in British Dialects*, paper delivered at Sociolinguistics Symposium 15, Newcastle, April 2004.

The Week in Westminster, BBC Radio 4, 16 July 2005.

Thoreau, H.D. (2006 [1849]) *A Week on the Concord and Merrimack Rivers* [online], The Project Gutenburg Etext, http://www.gutenburg.org/text/4232 (Accessed 3 May 2006).

Tripathi, P.D. (1992) 'The chosen tongue', *English Today*, vol. 32, no. 8, 4 October, pp. 3–11.

Trudgill, P. (1974) *The Social Differentiation of English in Norwich*, Cambridge, Cambridge University Press.

Trudgill, P. (1983a) 'Acts of conflicting identity: the sociolinguistics of British pop-song pronunciation' in Trudgill, P. (ed.) *On Dialect: Social and Geographical Perspectives*, Oxford, Blackwell.

Trudgill, P. (1983b) *Sociolinguistics: An Introduction to Language and Society* (revised edn), Harmondsworth, Penguin.

Trudgill, P. (1983c) 'Standard and non-Standard dialects of English in the UK: problems and policies' in Stubbs, M. and Hillier, H. (eds.), *Readings on Language, Schools, and Classrooms*, London, Methuen.

Trudgill, P. (1986) *Dialects in Contact*, Oxford, Blackwell.

Trudgill, P. (1990) *The Dialects of English,* Oxford, Blackwell.

Trudgill, P. (1994) *Dialects*, London, Routledge.

Trudgill, P. (2002) *Sociolinguistic Variation and Change*, Edinburgh, Edinburgh University Press.

Trudgill, P. (2004) *New-Dialect Formation: The Inevitability of Colonial Englishes*, Edinburgh, Edinburgh University Press.

Trudgill, P. and Chambers, J. K. (eds) (1991) 'Introduction', *Dialects of English: Studies in Grammatical Variation,* London, Longman.

Trudgill, P. and Hannah, J. (1994) *International English* (3rd edn), London, Edward Arnold.

Verma, S.K. (1982) 'Swadeshi English: form and function' in Pride, J.B. (ed.) *New Englishes*, Rowley, MA, Newbury House.

Walker, J. (1968 [1791]) *A Critical Pronouncing Dictionary and Expositer of the English Language*, Menston, Scholar Press.

Walvin, J. (1993) *Black Ivory: A History of British Slavery*, London, Fontana.

Wardhaugh, R. (1987) *Languages in Competition: Dominance, Diversity and Decline,* Oxford, Blackwell in association with André Deutsch.

Wee Kiat (1992) *Women in Men's Houses*, Singapore, Landmark.

Wells, J.C. (1982) *Accents of English I: An Introduction*, Cambridge, Cambridge University Press.

Williams, G. (1985) *When was Wales?*, Harmondsworth, Penguin.

Willis, L. (2002) 'Language use and identity among African-Caribbean young people in Sheffield' in Gubbins, P. and Holt, M. (eds) *Beyond Boundaries: Language Identity in Contemporary Europe,* Clevedon, Multilingual Matters.

Woolard, K.A. (2004) 'Codeswitching' in Duranti, A. (ed.) *A Companion to Linguistic Anthropology,* Oxford, Blackwell.

Wright, S. (1996) 'Accents of English' in Graddol, D., Leith, D. and Swann, J. (eds) *English: History, Diversity and Change*, London, Rouledge/Milton Keynes, The Open university.

Acknowledgements
Grateful acknowledgement is made to the following sources:

Text

Pages 29–33: Crystal, D. (1988) The English Language Today, *The English Language*, Copyright © David Crystal, 1988. Reproduced by permission of Penguin Books Ltd; pages 74–7: Crystal, D. (2004) The Origins of Old English – Interlude 1 The Celtic Language Puzzle, *The Stories of English*, pp. 25, 29–33, Copyright © David Crystal, 2004, Penguin Books Ltd; page 111: Joyce, P. (1991) *Visions of the People*, Cambridge University Press; pages 113–16: Harris R, and Taylor, T.J. © 1989. *Landmarks in Linguistic Thought: From Socrates to Saussure*, pp. 167–71, Routledge. Reproduced by permission of Taylor and Francis Books UK; pages 149–52: *From The Other Tongue: English across Cultures*. Copyright 1982, 1992 by the Board of Trustees of the University of Illinois. Used with permission of the University of Illinois Press; pages 167–8: © Tom Leonard 1984 from *Intimate Voices* republished Etruscan Books Devon 2003; pages 222–3: Hewings, A. and Hewings, M. (2005). *Standards and Variety, Grammar and Context – An Advanced Resource Book*, pp. 79–80, Routledge. © 2005 Ann Hewings and Martin Hewings; pages 224–6: Beal, J., 1993, The Grammar of Tyneside and Northumbrian English, in Milroy, J. and Milroy, L., 1993, *Real English: The Grammar of English Dialects in the British Isles*, Longman Group Limited, Pearson Education Ltd; pages 263–8: Myers-Scotton, C., 1989, *Codeswitching with English types of switching, types of communities, World Englishes*, vol. 8. no. 3, pp. 333–46, Basil Blackwell Ltd, Blackwell Publishers Ltd.

Figures

Page 13: © Bart Roozendaal, Cartoon Stock, www.cartoonstock.com; page 17: Magnus John; page 22: Aislin © 1977. Reproduced by permission of Terry Mosher (Aislin), *The Gazette*, Montreal; page 45: First page of Bede's *Ecclesiastical History of the English People* Cotton ms Tiberius CII folio 5v, by permission of the British Library; page 49: Photograph by kind permission of Dick Leith; page 83: Science Photo Library; page 85: *The History of Troy*, Le Fevre, Raduz folio 16r, John Rylands University Library of Manchester; page 90: Science Photo Library; pages 92 and 94: Newton, I. (3rd edition, 1726), *Philosophiae Naturalis Principia Mathematica* 8703F8 T. P. 9071036, by permission of the British Library and Hooke, R., 1665, *Micrographia: Or some physiological descriptions of minute bodies made by magnifying glasses with observations and inquiries thereupon* 435e19 T. P. 8972506, by permission of the British Library; page 94: By permission of the Syndics of Cambridge University Library; page 99: STC 15614, *An Introdvction of the Eyght Partes of Latine Speache*, folio A5r, by permission of The Folger Shakespeare Library;

page 101: Mary Evans Picture Library; page 136: Miriam Holden Collection, Department of Rare Books and Special Collections. Princeton University Library; page 141: © Corbis; page 157: Mary Evans Picture Library Ltd; page 162: Topham Picturepoint; page 166: © Getty Images/Bert Hardy; page 195: Trudgill, P. (1983) Language and Social Class, *Sociolinguistics: An Introduction to Language and Society*, Penguin Books Ltd; page 196: Downes, W. (1988) At the intersection of social factors, *Language and Society*, Cambridge University Press;   page 231: Trudgill, P. 1986, *Dialects in Contact*, p. 8, Basil Blackwell Ltd, Blackwell Publishers Ltd.

Illustrations

Page 228: Bryan McAllister.

Every effort has been made to contact copyright holders. If any have been inadvertently overlooked the publishers will be pleased to make the necessary arrangements at the first opportunity.

ndex